THE EVERYTHING® PRESSURE COOKER COOKBOOK

Dear Reader,

Like you, I'm always looking for ways to improve how I prepare food—and how it tastes. Using a pressure cooker helps me do just that.

A pressure cooker not only lets me take inexpensive cuts of meat and turn them into succulent entrées, it also saves me time. In the summer, it provides a way to simulate baking without raising the temperature in the kitchen by heating up the oven.

Today's assortment of safe pressure cookers adds to their versatility. Pressure cookers are available in four-, six-, and eight-quart pressure saucepans, as pressure skillets and braisers, pressure stockpots and canners, and countertop models.

This is my fifth cookbook for the *Everything*® series. I truly enjoy finding innovative methods for fixing and adapting traditional methods to create tasty food. I'm fortunate that I get to pass that information along through the recipes in my cookbooks. The recipes were tested using the Cuisinart six-quart programmable electric pressure cooker and an assortment of Kuhn Rikon Duromatic and B/R/K models. (See Appendix B for information on pressure cooker manufacturers.)

Throughout the book I provide tips and suggestions to help you cook an endless assortment of family-friendly dishes. My sincere wish is that the time you spend cooking will be more enjoyable because I've helped make the food that comes out of your kitchen not only delicious but also easier to prepare.

Pamela Rice Hahn

Welcome to the EVERYTHING® Series!

These handy, accessible books give you all you need to tackle a difficult project, gain a new hobby, comprehend a fascinating topic, prepare for an exam, or even brush up on something you learned back in school but have since forgotten.

You can choose to read an *Everything*® book from cover to cover or just pick out the information you want from our four useful boxes: e-questions, e-facts, e-alerts, and e-ssentials.

We give you everything you need to know on the subject, but throw in a lot of fun stuff along the way, too.

We now have more than 400 *Everything*® books in print, spanning such wide-ranging categories as weddings, pregnancy, cooking, music instruction, foreign language, crafts, pets, New Age, and so much more. When you're done reading them all, you can finally say you know *Everything*®!

QUESTION

Answers to common questions

FACT

Important snippets of information

ALERT

Urgent warnings

ESSENTIAL

Quick handy tips

PUBLISHER Karen Cooper

DIRECTOR OF ACQUISITIONS AND INNOVATION Paula Munier

MANAGING EDITOR, EVERYTHING® SERIES Lisa Laing

COPY CHIEF Casey Ebert

ACQUISITIONS EDITOR Katrina Schroeder

DEVELOPMENT EDITOR Elizabeth Kassab

EDITORIAL ASSISTANT Hillary Thompson

EVERYTHING® SERIES COVER DESIGNER Erin Alexander

LAYOUT DESIGNERS Colleen Cunningham, Elisabeth Lariviere, Ashley Vierra, Denise Wallace

Visit the entire Everything® series at *www.everything.com*

THE
EVERYTHING®
PRESSURE COOKER COOKBOOK

Pamela Rice Hahn

Avon, Massachusetts

To all my visitors at CookingWithPam.com

An Everything® Series Book.
Everything® and everything.com® are registered trademarks of F+W Media, Inc.

Published by Adams Media, a division of F+W Media, Inc.
57 Littlefield Street, Avon, MA 02322 U.S.A.
www.adamsmedia.com

ISBN 10: 1-4405-0017-7
ISBN 13: 978-1-4405-0017-6

Printed in the United States of America.

J   I   H   G   F   E   D   C   B   A

Library of Congress Cataloging-in-Publication Data
is available from the publisher.

This book is available at quantity discounts for bulk purchases.
For information, please call 1-800-289-0963.

Contents

Introduction ix

1   Pressure Cooker Primer 1

2   Chutneys, Preserves, Jams, and Condiments 9

3   Appetizers and Party Fare 22

4   Sauces. 35

5   Breakfast and Brunch. 45

6   Chicken. 54

7   Turkey 67

8   Beef 80

9   Pork. 93

10 Ground Meat 105

11 Fish and Seafood 116

12 International Flavors. 128

13 Soups 143

14 Stews and Chowders 157

15 Vegetarian 170

16 Pasta, Legumes, and Grains. 182

17 Rice and Risotto 195

18 Stovetop Casseroles. 210

19 Foods Worth the Extra Effort 221

20 Side Dishes. 235

21 Out-of-the-Ordinary Vegetables 246

22 Fabulous Fruits. 254

23 Custards, Steamed Puddings, and Desserts 266

Appendix A: Ingredient Sources 282
Appendix B: Equipment Sources. 283
Appendix C: Pressure Cooking Time Charts 284
Index. 291

Acknowledgments

For their help and support, I would like to thank everyone at Adams Media. For all of their hard work and perseverance, I would like to thank my agents, Sheree Bykofsky and Janet Rosen. Special thanks also go to my daughter, Lara Sutton; her husband, Randy; and the other joys in my life: Taylor, Charles, and Courtney; Ann, Andrew, Dennis, and Tony Rice; my mother; my sisters Kim, Tam, and Connie and their families, with special thanks to my nephew Brian Teeters; and Eric J. Ehlers, David Hebert, everybody at ProudPatriots.org, and my other online friends.

Introduction

THE PRESSURE COOKER MAKES it possible for you to prepare great-tasting food in ways that save you time and effort.

Pressure cookers aren't a new phenomena. In fact, pressure cookers were especially popular in the 1950s. Back in those days, the typical pressure cooker had a noisy rocking pressure valve on the lid. But because a pressure cooker didn't have an emergency mechanism in place to prevent the cooker from building up too much pressure, it had the tendency to have accidents. Those accidents forced the food inside the pressure cooker out. In other words, that sizzling hot food became sloppy, hot, airborne projectiles. Therefore, while it may not be technically correct to say that the pressure cooker would explode, the accident pretty much amounted to the same result. It's bad enough that you have to wash the dishes after you fix a meal; you don't want to have to wash gunk off of the ceiling, walls, and floors, too.

As you'll learn in Chapter 1, today's new generation of pressure cookers are much safer and easier to use. You'll find evidence of that when you take a quick look at this book. When you do, you'll see that there are recipes for food that can take you from breakfast to lunch to dinner. You can also make snacks, desserts, and dishes for special occasions.

While every effort was made to create foolproof recipes for this book, it's impossible to anticipate every factor that can affect cooking times. For example, a pressure cooker filled with cold, dense food is going to take longer to come to pressure than one that has room temperature or warm food. Regardless of the cooking method, ingredients at room temperature will cook faster than those just out of the refrigerator, and even faster than those fresh from the freezer. Granted, with the exception of some uses for the microwave oven, any food will cook faster in a pressure cooker than it will using any other method. But because it's impossible to predict the overall temperature of the food in all situations when it goes into the pressure cooker, overall cooking times aren't given. In other words, while each recipe will explain how long the food should remain at pressure, it won't state how long it will take that food to come to pressure, because it's impossible to predict.

Convenience isn't a constant either. A pressure cooker isn't practical in every situation, but it is a helpful substitute for other appliances. For example, the oven isn't always practical in the summer, so there are many instances when you can create a similar—if not identical—result in the pressure cooker. Most often, you will be able to achieve this in less time, and you'll always be able to do it without heating up the kitchen. Pressure cookers are perfect for those occasions when you need to do other chores around or away from the house, and the stovetop certainly isn't practical even for the most organized master at multitasking. At these times, an electric programmable countertop pressure cooker is the more practical solution. Different methods will suit your needs at different times—even when it comes to pressure cooker practicality.

Just like when you fix something using any other cooking method, adapting a recipe for the pressure cooker doesn't mean that there is only one correct way to fix each dish. For that reason, this book also includes sidebars that have bonus recipes, tips, and suggestions on how to alter some of the recipes.

Last but not least, it is also worth noting that the exact measurement for salt is seldom given in this book. Unless otherwise indicated, when a recipe calls for salt, sea salt was used to test the recipe. The recipes are designed according to personal preference, so as little salt as possible was added during the cooking process with the assumption that gray sea salt would be available at the table to season the food.

CHAPTER 1

Pressure Cooker Primer

Pressure cookers cook food up to 70 percent faster than conventional methods. Steam trapped in the pot builds up pressure, which creates a hotter cooking temperature. The pressure bears down on the surface of the liquid, which isn't able to break down the molecules to create more steam; this produces more heat. The end result is that the pressure raises the boiling point. The tight seal on the cooker also helps seal in vitamins and minerals and prevents the cooker from boiling dry during the cooking process.

A Brief History of Pressure Cookers

In 1679, a French physicist named Denis Papin invented what he called a steam digester by firmly securing a lid onto a cast iron pot. About 200 years after that, another Frenchman invented a way to preserve foods under high pressure. Home pressure canners were introduced in North America by National Presto Industries in 1915. By the 1940s, numerous manufacturers were selling pressure saucepans.

FACT

Large pressure cookers with the capacity to hold jars used in home canning are called pressure canners. Laboratories and hospitals sterilize materials using a type of pressure cooker known as an autoclave. Pressure cookers used in the food industry are often referred to as retorts.

Most of the recent innovations in pressure cookers were invented by European manufacturers. In the United States, pressure cooker popularity declined in the 1970s as many cooks switched to microwave ovens. Europeans tended to rely on pressure cookers as their preferred way to fix food quickly.

Today's improved pressure cookers usually feature a stationary pressure regulator that's either a fixed weight or a spring valve. The pressure regulator keeps the pressure even in the cooker by occasionally releasing a burst of steam. The pressure regulator also provides an easy way to quick release the pressure at the end of the pressure cooking time; this is usually done by pressing a button or flipping a pressure-release switch.

New pressure cookers have backup pressure release mechanisms that prevent the excess pressure accidents that were associated with older models. They also have safety features that cause the lid to remain locked into place until after all of the pressure has been released.

Equipment Considerations

Your cooking equipment can make a difference in how easy it is to prepare foods. Buy the best you can afford. Better pan construction equals more even heat distribution, which translates to reduced cooking time and more even cooking.

Food will burn more easily in an inexpensive pan with a thinner pan bottom. How well your cooking pan conducts the heat will make a difference in how high you set the burner temperature. With some practice, you'll soon learn the perfect heat settings for your pressure cooker: It might take a medium-high setting to sauté food in an inexpensive pressure cooker and a lot more stirring to prevent the food from burning, but you can accomplish the same task in a heavier pan when it's over medium heat, and with less frequent stirring.

ALERT

Read the instruction manual that came with your pressure cooker. Never exceed the fill line for your pressure cooker; adjust the recipe or prepare it in two batches if you need to. Overfilling the pressure cooker can cause it to explode, so be careful!

On the flipside, a heavier pan will retain the heat longer once it's removed from the burner than will an inexpensive one, so to prevent it from overcooking, food cooked to perfection in a heavier pan must be moved to a serving dish more quickly. This is especially true of foods like gravy that tend to thicken the longer they sit; gravy can turn from a succulent liquid to one big lump if it stays on the heat too long.

Pressure Release Methods

The ways pressure is released from the pressure cooker are:

- **The natural release method**, which refers to turning off the heat under the pressure cooker and either removing the pan from the heat or letting the pan remain on the burner, and then waiting until the pressure cooker has cooled sufficiently for all of the pressure to be released.
- **The quick release method**, which refers to using the valve on the pressure cooker to release the pressure.

- **The cold water release method**, which occurs when the pan is carried to the sink and cold water from the tap is run over the lid of the pressure cooker (but not over the valve!) until the pressure is released.

ALERT

The cold water release method isn't suggested in any of the recipes in this book; however, if you find that your pressure cooker retains too much heat after the quick release method when you prepare foods that only require a short cooking time—like certain vegetables, risotto, or polenta—try using the cold water release method the next time you fix that food.

Explanation of Cooking Methods

Cooking terms that you'll encounter in this book are:

- **Bain-marie**, or water bath, is a method used to make custards and steamed dishes by surrounding the cooking vessel with water; this helps maintain a more even cooking temperature around the food.
- **Baking** involves putting the food in a preheated oven; the food cooks by being surrounded by the hot, dry air of your oven. In the pressure cooker, foods that are traditionally baked (like a cheesecake, for example) are baked in a covered container that's placed on a rack submerged in water. The water in the bottom of the pressure cooker creates the steam that builds the pressure and maintains the heat inside the pressure cooker. The cover over the pan holding the food maintains the dry environment inside.
- **Braising** usually starts by browning a less expensive cut of meat in a pan on top of the stove and then covering the meat with a small amount of liquid, adding a lid or covering to the pan, and slowly cooking it. Braising can take place on the stovetop, in the oven, or in a slow cooker or pressure cooker. The slow-cooking process tenderizes the meat. The cooking environment in the pressure cooker greatly reduces the braising time needed. For example, a roast that would normally take two and a half to three hours in the oven or on the stove only requires forty-five to sixty minutes in the pressure cooker.

- **Deglazing** refers to the process of ridding a pan of any excess remaining fat by putting it over a medium-high heat and then adding enough cooking liquid to let you scrape up any browned bits stuck to the bottom of the pan. Doing this step before you add the other ingredients for your sauce or gravy gives the end result more flavor and color.
- **Poaching** is accomplished by gently simmering ingredients in broth, juice, water, wine, or other flavorful liquids until they're cooked through and tender.
- **Roasting**, like baking, is usually done in the oven, but generally at a higher oven temperature. Roasting meat in the moist environment inside a pressure cooker requires some trial and error because you can't rely on a programmable meat thermometer to tell you when the meat has reached the desired internal temperature. The upside is that the meat will roast much quicker when browned and then placed on the rack in a pressure cooker, and, even if it's cooked beyond your preferred preference, the meat will still be more moist than it would be if you had cooked it to that point in the dry environment of an oven.
- **Sautéing** is the method of quickly cooking small or thin pieces of food in some oil or butter that has been brought to temperature in a sauté pan (or in the pressure cooker) over medium to medium-high heat.
- **Steaming** is the cooking method that uses the steam from the cooking liquid to cook the food.
- **Stewing**, like braising, involves slowly cooking the food in a liquid; however, stewing involves a larger liquid-to-food ratio. In other words, you use far more liquid when you're stewing food. Not surprisingly, this method is most often used to make stew.
- **Stir-frying** is a cooking process similar to sautéing that's used to cook larger, bite-sized pieces of meat or vegetables in oil.

ESSENTIAL

Tempering is the act of gradually increasing the temperature of one cooking ingredient by adding small amounts of a hotter ingredient to the first. For example, tempering beaten eggs by whisking small amounts of hot liquid into them before you add the eggs to the cooking pan lets them be mixed into the dish; tempering prevents them from scrambling instead.

Pressure Cooker Tips and Troubleshooting Pointers

There will be a learning curve with each pressure cooker that you use. You also need to keep in mind that the same pressure cooker will behave differently on different stovetops. For example, electric burners usually retain heat longer than do gas burners; therefore, if you need to reduce the pressure when cooking over an electric burner, after you adjust the burner setting, you may need to lift the cooker off of the heat.

Also, as mentioned earlier in this chapter, pressure cookers are like any other pan in your kitchen: There's less chance that foods will burn or stick to the bottom of better pans with thicker pan bottoms. If burning is a problem with your pressure cooker, you can try one of these solutions:

- Add more liquid the next time you make that recipe.
- Begin to heat or bring liquids to a boil before you lock on the lid.
- Bring the cooker up to pressure over a lower heat.
- Use a heat diffuser.

There will be times when the pressure cooker will come to pressure almost immediately and other times when it can take twenty minutes or more to do so. Keep in mind that it can delay the time it takes the cooker to reach the desired pressure when you are cooking a much higher ratio of food to liquid or if the food was very cold when you began the cooking process.

After you've worked with your pressure cooker, you'll come to recognize the signs that the cooker is about to reach pressure by the sounds it makes. (The cooker will usually release some steam before the pressure gasket finally settles into place.) If the pressure cooker fails to come to pressure, chances are:

- The gasket isn't allowing for a tight seal. Coating the gasket in vegetable oil will sometimes help solve this problem. If it doesn't, you'll need to replace the gasket.

- The lid isn't properly locked into place.
- Something is clogging the pressure regulator. You'll need to use the quick release method so you can remove the lid and then follow the manufacturer's directions for cleaning the gasket before you can proceed.
- There isn't sufficient liquid in the cooker. If you believe this to be the case, you'll need to test the pressure by using the quick release method so that you can remove the lid, then add more liquid, lock the lid back into place, and try again.
- You have too much food in the pressure cooker. You'll need to remove some of the food and try again.

ALERT

If liquid or foam is released from the vent, remove the pressure cooker from the heat and wait until the pressure is released naturally. This problem can occur when the pressure cooker is filled beyond capacity; in this case, remove some of the ingredients before proceeding. Another possibility is that you're cooking a food that foams. Adding additional oil and cleaning the area around the pressure regulator should alleviate the problem.

Tips for Using This Cookbook

Don't be afraid to experiment a little with the recipes in this cookbook. Swap your favorite ingredients for those you're not too fond of. Adjust cooking times and measurements to suit your preferences. Keep in mind that the browning and sautéing times given in the recipes are suggestions. Once you become familiar with your pressure cooker's quirks, you'll be able to gauge the correct burner temperature and the amount of time you will need to sauté or brown foods on your own.

ESSENTIAL

As you prepare the dishes in this cookbook, make notes in the margins about which ones you, your family, and your friends preferred. Don't rely on your memory: If you think a recipe would benefit by adding a bit more seasoning, then note that too. Making such notes now will mean that someday, when you're ready to write out recipe cards, you'll be able to have an entire pressure cooker section in the recipe box.

As you get more comfortable with your pressure cooker, you can try adapting conventional recipes to use with the pressure cooker. Just remember to add the nonliquid ingredients first. For example, for a stew you'd add the meat and vegetables first and only add as much of the liquid called for in the recipe to cover the food and bring the liquid level up to the fill line. You can stir in more liquid later. Choose your cooking time based on what's required to cook the meat.

CHAPTER 2

Chutneys, Preserves, Jams, and Condiments

Cranberry-Apple Chutney
10

Fresh Tomato Chutney
11

Green Tomato Chutney
12

Sweet Onion Relish
12

Strawberry Jam
13

Dried Apricot Preserves
14

Mixed Citrus Marmalade
15

Rainbow Bell Pepper Marmalade
16

Corn Maque Choux
17

Mango Chutney
17

Thanksgiving Jam
18

Blueberry Jam
19

Mincemeat
20

Peach and Toasted
Almond Preserves
21

Cranberry-Apple Chutney

Chutney is an Indian dish that was introduced to the rest of the world by the British.

INGREDIENTS | SERVES 16

1 12-ounce bag cranberries

1 cup light brown sugar, packed

1 small sweet onion, peeled and diced

1 jalapeño pepper, seeded and minced

2 tablespoons fresh ginger, peeled and grated

1 clove garlic, minced

1 teaspoon yellow mustard seed

1 3-inch stick of cinnamon

1 teaspoon lemon juice

¼ teaspoon salt

3 pounds tart cooking apples

Optional: Ground ginger to taste

Optional: Ground cinnamon to taste

For Best Results

Placing the apples over the cranberry mixture prevents the cranberries from foaming as they cook, which could clog the pressure cooker vent. Serve this chutney with roast pork or turkey. If you'd like to make cranberry-pear chutney, substitute 3 pounds of peeled and cored ripe Bartlett pears for the apples.

1. Rinse and pick over the cranberries. Add the cranberries, brown sugar, onion, jalapeño, ginger, garlic, mustard, cinnamon stick, lemon juice, and salt to a 5- to 7-quart pressure cooker. Cook over medium heat until the sugar dissolves, stirring occasionally.

2. Peel and core the apples; cut into strips, 1 inch in length. Place the apples in a layer over the cranberry mixture in the pressure cooker. Do not stir the apples into the mixture.

3. Lock the lid in place and bring to high pressure. Cook on high pressure for 1 minute. Remove from the heat and quick-release the pressure.

4. Remove the cinnamon stick. Taste for seasoning and add ground ginger and ground cinnamon if desired.

5. Store in a covered container in the refrigerator for up to 2 weeks. Serve heated or chilled.

Fresh Tomato Chutney

For a change of pace, you can spread this chutney over Indian chapati bread, flat bread, or pizza crust; top with goat cheese; and bake.

INGREDIENTS | **YIELD: 2 PINTS**

4 pounds ripe tomatoes

1 1-inch piece fresh ginger root

3 cloves garlic

1¾ cups white sugar

1 cup red wine vinegar

2 onions, diced

¼ cup golden raisins

¾ teaspoon ground cinnamon

½ teaspoon ground coriander

¼ teaspoon ground cloves

¼ teaspoon ground nutmeg

¼ teaspoon ground ginger

1 teaspoon chili powder

1 pinch paprika

1 tablespoon curry paste

1. Puree the peeled tomatoes and fresh ginger in a blender or food processor.

2. Pour the pureed tomato mixture into the pressure cooker. Stir in the remaining ingredients. Stir to mix, lock the lid into place, and cook at low pressure for 10 minutes. Remove from heat and allow pressure to release naturally. Refrigerate in a covered container until ready to use. Serve chilled or at room temperature.

Peeling Fresh Vine-Ripened Tomatoes

Add enough water to a saucepan to cover the tomatoes; bring to a boil over medium-high heat. Use a slotted spoon to submerge the tomatoes in the boiling water for 1 minute, or until their skins begin to crack and peel. Use the slotted spoon to remove the tomatoes from the water and plunge them into ice water. The peelings will slip right off.

Green Tomato Chutney

If you prefer spicy chutney, you can substitute an Anaheim and 4 small red chili or jalapeño peppers for the red bell peppers.

INGREDIENTS | YIELD: 5 CUPS

2 pounds green tomatoes, stems removed and diced

1 white onion, peeled, quartered lengthwise, and thinly sliced

2 red bell peppers, seeded and diced

¼ cup currants

2 tablespoons fresh ginger, grated

¾ cup dark brown sugar, firmly packed

¾ cup white wine or white distilled vinegar

Pinch sea salt

1. Put all ingredients in the pressure cooker; stir to mix. Lock on the lid and bring to low pressure. Cook on low pressure for 10 minutes. Remove from the heat and allow pressure to release naturally.

2. Cool and refrigerate overnight before serving. Can be stored in a covered container in the refrigerator for 2 months.

Sweet Onion Relish

Use sweet onions like Vidalia, Candy, First Edition, Maui, or Walla Walla for this relish.

INGREDIENTS | YIELD: 4 CUPS

4 medium sweet onions

water

¾ cup golden raisins

1 cup honey

1 tablespoon cider vinegar

Pinch salt

1. Peel and thinly slice onions. Add onions to the pressure cooker and pour in water to cover. Bring to a boil over high heat; drain immediately and discard water.

2. Return onions to pressure cooker; stir in raisins, honey, vinegar, and salt until honey is evenly distributed throughout onion slices.

3. Lock on lid, bring to high pressure, and cook for 5 minutes. Reduce heat and maintain low pressure for an additional 10 minutes. Remove from heat and allow pressure to release naturally.

4. Remove lid and stir relish. If relish needs thickening, return pan to heat, bring to a gentle boil for 5 minutes. Can be served warm or stored in a covered container in the refrigerator for up to 4 weeks.

Strawberry Jam

In addition to the usual uses for fruit spread, this jam is the perfect addition to some plain yogurt or as an ice cream topping.

INGREDIENTS | YIELD: 4 CUPS

4 cups strawberries

3 cups granulated cane sugar

¼ cup fresh lemon juice

1. Rinse and hull the strawberries, then quarter or halve them. Add to the pressure cooker. Stir in the sugar. Set aside for 1 hour or until the strawberries are juicy.

2. Use a potato masher to crush the fruit and mix in the sugar until the sugar is dissolved. Stir in the lemon juice.

3. Lock the lid in place. Bring the cooker to full pressure and cook for 7 minutes. Remove from the heat and allow pressure to release naturally.

4. Remove the lid. Return to heat and bring to a full boil over medium-high heat. Boil for 3 minutes or until jam reaches the desired gel state.

5. Skim off and discard any foam. Ladle into hot, sterilized glass containers or jars, leaving ½ inch of headspace. Seal the containers or jars. Cool and refrigerate for a week or freeze. (If you prefer, you can follow the instructions that came with your canning jars and process the preserves for shelf storage.)

Dried Apricot Preserves

Never fill the pressure cooker more than half full when making preserves, chutneys, or other fruit dishes.

INGREDIENTS | YIELD: 7 CUPS

4 cups dried apricots, chopped

2 cups water

5 black peppercorns

5 cardamom pods

2 (3-inch) cinnamon sticks

2 star anise

½ cup lemon juice

4 cups granulated cane sugar

Determining the Gel Point

Test a small amount of preserves by spooning it onto an ice-cold plate. It's reached the gel point when it's as thick as you desire. A softer set is ideal for use in sauces; if you prefer a firm, jamlike consistency, you may need to continue to boil the mixture for up to 20 minutes.

1. Add the apricots to a bowl or to the pressure cooker. Pour in the water, cover, and let the apricots soak for 24 hours.

2. Wrap the peppercorns, cardamom pods, cinnamon sticks, and star anise in cheesecloth and secure with a string. Add to the pressure cooker along with the apricots, soaking water, and lemon juice. Lock the lid into place. Bring to pressure and cook on low pressure for 10 minutes. Remove from the heat and allow pressure to release naturally.

3. Uncover the pressure cooker. Remove and discard the cheesecloth spice bag and stir in the sugar.

4. Return the pressure cooker to the heat and bring to a rapid boil over medium-high heat. Boil covered for 2 minutes and uncovered for 2 minutes or until the apricot mixture reaches the gel point.

5. Skim off and discard any foam. Ladle into hot, sterilized glass containers or jars, leaving ½ inch of headspace. Seal the containers or jars. Cool and refrigerate for a week or freeze. (If you prefer, you can follow the instructions that came with your canning jars and process the preserves for shelf storage.)

Mixed Citrus Marmalade

Jam sugar contains pectin, the soluble dietary fiber extracted from citrus fruits used as a gelling agent for jams, jellies, and marmalades.

INGREDIENTS | YIELD: 4 CUPS

1 large orange

1 lime

2 lemons

2 clementines or satsumas

1 pink grapefruit

3 cups water

4 pounds jam sugar

Sugar Crystals and the Gelling Process

After you've added sugar, putting the lid back on the pressure cooker once the mixture comes to a boil creates steam inside the cooker that will cause any sugar clinging to the sides of the pan to wash down into the mixture. Even one lone sugar crystal can set off a chain reaction that will cause the entire mixture to crystallize rather than remain in its gelled state.

1. Wash the fruit in hot water to remove any wax. Remove the zest from the orange, lime, and lemons; add to the pressure cooker. Quarter all fruit and place in a large (doubled) piece of cheesecloth; twist the cheesecloth to squeeze out the juice into the pressure cooker. Tie the cheesecloth over the fruit and seeds and add it to the pressure cooker along with half of the water. Lock the lid in place and bring the pressure cooker to high pressure; cook on high for 10 minutes. Remove from the heat and allow pressure to release naturally.

2. Remove the lid from the pressure cooker. Place the cooker over medium heat and add the remaining water and sugar. Bring to a boil, stirring continuously until all the sugar has dissolved.

3. While the mixture continues to boil, place the lid back on the cooker (but do not lock it into place). Leave the lid in place for 2 minutes, remove it, and then continue to let the mixture boil for 8 minutes or until the desire gel point is reached.

4. Skim off and discard any foam. Ladle into hot, sterilized glass containers or jars, leaving ½ inch of head space. Seal the containers or jars. Cool and refrigerate for a week or freeze until needed. (If you prefer, you can follow the instructions that came with your canning jars and process the preserves for shelf storage.)

Rainbow Bell Pepper Marmalade

Serve Rainbow Bell Pepper Marmalade as a relish for meat or on top of cream cheese on crackers.

INGREDIENTS | YIELD: 2 CUPS

1 large green bell pepper
1 large red bell pepper
1 large yellow bell pepper
1 large purple or orange bell pepper
1 small yellow, white, or sweet onion
Water
2 cups granulated cane sugar
Pinch salt
2 tablespoons balsamic vinegar

1. Wash, quarter, and seed the bell peppers; cut them into thin slices or dice them. Peel, quarter, and thinly slice the onion. Add the peppers and onion to the pressure cooker.

2. Add enough water to the pressure cooker to cover the peppers and onion. Bring to a boil over high heat; drain immediately and discard the water.

3. Return the peppers and onion to the pressure cooker. Stir in the sugar, salt, and vinegar. Bring to high pressure and cook for 5 minutes. Remove pan from the heat and let sit for 5 minutes.

4. Quick-release any remaining pressure. Remove the lid and return the pan to the heat. Simmer briskly over medium-high heat for 6 minutes or until the mixture is thickened. Once cooled, store in a covered container in the refrigerator overnight before using.

Corn Maque Choux

You can use drained canned corn, fresh corn cut from the cob, or thawed frozen corn in this recipe.

INGREDIENTS | SERVES 4

3 tablespoons butter

2 small onions, peeled and diced

1 small green bell pepper, seeded and diced

½ cup celery, diced

2 cloves garlic, peeled and minced

4 cups whole kernel corn

2 Roma tomatoes, peeled, seeded, and diced

½ cup cilantro leaves, chopped, plus additional for garnish

⅛ teaspoon cayenne pepper

½ cup tomato juice

Salt, to taste

Freshly ground black pepper, to taste

1. Melt the butter in the pressure cooker over medium heat. Add the onion, bell pepper, and celery; sauté for 3 minutes or until the vegetables are soft. Add the minced garlic and sauté an additional 30 seconds.

2. Stir in the corn, tomatoes, chopped cilantro, cayenne pepper, tomato juice, salt, and pepper. Lock the lid into place and bring to low pressure; maintain pressure for 3 minutes.

3. Remove from heat and quick-release the pressure. Use a slotted spoon to immediately transfer the corn and vegetables to a serving bowl. Taste for seasoning and add additional salt and pepper if needed. Garnish with cilantro and serve.

Mango Chutney

This versatile chutney is good with Indian foods, greens or grains, meats and poultry, and even over ice cream.

INGREDIENTS | YIELD: 2 CUPS

2 almost ripe mangoes

2 small serrano or jalapeño peppers

1 large clove garlic

2 teaspoons fresh ginger, grated

6 unsweetened dried plums, coarsely chopped

¾ cup dark brown sugar, firmly packed

¾ cup raw cane sugar or turbinado sugar

1 cup white wine vinegar

2 teaspoons mustard powder

Pinch salt

1. Peel mangoes. Remove the pit and cut the fruit into small pieces. Seed and mince the peppers. Peel and mince the garlic. Add the mangoes, peppers, and garlic to the pressure cooker along with the remaining ingredients. Stir to combine.

2. Lock the lid into place. Bring to high pressure and cook for 5 minutes. Remove from heat and let sit for 7 minutes. Quick-release remaining pressure. Remove the lid, return the pan to the heat, and bring to a boil; boil briskly for 10 minutes. Cover and refrigerate overnight before using. Can be stored covered in the refrigerator for up to 6 weeks.

Thanksgiving Jam

This recipe makes enough of this festive jam to last through the entire holiday—with some left over for gifts.

INGREDIENTS | YIELD: 6 CUPS

1 pound cranberries

1 pound strawberries, hulled and diced

8 ounces blueberries

4 ounces rhubarb, diced

4 ounces dried black currants or raisins

1 lemon

6 cups granulated cane sugar

¼ cup water

Pinch salt

Holiday Jam Sauce for Leftover Turkey

Mix some Dijon mustard into some Holiday Jam and spread it over leftover turkey before you reheat it. The distinct flavor of the Dijon mustard combined with its ability to act as an emulsifier (so that it's completed blended into the jam) turns the combination into a succulent sauce.

1. Add the cranberries, strawberries, blueberries, rhubarb, currants or raisins, and lemon zest and juice to the pressure cooker. Stir in the sugar. Set aside for 1 hour, until the fruit is juicy.

2. Stir in the water and salt. Put the cooker over medium-high heat and bring the mixture to a boil. Lock the lid into place and bring the cooker to high pressure. Lower the heat to medium-low or sufficient heat to maintain the pressure for 10 minutes.

3. Remove from the heat and allow pressure to release naturally.

4. Remove the lid and return the pressure cooker to the heat. Bring to a boil. Boil rapidly for 3 minutes or until the gel point is reached. Skim off and discard any foam. Ladle into hot, sterilized glass containers or jars, leaving ½ inch of head space. Seal the containers or jars. Cool and refrigerate for a week or freeze. (If you prefer, you can follow the instructions that came with your canning jars and process the jam for shelf storage.)

Blueberry Jam

You can substitute a 6-ounce bottle of pectin for the dry pectin.

INGREDIENTS | **YIELD: 4 CUPS**

4 cups blueberries

4 cups granulated cane sugar

1 cup orange juice

1 teaspoon orange zest

Pinch freshly ground nutmeg

Pinch salt

1 1¾-ounce package dry pectin

1. Add the blueberries, sugar, orange juice, orange zest, nutmeg, and salt to the pressure cooker. Stir to combine.

2. Lock on the lid and bring to low pressure. Maintain pressure for 3 minutes. Remove from the heat and allow pressure to release naturally.

3. Remove the lid. Either process in a food mill to separate the pulp from the skins or push the blueberry mixture through a strainer.

4. Return the pulp to the pressure cooker. Place over medium-high heat, stir in the pectin, and bring mixture to a rolling boil, stirring constantly. Continue to boil and stir for 1 minute.

5. Skim off and discard any foam. Ladle into hot, sterilized glass containers or jars, leaving 1 inch of headspace. Seal the containers or jars. Cool and refrigerate for up to 5 weeks or freeze for up to 8 months. (If you prefer, you can follow the instructions that came with your canning jars and process the preserves for shelf storage.)

Mincemeat

Use mincemeat as a condiment or in mincemeat pie.

INGREDIENTS | **YIELD: 5 CUPS**

2½ pounds pears

1 tart green apple

1 lemon

1 orange

1 cup golden raisins

½ cup dried cranberries or currants

½ cup light brown sugar, firmly packed

1 teaspoon ground cinnamon

½ teaspoon ground ginger

¼ teaspoon ground cloves

¼ teaspoon ground nutmeg

Pinch salt

½ cup walnuts or pecans, chopped and toasted

½ cup brandy or cognac

Mincemeat Seasoning

Seasoning is an arbitrary thing. You'll want to add some of the spices to the mincemeat before you cook it, but if you prefer to taste for seasoning and then increase the spices according to your taste, use half of the spices during the cooking process and add more later if desired.

1. Peel, core, and dice the pears and apple. Wash the lemon and orange to remove any waxy coating. Add to the pressure cooker along with lemon zest and juice, orange zest and juice, raisins, cranberries or currants, brown sugar, cinnamon, ginger, cloves, nutmeg, and salt. Stir to combine.

2. Lock the lid into place and bring to high pressure; maintain pressure for 10 minutes. Remove from heat and allow pressure to release naturally.

3. Return to heat and bring to a simmer. Simmer for 10 minutes or until mixture is very thick. Stir in the nuts and brandy or cognac. Continue to simmer for an additional 5 minutes.

4. Ladle into hot, sterilized glass containers or jars, leaving ½ inch of headspace. Seal the containers or jars. Cool and then refrigerate for a week or freeze. (If you prefer, you can follow the instructions that came with your canning jars and process the preserves for shelf storage.)

Peach and Toasted Almond Preserves

Toasting the almonds is an important step that enhances the rich flavor of these preserves.

INGREDIENTS | **YIELD: 4 CUPS**

6 fresh ripe peaches

1 cup water

1 8-ounce package dried apricots, diced

½ cup toasted almonds

1¼ cups orange juice

¼ cup lemon juice

4½ cups granulated cane sugar

2 whole cloves

1 3-inch cinnamon stick

Pinch salt

1 1¾-ounce package pectin powder

Toasting Nuts

Preheat oven to 350°F. Place nuts on a shallow baking pan. Stirring occasionally, bake for 8 minutes or until the nuts are fragrant and golden brown. You can also toast nuts in a frying pan over medium-high heat. Stir and shake the pan constantly for 5 minutes or until nuts are golden brown.

1. Use a skewer or toothpick to poke several holes in each of the peaches. Place the peaches in the pressure cooker and pour the water over them. Lock on the lid on the pressure cooker. Bring to high pressure and maintain for 3 minutes.

2. Quick-release the pressure and remove the lid. Use a slotted spoon to move the peaches to a large bowl of ice water or to a bowl under cold running water. Peel the peaches and then cut them into small pieces, discarding the pits.

3. Add the peaches, apricots, almonds, orange juice, lemon juice, sugar, cloves, cinnamon stick, and salt to water remaining in the pressure cooker. Stir to combine. Lock on the lid and bring to high pressure; maintain pressure for 2 minutes.

4. Remove the pressure cooker from the heat. Quick-release the pressure and remove the lid. Remove the cloves and cinnamon stick; discard. Stir the pectin into the fruit mixture. Return to the heat and bring to a rolling boil over medium-high heat, stirring constantly.

5. Skim off and discard any foam. Ladle into hot, sterilized glass containers or jars, leaving 1 inch of headspace. Seal the containers or jars. Cool and then refrigerate for up to 5 weeks or freeze for up to 8 months. (If you prefer, you can follow the instructions that came with your canning jars and process the preserves for shelf storage.)

CHAPTER 3

Appetizers and Party Fare

Hummus
23

Baba Ghanoush
24

Savory Cheesecake
24

Dhal
26

Taco Chips Dip
27

Black Bean Dip
28

Chilled Cantaloupe
and Potato Soup
29

Stuffed Grape Leaves
30

Caribbean Relish
31

Mini Cabbage Rolls
32

Savory Sun-Dried
Tomato Cheesecake
33

South of the Border Chicken Dip
34

Hummus

Serve hummus with toasted pita chips or as a vegetable dip. Punch up the flavor with some dried spearmint and freshly ground black pepper if desired.

INGREDIENTS | YIELD: ABOUT 2 CUPS

1 cup chickpeas

2 teaspoons vegetable oil

4 cups water

1 teaspoon dried parsley

1 clove garlic, peeled and minced

2 tablespoons tahini

Salt, to taste

2 tablespoons lemon juice

¼ cup extra virgin olive oil or sesame oil

Optional: 6 tablespoons water or cooking liquid

Tahini

Tahini, sometimes also referred to as tahini paste, is sesame seed butter. It's available in toasted or untoasted varieties. It is a very common ingredient in Middle Eastern dishes, including hummus. You can substitute creamy peanut butter for the tahini if desired; like peanut butter, tahini contains very little saturated fat.

1. Add the chickpeas, vegetable oil, and 4 cups of water to the pressure cooker. Lock the lid into place; bring to high pressure and maintain for 40 minutes. Remove from the heat and allow pressure to release naturally. Remove the lid and check that the beans are soft and cooked through. Drain the beans if they're cooked through; if not, lock the lid back into place and cook the beans on high pressure for another 5 to 10 minutes.

2. Add the drained, cooked beans, parsley, garlic, tahini, salt, and lemon juice to a food processor or blender. Pulse to combine. Remove the lid and scrape down the sides of the food processor or blender bowl.

3. Reattach the lid to the food processor or blender, and add the olive oil with the machine running. Process until smooth, adding water or reserved cooking liquid a tablespoon at a time if necessary.

Baba Ghanoush

Serve with toasted pita chips or as a vegetable dip.

INGREDIENTS | YIELD: 1½ CUPS

1 tablespoon olive or sesame oil
1 large eggplant
4 cloves garlic, peeled and minced
½ cup water
3 tablespoons fresh parsley
½ teaspoon salt
2 tablespoons fresh lemon juice
2 tablespoons tahini
1 tablespoon extra virgin olive oil

1. Add the olive or sesame oil to the pressure cooker and bring to temperature over medium heat. Peel and dice the eggplant and add it to the pressure cooker. Sauté the eggplant in the oil until it begins to get soft. Add the garlic and sauté for 30 seconds. Add the water.

2. Lock on the lid. Bring to high pressure; maintain pressure for 4 minutes. Remove the pan from the heat, quick-release the pressure, and remove the lid.

3. Strain the cooked eggplant and garlic and add to a food processor or blender along with the parsley, salt, lemon juice, and tahini. Pulse to process. Scrape down the side of the food processor or blender container if necessary. Add the extra virgin olive oil and process until smooth.

Savory Cheesecake

For this dish, you'll need a pressure cooker that's large enough to accommodate a 7-inch springform pan placed on a trivet or rack. (For 8 main dish servings, serve this savory cheesecake with a green salad, crusty bread, and fresh fruit.)

INGREDIENTS | SERVES 16

2 teaspoons unsalted butter, melted
¼ cup toasted walnuts, finely chopped
3 8-ounce packages cream cheese
3 large eggs
2 teaspoons fresh lemon juice
1 teaspoon sage
⅛ teaspoon freshly ground white pepper
1 cup Gorgonzola cheese, crumbled
2 cups hot water

1. Coat the bottom and sides of a 7-inch springform pan with melted butter. Place a 16" × 16" piece of plastic wrap on top of an equal-sized piece of aluminum foil. Put the springform pan in the center of the plastic wrap–topped foil; form and crimp the foil around the springform pan to seal the bottom of the pan.

2. Pour the walnuts into the pan; turn the pan so that the walnuts cling to the butter and coat the bottom and sides of the pan.

Savory Cheesecake (*continued*)

3. Cut the cream cheese into 1-inch squares and add to a food processor; process until smooth. Add the eggs, lemon juice, sage, and pepper. Process for 1 minute, scrape down the bowl, and then process until smooth. Add the Gorgonzola cheese and pulse to mix the cheese into the cream cheese mixture. Pour the mixture into the springform pan.

4. Place a trivet or rack on the bottom of the pressure cooker. Pour in the hot water. Crisscross two 24" × 2" strips of foil on the counter and place the springform pan in the center. Cover the cheesecake mixture with a piece of foil treated with nonstick spray; lightly crimp this foil topper to keep in place over the pan. Bring the ends of the foil strips up over the springform pan; hold on to the strips and use them to lower the pan into the pressure cooker until it rests on the rack or trivet.

5. Lock on the lid and bring to high pressure; maintain the pressure for 16 minutes. Remove from the heat and allow pressure to release naturally. Remove the lid and lift the cheesecake from the pan. Remove the foil cover from the springform pan. Carefully use a piece of paper towel to sop up any moisture that may have accumulated on top of the cheesecake. Let the cheesecake cool to room temperature, then refrigerate overnight. To serve, remove the cheesecake from the springform pan, cut into pieces, and allow to come to room temperature.

Dhal

Serve spread on toasted flatbread or as a vegetable dip.

INGREDIENTS | YIELD: 2 CUPS

1 tablespoon olive oil

1 teaspoon unsalted butter

1 small onion, peeled and diced

2 teaspoons fresh ginger, grated

1 serrano chili pepper, seeded and finely diced

1 clove garlic, peeled and minced

½ teaspoon garam masala

¼ teaspoon ground turmeric

½ teaspoon dry mustard

1 cup dried yellow split peas

2 cups water

¼ cup plain yogurt or sour cream

2 tablespoons fresh cilantro, minced

1. Add the oil and butter to the pressure cooker and bring to temperature over medium heat. Add the onion, ginger, and chili; sauté for 3 minutes or until soft. Add the garlic, garam masala, turmeric, and dry mustard; sauté for an additional minute. Stir in the split peas. Pour in the water.

2. Lock on the lid. Bring the pressure cooker to high pressure; maintain for 8 minutes. Remove from the heat and allow pressure to release naturally. Transfer the cooked split pea mixture to a bowl; stir until cooled.

3. Add the yogurt or sour cream; whisk until smooth. Stir in the cilantro.

Veggie Wraps

Spread dhal over a soft tortilla, pita, or other flatbread and top with grilled vegetables, such as zucchini and red onions. Add couscous or cheese for even more taste. Roll up and serve. Whole wheat low-carb tortillas have extra fiber, so look for those at your grocery store.

Taco Chips Dip

Spoon Taco Chips Dip over shredded iceberg lettuce. Top with grated Monterey jack cheese, guacamole, and sour cream. Serve with baked tortilla chips.

INGREDIENTS | SERVES 16

1 cup dried kidney beans

2 cups water

¼ cup olive oil

1 large onion, peeled and diced

1 pound ground beef or turkey

2 cloves garlic, peeled and minced

1 8-ounce can tomato sauce

1 cup beef broth

1 tablespoon light brown sugar

2 teaspoons chili powder

1 teaspoon ground cumin

Optional: Dried red pepper flakes, to taste

Salt, to taste

Sodium-Free Version

You can eliminate the salt entirely from this dish if you substitute Mrs. Dash® Southwest Chipotle or Tomato Basil Garlic seasoning blend for some of the chili powder and the dried red pepper flakes. Use Mrs. Dash Extra Spicy seasoning blend if you prefer a hot, spicy dip.

1. Put the beans and water in a covered container and let soak at room temperature overnight. When ready to prepare the dip, drain the beans.

2. Bring the olive oil to temperature in the pressure cooker. Add the onion and sauté for 3 minutes or until softened. Add the ground beef or turkey; stir and break apart until the meat is no longer pink. Drain off any fat rendered from the meat. Add the garlic and stir into the meat.

3. Add the beans, tomato sauce, broth, brown sugar, chili powder, cumin, and red pepper flakes if using. Stir well.

4. Lock the lid into place and bring to high pressure; maintain pressure for 10 minutes. Remove from the heat and allow pressure to release naturally for 10 minutes. Quick-release any remaining pressure and remove the lid. Stir the dip, crushing the beans into the mixture. For a smooth dip, use an immersion blender or transfer the dip to a food processor or blender and process. Taste for seasoning and add salt if needed. Serve warm.

Black Bean Dip

To give this dip a little kick, you can substitute canned jalapeño peppers for the mild green chilies. Serve with corn chips or baked tortilla chips.

INGREDIENTS | SERVES 12

1 cup dried black beans

2 cups water

4 slices bacon, finely diced

1 tablespoon olive oil

1 small onion, peeled and diced

3 cloves garlic, peeled and minced

1 14½-ounce can diced tomatoes

2 4-ounce cans mild green chilies, finely chopped

1 teaspoon chili powder

½ teaspoon dried oregano

¼ cup fresh cilantro, finely chopped

Salt, to taste

1 cup Monterey jack cheese, grated

1. Add the beans and water to a container; cover and let the beans soak overnight at room temperature.

2. Add the bacon and oil to the pressure cooker. Fry over medium-high heat until the bacon is almost done. Add the onion; sauté for 3 minutes or until the onion is soft. Add the garlic and sauté for 30 seconds.

3. Drain the beans and add them to the pressure cooker along with the tomatoes, chilies, chili powder, and oregano. Stir well, scraping up any bacon bits clinging to the bottom of the cooker. Lock the lid into place. Bring to high pressure; maintain pressure for 12 minutes. Remove from heat and allow pressure to release naturally for 10 minutes.

4. Quick-release any remaining pressure. Remove the lid. Transfer the cooked beans mixture to a food processor or blender. Add the cilantro and process until smooth. Taste for seasoning; add salt if desired.

5. Transfer the dip to a bowl or fondue pot. Stir in the cheese. Serve warm.

Chilled Cantaloupe and Potato Soup

This soup is a great addition to a summer meal. Serve with spring rolls or a club sandwich.

INGREDIENTS | SERVES 8

3 large potatoes
1 jalapeño pepper
½ teaspoon salt
4 cups milk
1 large cantaloupe
1 tablespoon freshly squeezed lime juice
¼ cup sliced almonds, toasted
8 sprigs fresh cilantro
1 lime, cut into 8 thin rounds

1. Peel and dice the potatoes. Seed and halve the jalapeño. Add the potatoes, jalapeño, salt, and milk to the pressure cooker. Lock on the lid and bring to low pressure; maintain pressure for 10 minutes. Remove from the heat and allow pressure to release naturally.

2. Remove the lid. Use a slotted spoon or tongs to remove the jalapeño halves; discard. Transfer the cooked potato mixture to a blender or food processor.

3. Discarding the seeds and rind, cut the cantaloupe into small chunks. Add to the food processor. Puree. Transfer the soup to a covered container and refrigerate for at least 5 hours or overnight.

4. Just prior to serving, stir in the lime juice. Taste and adjust seasoning if necessary. Divide the soup into bowls. Garnish each with some toasted almonds, a cilantro sprig, and a lime round.

Stuffed Grape Leaves

A medium (about 5-ounce) lemon will yield about 2 teaspoons
of lemon zest and 2–3 tablespoons of juice.

INGREDIENTS | SERVES 16

⅓ cup olive oil

4 scallions, minced

⅓ cup fresh mint, minced

⅓ cup fresh parsley, minced

3 cloves garlic, peeled and minced

1 cup long-grain white rice

2 cups chicken broth

1 teaspoon salt

¼ teaspoon freshly ground black pepper

½ teaspoon lemon zest, grated

1 16-ounce jar grape leaves

2 cups water

½ cup fresh lemon juice

Dolmades

Stuffed Grape Leaves are often referred to as dolmades. Some versions call for spiced ground lamb or other ground meat to be added to the filling. Because these simply have a rice and herb filling, you can serve them as appetizers or as a side dish.

1. Bring the oil to temperature in the pressure cooker over medium-high heat. Add the scallions, mint, and parsley; sauté for 2 minutes or until the onions are soft. Add the garlic and sauté for an additional 30 seconds. Add the rice and stir-fry in the sautéed vegetables and herbs for 1 minute. Add the broth, salt, pepper, and lemon zest; stir to mix. Lock the lid into place. Bring to high pressure; maintain pressure for 8 minutes.

2. Quick-release the pressure. Remove lid and transfer the rice mixture to a bowl.

3. Drain the grape leaves. Rinse them thoroughly in warm water and then arrange them rib side up on a work surface. Trim away any thick ribs. Spoon about 2 teaspoons of the rice mixture on each grape leaf; fold the sides of each leaf over the filling and then roll it from the bottom to the top. Repeat with each leaf. Pour the water into the pressure cooker. Place a steamer basket in the pressure cooker and arrange the stuffed grape leaves seam side down in the basket. Pour the lemon juice over the stuffed grape leaves and then press heavy plastic wrap down around them.

4. Lock the lid into place. Bring to high pressure; maintain pressure for 10 minutes.

5. Quick-release the pressure. Remove the lid. Lift the steamer basket out of the pressure cooker and, leaving the plastic in place, let the stuffed grape leaves rest for 5 minutes. Serve hot or cold with Lemon Dipping Sauce (page 32) if desired.

Caribbean Relish

*Think of this relish as hummus with a Caribbean flair. Serve with tomato relish
as a condiment for grilled chicken or pork, or as a dip for corn chips.*

INGREDIENTS | SERVES 12

1½ cups red or white kidney beans

7 cups water

2 teaspoons vegetable oil

Salt, to taste

2 tablespoons tahini paste

⅜ cup crushed pineapple, drained

4 cloves of garlic, peeled and minced

¼ teaspoon dried cumin

¼ teaspoon ground ginger

¼ teaspoon freshly ground white pepper

½ cup fresh cilantro, minced

Tomato Relish

Peel, seed, and dice 2 large tomatoes. Add
to bowl and mix them together with ½ cup
thawed frozen corn, ¼ cup extra virgin
olive oil, and 6 diced scallions. Season with
salt, freshly ground black pepper, and fresh
lime juice to taste. It also tastes great with
sandwiches.

1. Add the beans to the pressure cooker and pour 3 cups
   water over them or enough to cover the beans
   completely. Cover and let soak overnight. Drain and
   return to the pressure cooker. Pour 4 cups water over
   the beans. Add the oil. Lock the lid into place. Bring
   to high pressure; maintain pressure for 10 minutes.
   Remove from the heat and allow pressure to release
   naturally for 10 minutes.

2. Quick-release any remaining pressure. Remove the lid
   and, if the beans are cooked through, drain them. If
   additional cooking time is needed, lock the lid into
   place, return to high pressure, and cook for an
   additional 2–5 minutes.

3. Add the cooked beans, salt, tahini, pineapple, garlic,
   cumin, ginger, pepper, and cilantro to a blender or
   food processor. Pulse until mixed but still chunky.
   Transfer to a covered container and chill.

Mini Cabbage Rolls

You can improve the flavor of these cabbage rolls by adding diced roasted red pepper instead of raw red bell pepper.

INGREDIENTS | YIELD: 30

1 medium head savoy cabbage

1 cup water

1 pound lean ground beef

1 cup long-grain rice

1 red bell pepper, seeded and minced

1 medium sweet onion, peeled and diced

1 cup beef broth

⅓ cup extra virgin olive oil

2 tablespoon fresh mint, minced

1 teaspoon dried tarragon

Salt and freshly ground black pepper, to taste

2 cups water

2 tablespoons lemon juice

Lemon Dipping Sauce

You can make a lemon dipping sauce for the stuffed cabbage leaves or stuffed grape leaves by whisking 2 beaten eggs, 1 tablespoon olive oil, 2 tablespoons lemon juice, 2 teaspoons Dijon mustard, and 1 teaspoon granulated cane sugar in a heavy saucepan over low heat until the sauce is thick.

1. Wash the cabbage. Remove the large, outer leaves and set aside. Remove the remaining cabbage leaves and place them in the pressure cooker. Pour in the cup of water. Lock on the lid. Bring to low pressure; maintain the pressure for 1 minute. Quick-release the pressure. Drain the inner cabbage leaves in a colander and then move them to a cotton towel.

2. Add the ground beef, rice, bell pepper, onion, broth, oil, mint, tarragon, salt, and pepper to a bowl. Stir to combine.

3. Add the reserved cabbage leaves to the bottom of the pressure cooker.

4. Remove the stem running down the center of each steamed cabbage leaf and tear each leaf in half lengthwise. Place 1 tablespoon of the ground beef mixture in the center of each cabbage piece. Loosely fold the sides of the leaf over the filling and then fold the top and bottom of the leaf over the folded sides. As you complete them, place each stuffed cabbage leaf in the pressure cooker.

5. Pour the water and lemon juice over the stuffed cabbage rolls. Lock the lid into place and bring to high pressure; maintain pressure for 15 minutes. Remove from the heat and allow pressure to release naturally. Carefully move the stuffed cabbage rolls to a serving platter, piercing each one with a toothpick if serving as appetizers.

Savory Sun-Dried Tomato Cheesecake

You can freeze this cheesecake for up to 3 months, so it makes the perfect make-ahead addition for a cheese plate. Thaw a wedge of the cheesecake in the refrigerator and then serve at room temperature spread on crackers or thin slices of crusty bread.

INGREDIENTS | YIELD: 1 7-INCH CHEESECAKE

3 tablespoons butter, melted

⅓ cup bread crumbs or savory cracker crumbs

½ cup sun-dried tomatoes in oil

6 cloves garlic, peeled and minced

1 teaspoon dried oregano

3 large eggs

3 tablespoons all-purpose flour

2 8-ounce packages cream cheese

¾ cup sour cream

½ cup scallion, diced

2 cups hot water

1. Coat the sides and bottom of a 7-inch springform pan with melted butter. Evenly distribute the crumbs over the bottom and sides of the pan. Place a 16" × 16" piece of plastic wrap on top of an equal-sized piece of aluminum foil. Put the springform pan in the center of the plastic wrap–topped foil; form and crimp the foil around the springform pan to seal the bottom of the pan.

2. Drain the tomatoes, leaving 1 tablespoon oil, and add to a food processor along with the garlic, oregano, eggs, flour, cream cheese, and ¼ cup sour cream. Puree until smooth. Stir in the scallions. Pour into the springform pan. Cover with foil; crimp to seal.

3. Place a trivet or rack on the bottom of the pressure cooker. Pour in the hot water. Use two 24-inch lengths of aluminum foil folded in half lengthwise twice to create 24" × 2" strips of foil. Crisscross the foil strips on the counter and place the springform pan in the center. Bring the ends of the foil strips up over the springform pan; hold on to the strips and use to lower the pan into the pressure cooker until it rests on the rack or trivet.

4. Lock the lid into place and bring to high pressure; maintain for 20 minutes. Remove from the heat and let rest for 7 minutes before quick-releasing any remaining pressure. Remove the lid and let the cheesecake continue to cool in the pressure cooker until all of the steam has dissipated.

5. Use the foil strips to lift the pan from the pressure cooker. Remove the foil lid. Sop up any moisture with a paper towel. Cool. Spread the remaining ½ cup sour cream over the top.

South of the Border Chicken Dip

You can adjust the heat of this dip depending on what type of salsa or chili powder you use. Alternatively, to add more heat you can add some crushed red pepper flakes and use jalapeño-jack cheese.

INGREDIENTS | SERVES 24

3 slices bacon, diced

2 tablespoons olive oil

1 medium white onion, peeled and diced

3 cloves garlic, peeled and minced

½ cup fresh cilantro, minced

⅓ cup salsa

¼ cup ketchup

½ cup chicken broth

1 teaspoon chili powder

1 pound chicken breast tenders, finely diced

Optional: 1 tablespoon all-purpose flour

1 cup Monterey jack cheese, grated

½ cup sour cream

Salt and freshly ground black pepper, to taste

1. Add the bacon and oil to the pressure cooker; bring to temperature and add the onion, garlic, and cilantro. Sauté for 3 minutes or until the onion is soft. Stir in the salsa, ketchup, broth, chili powder, and diced chicken. Lock the lid into place and bring to low pressure; maintain pressure for 6 minutes.

2. Remove the lid and simmer over medium heat to thicken the sauce. If needed, whisk the flour into the dip, bring to a boil, and then simmer for 2 minutes or until the flour taste is cooked out. Lower the heat and add the cheese, stirring constantly until it is melted into the dip. Fold in the sour cream. Taste for seasoning and add salt and pepper if desired. Serve warm with baked corn or flour tortilla chips.

CHAPTER 4

Sauces

Quick Demi-Glace
36

Bolognese Sauce
37

Chicken and Spinach
Curry Sauce
38

Country Barbeque Sauce
38

Plum Sauce
39

Kansas City–Style
Barbeque Sauce
40

Memphis-Style Barbeque Sauce
40

Cranberry-Applesauce
41

Fresh Tomato Sauce
41

Spaghetti Meat Sauce
42

Marinara Sauce
43

Sausage and Mushroom Sauce
44

Quick Demi-Glace

Quick is a relative term in this case. This demi-glace version takes several hours to make rather than more than an entire day of simmering sauces on the stovetop. This version omits the tomatoes, leaving you with the option of whisking in some sautéed tomato paste when a tomato back note is needed.

INGREDIENTS | YIELD: 1 CUP

1½ pounds veal bones
1½ pounds beef bones
1 pound chicken backs
Water
1 tablespoon vegetable oil
1 medium white onion, peeled and diced
1 large carrot, peeled and diced
1 celery stalk with leaves, diced
1 tablespoon dried parsley
½ teaspoon dried thyme
½ teaspoon whole black peppercorns
1 bay leaf

Defining Demi-Glace

Traditionally, the highly concentrated, rich half-glaze sauce known as demi-glace is created by reducing equal amounts of veal stock and brown sauce, the latter being one of the French mother sauces made by simmering brown roux, brown stock, bacon, aromatics (onions, celery, carrots), a bouquet garni (bay leaf, thyme, parsley, celery stalk, and peppercorns wrapped inside leek greens), and tomatoes.

1. Trim the bones of any fat, but leave some meat attached to them. Discard any chicken skin and chop the backs into 3-inch pieces.

2. Preheat the broiler. Arrange the bones in a roasting pan; place the pan in the oven about 6 inches away from the source of heat. Broil for 15 minutes on both sides. Add the chopped chicken backs to the pan and return the pan to the oven. Broil for another 15 minutes.

3. Discard the fat from the roasting pan. Place the pan over two burners on medium-high heat until the pan sizzles. Pour in 2 cups of water and stir it into the bones, scraping up the browned bits on the bottom of the roasting pan. Remove from heat.

4. Add the oil to the pressure cooker and bring to temperature. Add onion, carrot, celery, parsley, thyme, and peppercorns; sauté for 3 minutes. Add the bay leaf. Transfer the bones and water to the pressure cooker. Add additional hot water so that the water level is an inch above the bones. (Note: The bones and water should not fill the pressure cooker beyond two-thirds full.)

5. Lock the lid into place and bring to high pressure; maintain for 1½ hours. Remove from heat and allow pressure to release naturally. Strain the stock into a stockpot. Let rest for 10 minutes and then skim off and discard any fat. Place the stockpot over high heat and bring to a boil. Reduce the heat, but maintain and boil for an hour or until the liquid is dark brown and thick. Chilled demi-glace can be cut into cubes, wrapped in plastic, and stored in the refrigerator for 2 weeks, and can be frozen indefinitely in freezer bags.

Bolognese Sauce

*This rich meat sauce is the perfect topping for fettuccine. Serve
with a tossed salad and crusty, warm garlic bread.*

INGREDIENTS | YIELD: 4 CUPS

1 tablespoon unsalted butter

1 medium sweet onion, peeled and diced

1 medium carrot, peeled and diced

1 stalk celery with leaves, diced

1 clove garlic, peeled and minced

8 ounces ground round

8 ounces ground pork

8 ounces ground veal

2 tablespoons tomato paste

½ cup dry white wine

1 14½-ounce can diced tomatoes

1 bay leaf

½ cup heavy cream

Salt and freshly ground black pepper, to taste

A Less Expensive Alternative

Omit the ground veal and instead use 12 ounces each of ground round and ground pork. Stir ¾ teaspoon of Minor's Veal Base (*www.soupbase.com*) into the meat when you add the canned tomatoes. The veal base will add some sodium, so taste the sauce before you add any salt, or consider using no-salt-added canned tomatoes.

1. Melt the butter in the pressure cooker over medium-high heat. Add the onion, carrot, and celery; sauté for 3 minutes or until the vegetables begin to soften. Add the garlic and ground meat. Fry for about 5 minutes or until the meat loses its pink color, breaking the meat apart as you do so. Drain and discard any rendered fat. Stir in the tomato paste and sauté for 1 minute. Stir in the white wine and boil for about 2 minutes.

2. Stir in the undrained tomatoes. Add the bay leaf. Lock the lid into place and bring to high pressure; maintain pressure for 15 minutes.

3. Remove from heat and quick-release the pressure. Remove the lid. Return the pan to medium-high heat and bring to a boil. Stir in the cream, continuing to cook for about 5 minutes. Taste for seasoning and add salt and pepper as needed.

Chicken and Spinach Curry Sauce

The chicken and spinach create a layer in the pressure cooker that keeps the pasta sauce from burning on the bottom of the pan.

INGREDIENTS | SERVES 6

½ cup chicken broth or water

1 pound boneless, skinless chicken, cut into 1-inch pieces

2 10-ounce packages frozen spinach, rinsed of any ice crystals

1½ cups pasta sauce

1 tablespoon mild curry powder

2 tablespoons applesauce

Salt and freshly ground black pepper, to taste

6 cups cooked rice

Optional: Fresh cilantro

1. Add the broth and chicken to the pressure cooker and place the frozen spinach on top. Mix the pasta sauce with the curry powder and pour it over the spinach. Do not mix the sauce into the other ingredients.

2. Lock the lid in place. Bring to high pressure over medium heat; maintain the pressure for 5 minutes. Quick-release the pressure. Carefully remove the lid, add the applesauce, and stir well. If the moisture from the spinach thinned the sauce too much, simmer uncovered for 5 minutes or until the sauce is the desired consistency. Taste the sauce and add more curry powder, salt, and pepper if needed. Serve over cooked rice. Garnish with cilantro if desired.

Country Barbeque Sauce

You can use this barbeque sauce as a serving sauce served on the side, a dipping sauce, or a grilling wet-mop sauce.

INGREDIENTS | YIELD: ABOUT 5 CUPS

4 cups ketchup

½ cup apple cider vinegar

½ cup Worcestershire sauce

½ cup light brown sugar, firmly packed

¼ cup molasses

¼ cup prepared mustard

2 tablespoons barbeque seasoning

1 teaspoon freshly ground black pepper

Optional: 1 tablespoon liquid smoke

Optional: 2 tablespoons hot sauce, or to taste

Optional: Salt, to taste

Add all ingredients to the pressure cooker. Stir to mix. Lock the lid into place. Bring to low pressure; maintain for 20 minutes. Remove from heat and quick-release the pressure. Taste for seasoning and add the desired amount of optional seasoning. Ladle into sterilized glass jars; cover and store in the refrigerator for up to 3 months.

Plum Sauce

Plum sauce is often served with egg rolls. It's also delicious if you brush it on chicken or pork ribs; doing so near the end of the grilling time will add a succulent glaze to the grilled meat.

INGREDIENTS | **YIELD: 4 CUPS**

8 cups (about 3 pounds) plums, pitted and cut in half

1 small sweet onion, peeled and diced

1 cup water

1 teaspoon fresh ginger, peeled and minced

1 clove garlic, peeled and minced

¾ cup granulated sugar

½ cup rice vinegar or cider vinegar

1 teaspoon ground coriander

½ teaspoon salt

½ teaspoon cinnamon

¼ teaspoon cayenne pepper

¼ teaspoon ground cloves

1. Add the plums, onion, water, ginger, and garlic to the pressure cooker. Lock the lid into place and bring to low pressure; maintain for 5 minutes. Remove from the heat and quick-release the pressure.

2. Use an immersion blender to pulverize the contents of the pressure cooker before straining it, or press the cooked plum mixture through a sieve.

3. Return the liquefied and strained plum mixture to the pressure cooker and stir in sugar, vinegar, coriander, salt, cinnamon, cayenne pepper, and cloves. Lock the lid into place and bring to low pressure; maintain for 5 minutes. Remove from heat and quick-release the pressure. Remove the lid and check the sauce; it should have the consistency of applesauce. If it isn't yet thick enough, place the uncovered pressure cooker over medium heat and simmer until desired consistency is achieved.

Kansas City–Style Barbeque Sauce

Pan-toasting the smoked paprika before you add the other ingredients will intensify its smoky flavor.

INGREDIENTS | YIELD: 4 CUPS

2 tablespoons smoked paprika

3½ cups ketchup

½ cup light brown sugar

¼ cup molasses

¼ cup white distilled or white wine vinegar

¼ teaspoon cayenne pepper

1 tablespoon onion powder

1½ teaspoons celery seed

1 teaspoon celery salt

1½ teaspoons garlic powder

1 teaspoon ground cumin

2 teaspoons mustard powder

1½ teaspoons chili powder

1 teaspoon fresh lemon juice

1 teaspoon freshly ground black pepper

¼ teaspoon ground ginger

¼ teaspoon ground allspice

¼ teaspoon dried thyme

Add the smoked paprika to the pressure cooker. Lightly toast it over medium heat until it begins to release its smoked fragrance. Stir in the remaining ingredients. Lock on the lid and bring to low pressure; maintain pressure for 20 minutes. Quick-release the pressure. Allow sauce to cool and then refrigerate in a covered container for up to a week, or freeze until needed.

Memphis-Style Barbeque Sauce

Before you shape hamburger to fix on the grill, stir some of this barbeque sauce into the ground meat.

INGREDIENTS | YIELD: 4 CUPS

2 cups ketchup

1½ cups distilled white vinegar

¼ cup light brown sugar

2 tablespoons onion powder

¼ cup Worcestershire sauce

¼ cup prepared mustard

1 teaspoon freshly ground black pepper

Salt, to taste

Optional: Cayenne pepper or hot sauce, to taste

Add all ingredients except the salt and cayenne pepper or hot sauce to the pressure cooker. Lock on the lid and bring to low pressure; maintain pressure for 5 minutes. Quick-release the pressure. Stir the sauce and taste for seasoning; add salt and cayenne pepper or hot sauce if desired. Allow sauce to cool and then refrigerate in a covered container for up to a week or freeze until needed.

Cranberry-Applesauce

Don't substitute margarine for the butter in this recipe. Also, make sure that the ingredients don't go above the halfway mark on the pressure cooker. Serve this spiced sauce over cooked pork or ham.

INGREDIENTS | SERVES 8

4 medium tart apples

4 medium sweet apples

1 cup cranberries

Zest and juice from 1 large orange

½ cup dark brown sugar

½ cup granulated cane sugar

1 tablespoon unsalted butter

2 teaspoons ground cinnamon

½ teaspoon ground cloves

¼ teaspoon freshly ground black pepper

⅛ teaspoon salt

1 tablespoon fresh lemon juice

1. Peel, core, and grate the apples. Wash the cranberries. Add the cranberries to the pressure cooker and top with grated apples. Add the remaining ingredients.

2. Lock the lid into place and bring to low pressure; maintain pressure for 5 minutes. Remove from heat and allow pressure to release naturally. Remove the lid; lightly mash the apples with a fork. Stir well. Serve warm or chilled.

Fresh Tomato Sauce

You can use this sauce immediately, refrigerate it in a covered container for up to a week, or freeze it for 6 months.

INGREDIENTS | YIELD: 4 CUPS

2 tablespoons olive oil

2 cloves garlic, peeled and minced

2½ pounds fresh, vine-ripened tomatoes

1 teaspoon dried parsley

1 teaspoon dried basil

1 tablespoon balsamic vinegar

½ teaspoon granulated cane sugar

Salt, to taste

Freshly ground black pepper, to taste

1. Add the oil to the pressure cooker and bring to temperature over medium heat. Add the garlic; sauté for 30 seconds.

2. Peel and dice the tomatoes. Add them to the pressure cooker along with any juice from the tomatoes and the remaining ingredients.

3. Lock the lid in place and bring to low pressure; maintain for 10 minutes. Remove from the heat and allow pressure to release naturally.

4. Remove the lid and stir the sauce. If you prefer a thicker sauce, return to the heat and simmer uncovered for 10 minutes or until it reaches the desired thickness.

Spaghetti Meat Sauce

Be sure to have freshly grated Parmigiano-Reggiano cheese available to sprinkle over the pasta and sauce.

INGREDIENTS | SERVES 6

1 pound lean ground beef

1 large sweet onion, peeled and diced

1 stalk celery, diced

1 medium green bell pepper, seeded and diced

1 clove garlic, peeled and minced

Salt and freshly ground black pepper, to taste

1 cup water

1 8-ounce can tomato sauce

⅛ teaspoon dried red pepper flakes

1 teaspoon dried parsley

½ teaspoon dried oregano

½ teaspoon dried basil

¼ teaspoon dried thyme

2 teaspoons sugar

1 6-ounce can tomato paste

1. Add the ground beef, onion, celery, and green bell pepper to the pressure cooker. Fry for 5 minutes over medium-high heat or until the fat is rendered from the meat. Drain and discard the fat. Stir in the remaining ingredients, except for the tomato paste.

2. Lock the lid into place. Bring the pressure cooker to low pressure; maintain pressure for 10 minutes.

3. Quick-release the pressure. Remove the lid and stir in the tomato paste. Simmer the sauce uncovered for 5 minutes or until desired thickness is reached. Serve hot over spaghetti.

Marinara Sauce

Serve warm Marinara Sauce over pasta, rice, or vegetables.

INGREDIENTS | SERVES 6

2 tablespoons olive oil

1 large sweet onion, peeled and diced

1 small red bell pepper, seeded and diced

1 large carrot, peeled and grated

4 cloves garlic, peeled and minced

1 tablespoon dried parsley

½ teaspoon dried ground fennel

1 teaspoon dried basil

1 bay leaf

Pinch dried red pepper flakes

¼ teaspoon salt

1 14½-ounce can diced tomatoes in sauce

½ cup chicken broth

1. Add the oil to the pressure cooker and bring to temperature over medium-high heat. Add the onion, bell pepper, and carrots; sauté for 3 minutes. Stir in the garlic and sauté an additional 30 seconds. Stir in the remaining ingredients.

2. Lock the lid into place. Bring the pressure cooker to low pressure; maintain for 10 minutes.

3. Quick-release the pressure. Remove the lid. Stir the sauce. Remove and discard the bay leaf. If desired, use an immersion blender to puree the sauce.

English Muffin Pizzas

Brush both sides of an English muffin with extra virgin olive oil. Arrange on a baking tray and place under the broiler for 2 minutes or until the slices just begin to brown. Spoon warm Marinara Sauce over the slices, sprinkle grated mozzarella and Parmigiano-Reggiano cheese over the sauce, and top with pepperoni slices. Broil until the cheese is melted and bubbly.

Sausage and Mushroom Sauce

You can use spicy or sweet Italian sausage in this sauce, whichever you prefer. Or you can compromise and use sweet Italian sausage and add a pinch of dried red pepper flakes to taste.

INGREDIENTS | YIELD: 5 CUPS

1 tablespoon olive oil

2 medium sweet onions, peeled and diced

8 ounces ground beef

1 pound Italian sausage

1 red bell pepper, seeded and diced

4 cloves garlic, peeled and minced

1 cup mushrooms, sliced

1 medium carrot, peeled and grated

2½ teaspoons dried oregano

1 teaspoon dried basil

½ teaspoon fennel seed

1 teaspoon granulated cane sugar

1 bay leaf

1 14½-ounce can plum tomatoes

2 cups tomato juice

½ cup red wine

¼ cup tomato paste

Salt and freshly ground black pepper, to taste

Improvised Vegetable Soup

Create a quick soup for 4 by simmering a cup of Sausage and Mushroom Sauce, 2 cups of beef or chicken broth, and a 12-ounce bag of frozen mixed vegetables over medium heat in a large saucepan until the mixture is brought to temperature. Stir in a cup of cooked macaroni. Add 8 ounces diced fully cooked smoked sausage if you're serving the soup as the main course. Serve with garlic bread and a tossed salad.

1. Bring the oil to temperature in the pressure cooker over medium-high heat. Add the onion and sauté for 2 minutes. Add the ground beef; fry for 5 minutes or until it renders its fat and loses its pink color. Drain and discard any fat.

2. Remove the casing from the Italian sausage; break the meat apart and add to the pressure cooker along with the bell pepper, garlic, mushrooms, and carrots. Sauté and stir for 3 minutes. Stir in the oregano, basil, fennel seed, and sugar. Add the bay leaf.

3. Dice or puree the plum tomatoes and juices in the blender. Stir into the meat mixture in the pressure cooker along with the tomato juice, wine, and tomato paste.

4. Lock the lid into place. Bring to high pressure; maintain for 20 minutes. Remove from the heat and quick-release the pressure.

5. Return to the heat; stir and simmer the sauce uncovered for a few minutes to thicken it. Taste for seasoning and add salt and pepper if needed.

CHAPTER 5

Breakfast and Brunch

Breakfast Hash
46

Country Ham with
Red-Eye Gravy
47

Steel-Cut Oats
47

Enjoy-Your-Veggies Breakfast
48

Country Sausage Gravy
49

Sausage Links Brunch
49

Hash Browns with Smoked
Sausage and Apples
50

Cornmeal Mush
51

Sausage Brunch Gravy
51

Sausage and Cheese Scramble
52

Irish Oatmeal with Fruit
53

Breakfast Hash

Country-style hash browns are a mixture of diced potatoes, onion, and bell peppers.

INGREDIENTS | SERVES 4

8 ounces ground sausage

⅓ cup water

1 1-pound bag frozen country-style hash browns, thawed

4 large eggs

1 cup Cheddar cheese, grated

Optional: Salsa

Optional: ¼ cup fresh cilantro, minced

Breakfast Hash Alternative

If you only have regular hash browns on hand, fry a small peeled and diced sweet onion and a small seeded and diced red or green bell pepper along with the sausage. Hash browns are easy to prepare and make a fantastic addition to any breakfast or brunch.

1. Add the sausage to the pressure cooker; fry it over medium heat until it's browned and cooked through, breaking it apart as you do so.

2. Drain and discard any rendered fat. Pour in the water, stirring it into the meat, scraping up any meat stuck to the bottom of the pan.

3. Stir in the hash browns. Lightly beat the eggs and evenly pour them over the sausage and hash browns mixture.

4. Lock the lid into place and bring to low pressure; maintain pressure for 4 minutes.

5. Remove from the heat and quick-release the pressure. Remove the lid, evenly sprinkle the cheese over the top of the hash, and cover the pressure cooker.

6. Let sit for 5 minutes to allow the cheese to melt. Serve warm. Top each serving with salsa and fresh cilantro if desired.

Country Ham with Red-Eye Gravy

*Red-eye gravy is akin to au jus (a dipping sauce) rather than
a traditional thickened gravy. Serve with biscuits.*

INGREDIENTS | SERVES 4

1 tablespoon lard or vegetable oil

4 4-ounce slices of country ham

¾ cup coffee

1 teaspoon sugar

Cajun-Style Red-Eye Gravy

Following the directions for the Country Ham with Red-Eye Gravy recipe, substitute a pound of cooked roast beef for the country ham. When you add the coffee, add cayenne pepper or hot sauce, to taste. Serve over cooked rice and butter beans or peas.

1. Heat the lard or oil in a pressure cooker. Add ham and fry on both sides for 2 minutes. Add coffee. Lock the lid into place, bring to low pressure, and maintain for 8 minutes.

2. Remove from heat and quick-release the pressure. Remove ham to a serving platter. Add the sugar to the pan and stir until it dissolves, scrapping the bottom of the pan as you do so. Pour over the ham and serve immediately.

Steel-Cut Oats

Steel-cut oats, whole grain groats that have been cut into only two or three pieces, are sometimes referred to as Irish oatmeal. They are high in B-vitamins, calcium, protein, and fiber.

INGREDIENTS | SERVES 2

4 cups water

1 cup steel-cut oats, toasted

1 tablespoon butter

Pinch salt

Toasting Steel-Cut Oats

Preheat the oven to 300°F. Place the steel-cut oats on a baking sheet. Bake for 20 minutes. Store toasted steel-cut oats in a covered container in a cool place. Toasting steel-cut oats will enhance the flavor and allow them to cook in half the time.

1. Place the rack in the pressure cooker; pour ½ cup water over the rack.

2. In a metal bowl that will fit inside the pressure cooker and rest on the rack, add the oats, butter, salt, and 3½ cups water. Lock the lid into place.

3. Bring to low pressure. For chewy oatmeal, maintain the pressure for 5 minutes. For creamy oatmeal, maintain pressure for 8 minutes.

4. Remove from the heat and allow pressure to release naturally. Use tongs to lift the metal bowl out of the pressure cooker.

5. Spoon the cooked oats into bowls; season and serve as you would regular oatmeal.

Enjoy-Your-Veggies Breakfast

Adding toasted nuts provides protein. If you want to add more, you can stir in some diced tofu when you add the water.

INGREDIENTS | SERVES 4

1 tablespoon olive or vegetable oil

1 small sweet onion, peeled and diced

2 large carrots, peeled and diced

2 medium potatoes, peeled and diced

1 stalk celery, diced

1 large red bell pepper, seeded and diced

1 tablespoon low-sodium soy sauce

¼ cup water

1 cup zucchini or summer squash, peeled and diced

2 medium tomatoes, peeled and diced

Freshly ground black pepper, to taste

Optional: Brown rice or whole grain tortilla

Optional: Sunflower seeds, pumpkin seeds, or slivered almonds, toasted

1. Add the oil to the pressure cooker and bring to temperature over medium heat. Add the onion; sauté for 2 minutes.

2. Stir in the carrots, potatoes, celery, and bell pepper; sauté for 2 minutes. Add the soy sauce and water.

3. Lock on the lid and bring to high pressure; maintain pressure for 2 minutes. Remove from the heat and quick-release the pressure.

4. Return to the heat and add the squash and tomatoes. Bring to high pressure and maintain for 1 minute. Remove from the heat and quick-release the pressure.

5. Taste for seasoning and add pepper, to taste. Serve over rice or as filling in sandwich wraps, topped with your choice of toasted nuts if desired.

Country Sausage Gravy

This type of gravy is referred to as sawmill gravy in some parts of the country and as milk gravy in others. Serve it over buttermilk biscuits and hash browns with eggs.

INGREDIENTS | SERVES 8

2 pounds ground pork sausage

2 tablespoons butter

¼ cup all-purpose flour

2 cups half-and-half

Salt and freshly ground black pepper, to taste

1. Add the sausage to the pressure cooker. Breaking it apart as you do so, fry over medium-high heat for 5 minutes or until the sausage begins to brown.

2. Lock the lid into place and bring to low pressure; maintain for 8 minutes. Remove from the heat and quick-release the pressure. Drain and discard most of the fat. Return the pressure cooker to medium-high heat. Add the butter and stir into the sausage until it's melted.

3. Sprinkle the flour over the meat and stir-fry it into the meat for a minute, stirring continuously. Whisk in the half-and-half a little at a time. Bring to a boil and immediately reduce the heat; maintain a simmer for 3 minutes or until the gravy thickens. Taste for seasoning and add salt and pepper.

Sausage Links Brunch

Sausage links smothered in maple syrup are the hallmark Midwestern breakfast. This dish has a more savory twist and gets even better if you top each serving with a fried egg.

INGREDIENTS | SERVES 4

1 pound pork sausage links

4 large potatoes, peeled and sliced thin

1 medium sweet onion, peeled and diced

1 16-ounce can creamed corn

¼ teaspoon pepper

¾ cup tomato juice

Salt, to taste

1. Add the sausage links to the pressure cooker and brown them over medium heat. Remove the sausages to a plate.

2. Layer the potatoes, onion, and corn in the cooker. Sprinkle on the pepper. Place sausage links on top of the corn.

3. Pour the tomato juice over the top of the other ingredients in the cooker. Lock the lid, bring to high pressure, and maintain for 7 minutes.

4. Remove from the heat and let sit for 10 minutes or until the pot returns to normal pressure. Taste for seasoning and add salt and additional pepper if needed.

Hash Browns with Smoked Sausage and Apples

To make your own hash browns, peel and grate 1 pound baking potatoes, squeeze out any excess water with a potato ricer, and fry the potatoes in oil until they're golden brown. This dish is good topped with a fried or poached egg.

INGREDIENTS | SERVES 4

2 tablespoons olive oil

2 tablespoons butter

1 12-ounce bag frozen hash brown potatoes

Salt and freshly ground pepper, to taste

6 ounces cooked smoked sausage, coarsely chopped

2 medium apples, such as Golden Delicious, cut into thin slices

Optional: 1 teaspoon cinnamon

Optional: 1–2 tablespoons toasted walnuts, chopped

Optional: 1–2 tablespoons maple syrup

1. Add the oil and butter to the pressure cooker and bring to temperature over medium heat.

2. Add the hash brown potatoes; sauté for 5 minutes, stirring occasionally, until they are thawed and just beginning to brown. Season with the salt and pepper.

3. Use a wide metal spatula to press the potatoes down firmly in the pan. Add the sausage and apples over the top of the potatoes.

4. Sprinkle the cinnamon over the apples, top with the toasted walnuts, and drizzle with the maple syrup if using.

5. Lock the lid in place and bring to low pressure; maintain pressure for 6 minutes. Remove from the heat and quick-release the pressure. Serve.

Cornmeal Mush

This is cornmeal that's cooked into a thick porridge. It makes for a tasty and inexpensive breakfast food.

INGREDIENTS | SERVES 6

1 cup yellow cornmeal
4 cups water
½ teaspoon salt
1 tablespoon butter

1. In a bowl, whisk the cornmeal together with 1 cup water and salt. Set aside.

2. Add the remaining water to the pressure cooker. Bring to a boil over medium heat. Stir cornmeal and water mixture into the boiling water. Add butter and stir continuously until the mixture returns to a boil.

3. Lock the lid into place. Bring to low pressure; maintain for 10 minutes. Remove from heat and quick-release the pressure. Spoon into bowls and serve with a sweetener and milk or cream, like oatmeal.

Sausage Brunch Gravy

This gravy substitutes aromatic vegetables for some of the sausage. Serve it over rice or buttermilk biscuits and hash browns with eggs.

INGREDIENTS | SERVES 8

1 pound ground pork sausage
1 small sweet onion, peeled and diced
1 green bell pepper, seeded and diced
1 red bell pepper, seeded and diced
2 tablespoons butter
¼ cup all-purpose flour
2 cups half-and-half
Salt and freshly ground black pepper, to taste

1. Add the sausage, onion, and diced bell peppers to the pressure cooker. Fry over medium-high heat and break sausage apart for 5 minutes or until it begins to brown.

2. Lock the lid into place and bring to low pressure; maintain for 10 minutes. Remove from the heat and quick-release the pressure. Remove the lid. Drain and discard any excess fat.

3. Return the pressure cooker to medium-high heat. Add the butter, stir into the sausage mixture until it's melted. Add the flour and stir-fry it into the meat for 1 minute, stirring continuously. Whisk in the half-and-half a little at a time.

4. Bring to a boil and then immediately reduce the heat; maintain a simmer for 3 minutes or until the gravy thickens. Taste for seasoning and add salt and pepper if needed.

Sausage and Cheese Scramble

Serve with toasted whole grain bread or biscuits spread with some honey-butter. Experiment with different types of cheese to find your favorite.

INGREDIENTS | SERVES 8

1 tablespoon olive oil or vegetable oil

1 large sweet onion, diced

1 green bell pepper, seeded and diced

1 red bell pepper, seeded and diced

1 yellow or orange bell pepper, seeded and diced

1 pound ground sausage

1 1-pound bag frozen hash browns, thawed

8 large eggs

¼ cup water or heavy cream

Optional: A few drops hot sauce

Salt and freshly ground pepper, to taste

½ pound Cheddar cheese, grated

1. Add the oil to the pressure cooker and bring it to temperature over medium-high heat.

2. Add the onion and diced bell peppers; sauté until the onion is transparent, about 5 minutes. Stir in the sausage and hash browns.

3. Bring to low pressure; maintain for 10 minutes. Remove from the heat and quick-release the pressure. Remove the lid. Drain and discard any excess fat.

4. Return the pan to medium heat. Whisk together the eggs, water or heavy cream, hot sauce (if using), and salt and pepper.

5. Pour the eggs over the sausage-potato mixture. Stir to combine and scramble the eggs until they begin to set.

6. Add the cheese and continue to scramble until the eggs finish cooking and the cheese melts.

7. If you prefer, instead of stirring the cheese into the mixture, you can top it with the cheese, then cover the pressure cooker and continue to cook for 1–2 minutes or until the cheese is melted. Serve immediately.

Irish Oatmeal with Fruit

You can substitute other dried fruit according to your tastes. Try prunes, dates, and cherries for different flavors. Adding butter to this recipe gives it additional flavor and helps prevent the oatmeal from foaming, which can clog the pressure release valve.

INGREDIENTS | SERVES 2

3 cups water

1 cup toasted steel-cut oats

2 teaspoons butter

1 cup apple juice

1 tablespoon dried cranberries

1 tablespoon golden raisins

1 tablespoon snipped dried apricots

1 tablespoon maple syrup

¼ teaspoon ground cinnamon

Pinch salt

Optional: Brown sugar or maple syrup

Optional: Chopped toasted walnuts or pecans

Optional: Milk, half-and-half, or heavy cream

Cooking Ahead

If you're not a morning person, you can make Irish Oatmeal with Fruit the night before. Once it's cooled, divide between two covered microwave-safe containers and refrigerate overnight. The next morning cover each bowl with a piece of paper towel to catch any splatters and then microwave on high for 1 to 2 minutes or until heated through.

1. Place the rack in the pressure cooker; pour ½ cup water over the rack.

2. In a metal bowl that will fit inside the pressure cooker and rest on the rack, add the oats, butter, 2½ cups water, apple juice, cranberries, raisins, apricots, maple syrup, cinnamon, and salt; stir to combine.

3. Lock the lid into place. Bring to low pressure. For chewy oatmeal, maintain the pressure for 5 minutes. For creamy oatmeal, maintain pressure for 8 minutes.

4. Remove from the heat and allow pressure to release naturally. Use tongs to lift the metal bowl out of the pressure cooker.

5. Spoon the cooked oats into bowls. Serve warm, topped with brown sugar or additional maple syrup, chopped nuts, and milk, half-and-half, or heavy cream.

CHAPTER 6

Chicken

Chicken Broth
55

Chicken Bordeaux
55

Chicken Masala
56

Chicken Cacciatore
57

Pesto Chicken
58

Satay-Flavored Chicken
58

Curried Chicken Salad
59

Ginger-Chili Chicken
60

Chicken Stuffed with
Apricots and Prunes
61

Chicken in Spiced Orange Sauce
62

Herbed Chicken in Lemon Sauce
62

Chicken Paprikash
63

Chicken in Sweet Onion Sauce
63

Chicken in Red Sauce
64

Chicken Piccata
65

East Indian Chicken
66

Chicken Broth

The chicken fat that will rise to the top of the broth and harden overnight in the refrigerator is known as schmaltz. You can save that fat and use it instead of butter for sautéing vegetables.

INGREDIENTS | YIELDS ABOUT 3 CUPS

3 pounds bone-in chicken pieces
1 large onion, peeled and quartered
2 large carrots, scrubbed
1 stalk celery
Salt and freshly ground black pepper, to taste
4 cups water

1. Add the chicken and onion to the pressure cooker. Cut the carrots and celery into several pieces; add them. Add the salt, pepper, and water.

2. Lock the lid into place and bring to low pressure; maintain pressure for 20 minutes. Remove from the heat and allow pressure to release naturally.

3. Strain, discarding the cooked vegetables. Remove any meat from the bones and save for another use; discard the skin. Cool the broth and refrigerate overnight.

4. Remove the hardened schmaltz. The resulting concentrated broth can be kept for 1 or 2 days in the refrigerator or frozen for up to 3 months.

Chicken Bordeaux

Serve Chicken Bordeaux with buttered egg noodles, cooked rice, or potatoes prepared your favorite way.

INGREDIENTS | SERVES 4

3 tablespoons vegetable oil
1 clove garlic, peeled and crushed
3 pounds chicken pieces
1 teaspoon cracked black pepper
1 cup dry white wine
1 14½-ounce can diced tomatoes
4 ounces mushrooms, sliced

1. Bring the oil to temperature in the pressure cooker over medium-high heat. Add garlic; sauté to infuse the garlic flavor into the oil. Remove garlic and discard.

2. Rub chicken with pepper. Arrange the chicken pieces skin side down in the pressure cooker. Pour in the wine and tomatoes. Add the mushrooms.

3. Lock the lid into place and bring to low pressure; maintain for 10 minutes. Remove from the heat and quick-release the pressure.

4. Remove chicken to a serving platter and keep warm. Return the pressure cooker to the heat and simmer the sauce until it thickens. Pour over the chicken.

Chicken Masala

Make this dish tomato free by omitting the chicken broth and drained tomatoes and substituting an undiluted can of condensed cream of chicken soup. Serve the finished dish over cooked rice with Indian flatbread and a cucumber salad.

INGREDIENTS | SERVES 4

2 tablespoons ghee or vegetable oil

1 stalk celery, finely diced

1 medium sweet onion, peeled and diced

1 large carrot, peeled and grated

1½ tablespoons garam masala

1 clove garlic, peeled and minced

⅓ cup flour

½ cup chicken broth

1 14½-ounce can diced tomatoes, drained

1 cup coconut milk

1 pound boneless, skinless chicken breasts, diced

1 cup frozen peas, thawed

Salt and freshly ground black pepper, to taste

Garam Masala Spice Blend

Make your own garam masala spice blend by mixing together 1 tablespoon ground coriander, 2 teaspoons ground cardamom, 1 teaspoon cracked black pepper, 1 teaspoon ground cinnamon, 1 teaspoon Charnushka, 1 teaspoon caraway, ½ teaspoon ground cloves, ½ teaspoon freshly ground China #1 ginger, and ¼ teaspoon ground nutmeg. Store in a covered container in a cool, dry place.

1. Add the ghee or oil to the pressure cooker and bring to temperature over medium heat.

2. Add the celery; sauté for 1 minute. Add the onion; sauté for 3 minutes or until the onion is transparent. Stir in the carrot, garam masala, and garlic; sauté for 1 minute.

3. Stir in the flour, then whisk in the chicken broth. Stir in the tomatoes, coconut milk, and chicken.

4. Lock the lid into place and bring to low pressure. Maintain pressure for 10 minutes. Remove from the heat and allow pressure to release naturally.

5. Remove the lid and stir. If the sauce is too thick, loosen it by stirring in chicken broth or coconut milk a tablespoon at a time.

6. Return pan to medium heat, stir in the peas, and cook until the peas are heated through. Taste for seasoning and add salt and pepper if needed.

Chicken Cacciatore

Serve Chicken Cacciatore with pasta or rice, garlic bread, and a tossed salad.

INGREDIENTS | SERVES 4

1 3-pound chicken, cut up
3 tablespoons all-purpose flour
½ teaspoon salt
⅛ teaspoon freshly ground pepper
2 tablespoons vegetable or olive oil
¼ cup diced salt pork
1 large onion, peeled and sliced
2 cloves garlic, peeled and minced
1 tablespoon dried parsley
2 teaspoons Mrs. Dash Classic Italian Medley Seasoning Blend
2 large carrots, peeled and diced
1 stalk celery, diced
1 14½-ounce can diced tomatoes
Salt and freshly ground pepper, to taste
½ cup white wine
1 6-ounce can tomato paste

Italian Medley Seasoning Blend

Mrs. Dash Classic Italian Medley Seasoning Blend is a mixture of garlic, basil, oregano, rosemary, parsley, marjoram, white pepper, sage, savory, cayenne pepper, thyme, bay leaf, cumin, mustard powder, coriander, onion, and red bell pepper. All of the Mrs. Dash blends are salt free, which makes them a healthy addition to any dish.

1. Trim and discard any extra fat from the chicken. Add the flour, salt, and pepper to a large zip-closure bag. Add the chicken, seal the bag, and shake to coat the chicken.

2. Bring the oil to temperature in the pressure cooker over medium-high heat. Add the salt pork and sauté until it begins to render its fat.

3. Add the meatier pieces of chicken, skin side down, and brown until crisp. Add the remaining ingredients except for the tomato paste.

4. Lock the lid into place. Bring to low pressure; maintain pressure for 20 minutes.

5. Remove the pan from the heat and quick-release the pressure. Place the chicken on a serving platter and keep warm.

6. Return the pan to the heat, stir the tomato paste into the sauce in pressure cooker, and simmer for 5 minutes or until thickened. Pour the sauce over chicken.

Pesto Chicken

There's already salt and pepper in the pesto, so there's none called for in this recipe. Have it on the table for those who want to add more.

INGREDIENTS | SERVES 4

3 pounds bone-in chicken thighs
⅓ cup pesto
½ cup chicken broth
1 large sweet onion, peeled and sliced
8 small red potatoes, peeled
1 1-pound bag baby carrots

1. Remove the skin and trim the chicken thighs of any fat; add to a large zip-closure bag along with the pesto. Seal and shake to coat the chicken in the pesto.

2. Add the broth and onions to the pressure cooker. Place the trivet or cooking rack on top of the onions. Arrange the chicken on the rack and then add the potatoes and carrots to the top of the chicken.

3. Lock the lid into place. Bring to high pressure; maintain pressure for 11 minutes. Remove the pressure cooker from the heat. Quick-release the pressure. Transfer the chicken, potatoes, and carrots to a serving platter. Use tongs to remove the trivet or cooking rack.

4. Remove any fat from the juices remaining in the pan, then strain the juices over the chicken and vegetables. Serve hot.

Satay-Flavored Chicken

Serve this chicken dish over cooked jasmine rice. Drizzle with the peanut sauce. Serve with Indian flatbread and a cucumber salad.

INGREDIENTS | SERVES 4

½ cup coconut milk
1 tablespoon fish sauce
2 teaspoons red curry paste
1 teaspoon light brown sugar
½ teaspoon ground turmeric
¼ teaspoon freshly ground black pepper
1 pound boneless, skinless chicken breasts, cut into bite-size pieces

1. Add all ingredients to the pressure cooker. Stir to mix. Lock the lid into place and bring to low pressure; maintain pressure for 10 minutes. Remove from the heat and allow pressure to release naturally.

2. Remove the lid, return pan to medium heat, and simmer until the sauce is thickened. Pour over cooked jasmine rice.

Curried Chicken Salad

If you prepare the chicken the night before and refrigerate it in its own broth, the chicken will be moist beyond belief.

INGREDIENTS | SERVES 6

1 medium sweet onion, peeled and quartered

1 large carrot, peeled and diced

1 stalk celery, diced

8 peppercorns

1 cup water

3 pounds chicken breast halves, bone-in and with skin

¼ cup mayonnaise

½ cup sour cream

2–3 tablespoons curry powder

Salt, to taste

½ teaspoon freshly ground black pepper

1½ cups apples, diced

½ cup seedless green grapes, halved

1 cup celery, sliced

1 cup slivered almonds, toasted

2 tablespoons red onion or shallot, diced

1. Add the onion, carrot, celery, peppercorns, water, and chicken to the pressure cooker.

2. Lock the lid into place and bring to high pressure; maintain pressure for 10 minutes.

3. Remove from heat; allow pressure to release naturally for 10 minutes and then quick-release any remaining pressure.

4. Use a slotted spoon to transfer chicken to a bowl. Strain the broth in the pressure cooker and then pour it over the chicken. Allow chicken to cool in the broth.

5. To make the salad, add the mayonnaise, sour cream, curry powder, salt, and pepper to a bowl. Stir to mix. Stir in the apples, grapes, celery, almonds, and red onion or shallot.

6. Remove the chicken from the bones. Discard the bones and skin. Dice the chicken and fold into the salad mixture. Chill until ready to serve.

Ginger-Chili Chicken

Serve these thighs and sauce with rice, topped with coleslaw on a hamburger bun, or rolled into flour tortillas with romaine leaves.

INGREDIENTS | SERVES 6

1 cup plain yogurt

1 clove garlic, peeled and minced

2 teaspoons fresh ginger, grated

¼ teaspoon cayenne pepper

3 pounds boneless, skinless chicken thighs

1 14½-ounce can diced tomatoes

8 teaspoons ketchup

½ teaspoon chili powder

4 tablespoons butter

1 teaspoon sugar

½ cup cashews, crushed

Salt and freshly ground black pepper, to taste

Optional: Plain yogurt or sour cream

Optional: A few drops of red coloring

1. Mix together the yogurt, garlic, ginger, and cayenne pepper in a bowl or zip-closure bag; add the chicken thighs and marinate for 4 hours.

2. Remove the chicken thighs from the marinade and add them to the pressure cooker along with the undrained diced tomatoes, ketchup, and chili powder.

3. Lock the lid into place and bring to low pressure; maintain pressure for 8 minutes. Quick-release the pressure.

4. Use a slotted spoon to move cooked chicken thighs to a serving platter and keep warm.

5. Use an immersion blender to puree the tomatoes. Whisk in the butter and sugar. Stir in the cashews. Taste for seasoning and add salt and pepper, to taste.

6. If the sauce is spicier than you'd like, stir in some plain yogurt or sour cream 1 tablespoon at a time until you're pleased with the taste. Add red food coloring if desired. Pour over the chicken thighs and serve.

Chicken Stuffed with Apricots and Prunes

To offset the sweetness of the fruit in this dish, serve with a tossed salad dressed with a sour cream or other creamy dressing and dinner rolls.

INGREDIENTS | SERVES 4

1 3-pound chicken

12 pitted prunes, snipped

8 dried apricots, snipped

½ small lemon, cut into 6 thin slices

1 tablespoon vegetable oil

¼ cup finely minced shallots

2 stalks celery, finely minced

1 tablespoon finely minced fresh ginger

1 cup chicken stock

¼ teaspoon salt or to taste

2 medium sweet potatoes, peeled and halved

1 tablespoon grated orange zest

¼ cup Grand Marnier liqueur or orange juice

1. If available, remove the giblets from the chicken cavity. Chop the gizzard, heart, and liver and mix them together with the prunes, apricots, and lemon slices. Add the mixture to the chicken cavity.

2. Bring the oil to temperature in the pressure cooker. Add the shallots and celery; sauté for 2 minutes. Stir in the ginger.

3. Place the chicken, breast side down, in the pressure cooker. Pour in the broth and add the salt. Place the sweet potatoes around the chicken.

4. Lock the lid into place and bring to low pressure; maintain pressure for 25 minutes. Remove the pan from the heat and quick release the pressure. Carefully move the sweet potatoes and chicken to a serving platter; keep warm.

5. Stir the orange zest and liqueur or orange juice into the pan juices. Return the pressure cooker to the heat; bring to a boil over medium-high heat. Cook until the alcohol burns off or the sauce thickens slightly. Either pour the sauce over the chicken and potatoes or transfer to a gravy boat to serve the sauce on the side.

Chicken in Spiced Orange Sauce

Serve Chicken in Spiced Orange Sauce over rice. Have soy sauce available at the table.

INGREDIENTS | SERVES 8

2 tablespoons butter

3 pounds boneless, skinless chicken thighs

1 teaspoon paprika

½ teaspoon salt

⅛ teaspoon cinnamon

⅛ teaspoon ginger

Pinch ground cloves

½ cup white raisins

½ cup slivered almonds

1½ cups orange juice

1 1-pound bag baby carrots, quartered

1 tablespoon cornstarch

¼ cup cold water

1. Bring the butter to temperature in the pressure cooker over medium heat. Add the chicken thighs and fry for 2 minutes on each side. Add the paprika, salt, cinnamon, ginger, cloves, raisins, almonds, orange juice, and carrots.

2. Lock the lid into place. Bring to low pressure; maintain pressure for 10 minutes. Quick-release the pressure; remove the lid.

3. Combine cornstarch with the water and whisk into the sauce. Stir and cook for 3 minutes or until the sauce is thickened and the raw cornstarch taste is cooked out of the sauce.

Herbed Chicken in Lemon Sauce

Instead of the Minor's chicken base you can substitute the amount of chicken bouillon granules needed to make a half cup of broth. Serve with roast potatoes or cooked rice.

INGREDIENTS | SERVES 4

2 tablespoons olive oil

1 pound boneless, skinless chicken breast

½ cup white wine

2 tablespoons fresh lemon juice

2 cloves garlic, peeled and minced

½ teaspoon Minor's natural chicken base

1 teaspoon Dijon mustard

1 teaspoon dried parsley

½ teaspoon dried basil

½ teaspoon dried rosemary

¼ teaspoon dried oregano

1. Bring the oil to temperature in the pressure cooker over medium heat. Cut the chicken into bite-size pieces. Add to the pressure cooker; stir-fry for 5 minutes.

2. Add the remaining ingredients; mix well. Lock the lid into place and bring to low pressure; maintain for 10 minutes. Remove from heat and quick-release pressure.

3. If the sauce needs thickening, use a slotted spoon to transfer the chicken to a serving bowl and keep warm. Return the pan to the heat and simmer, uncovered, for 5 to 10 minutes. Pour the sauce over the chicken and serve.

Chicken Paprikash

This simple recipe takes hardly any time or effort at all. Serve with buttered egg noodles.

INGREDIENTS | SERVES 4

2 tablespoons ghee or vegetable oil

1 medium sweet onion, peeled and diced

1 green bell pepper, peeled and diced

5 cloves garlic, peeled and minced

4 chicken breast halves

¼ cup tomato sauce

2 tablespoons Hungarian paprika

1 cup chicken broth

1 tablespoon flour

¾ cup sour cream

Salt and freshly ground black pepper, to taste

1. Bring the ghee or oil to temperature in the pressure cooker over medium-high heat. Add the onion and green pepper; sauté for 3 minutes. Stir in the garlic. Add the chicken pieces skin side down; brown.

2. Mix together the tomato sauce, paprika, and chicken broth. Pour over the chicken. Lock the lid into place. Bring to low pressure; maintain pressure for 10 minutes.

3. Remove the pan from the heat and quick-release the pressure. Transfer the chicken to a serving platter and keep warm. Return the pan to the heat.

4. Stir the flour into sour cream, then stir into the pan juices. Cook and stir. Simmer for 5 minutes. Salt and pepper to taste. Pour sauce over chicken.

Chicken in Sweet Onion Sauce

Your family will love this rich, succulent one-pot meal. (You'll love it because it's quick and easy.) Serve with a tossed salad and dinner rolls.

INGREDIENTS | SERVES 6

1 tablespoon olive oil

1 tablespoon butter or ghee

2 large sweet onions, peeled and diced

8 ounces fresh mushrooms, sliced

6 boneless, skinless chicken breasts

1 10¾-ounce can cream of mushroom soup

6 medium potatoes, peeled and sliced

1 1-pound bag of baby carrots

2 tablespoons heavy cream

1. Bring the oil and butter or ghee to temperature in the pressure cooker over medium heat. Add the onion; sauté for 2 minutes. Stir in the mushrooms; sauté for 3 minutes.

2. Add the chicken, mushroom soup, and vegetables to the pressure cooker. Lock lid in place and bring to low pressure; maintain pressure for 8 minutes. Remove from heat and let pressure release naturally.

3. Remove the lid and transfer the chicken and vegetables to a serving platter; keep warm. Return pan to heat and stir in cream. Simmer and then pour sauce over the chicken and vegetables on the serving platter.

Chicken in Red Sauce

Serve with a hearty tossed salad that includes chopped hard-boiled egg, dressed with lemon vinaigrette.

INGREDIENTS | SERVES 4

1½ tablespoons olive oil

4 chicken leg-thigh pieces

Salt and freshly ground pepper, to taste

2 cups water

1 tablespoon paprika

1 medium carrot, scrubbed and halved

1 stalk celery, halved

1 bay leaf

1 1-inch cinnamon stick

Pinch cayenne pepper

2 whole cloves

2 small yellow onions, peeled and halved

½ cup dry sherry

1 tablespoon fresh lemon juice

½ cup slivered almonds, toasted

Lemon Vinaigrette

Whisk 2 tablespoons fresh lemon juice together with ½ teaspoon Dijon mustard, ⅛ teaspoon dried thyme, a pinch of sugar, ⅛ teaspoon salt, and ⅛ teaspoon freshly ground black pepper. Slowly pour ½ cup extra virgin olive oil into the lemon juice mixture, whisking as you do so. Taste for seasoning and adjust.

1. Bring the oil to temperature in the pressure cooker over medium-high heat. Remove and discard the skin from the chicken pieces.

2. Add the chicken to the pressure cooker. Sprinkle the pieces with salt and pepper, to taste.

3. Add the water, paprika, carrot, celery, bay leaf, cinnamon, and cayenne pepper. Stick a whole clove into each onion half; add them to the pressure cooker.

4. Lock the lid in place and bring to low pressure; maintain for 12 minutes. Remove from the heat and let rest for 10 minutes. Quick-release any remaining pressure.

5. Transfer the chicken to a serving platter and keep warm. Remove and discard the carrot and celery pieces, bay leaf, cinnamon stick, and onion.

6. Return the pressure cooker to the heat. Add the sherry and bring to a boil over medium-high heat. Simmer for 3 minutes. Stir in the lemon juice. Pour the sauce over the chicken and top with the almonds.

Chicken Piccata

If you prefer a more intense lemon flavor, add a teaspoon or two of grated lemon zest to the sauce just before you return the pan to the heat to bring it to a boil.

INGREDIENTS | SERVES 6

2 tablespoons olive or vegetable oil

4 shallots, peeled and minced

3 cloves garlic, peeled and minced

6 chicken breast halves

¾ cup chicken broth

⅓ cup fresh lemon juice

1 tablespoon dry sherry

½ teaspoon salt

¼ teaspoon freshly ground white pepper

1 teaspoon dried basil

1 cup pimento-stuffed green olives, minced

2 tablespoons extra virgin olive oil

1 tablespoon butter

1 tablespoon all-purpose flour

¼ cup sour cream

¼ cup fontinella cheese, grated

Optional: 1 lemon, thinly sliced

1. Bring the oil to temperature in the pressure cooker over medium-high heat. Add the shallots; sauté for 3 minutes. Stir in the garlic.

2. Arrange the chicken breast halves in the pressure cooker, skin side down. Add the broth, lemon juice, sherry, salt, pepper, basil, and olives. Lock the lid into place. Bring to high pressure; maintain for 10 minutes.

3. Remove from the heat and quick-release the pressure. Use tongs to transfer the chicken to a broiling rack, arranging pieces skin side up.

4. Brush the skin with the extra virgin olive oil. Place under the broiler at least 6 inches from the heat and broil to crisp the skin while you finish the sauce.

5. In a small bowl, mix the butter and flour together to form a paste. Stir in 2 tablespoons of the pan juices.

6. Return the pressure cooker to the heat and bring to a boil over medium-high heat. Once it reaches a boil, stir in the flour mixture.

7. Reduce heat to maintain a simmer for 3 minutes or until the mixture is thickened and the raw flour taste is cooked out of the sauce. Stir in the sour cream.

8. Move the chicken from the broiling rack to a serving platter. Pour the sour cream sauce over the chicken. Sprinkle the cheese over the top. Garnish with lemon slices if desired.

East Indian Chicken

Serve with cooked rice or couscous and a cucumber salad. Make a tangy vinaigrette for the salad with equal parts rice vinegar and chili sauce, a little sesame oil, and sugar, garlic powder, salt, and pepper to taste.

INGREDIENTS | **SERVES 6**

1 cup water

½ cup plain yogurt

1 tablespoon lemon juice

2 cloves garlic, peeled and minced

2 teaspoons grated fresh ginger or ½ teaspoon ground ginger

1 teaspoon turmeric

¼ teaspoon salt

1 teaspoon paprika

1 teaspoon curry powder

¼ teaspoon freshly ground black pepper

6 boneless, skinless chicken breasts

2 teaspoons cornstarch

2 teaspoons cold water

1. Mix water, yogurt, lemon juice, garlic, ginger, turmeric, salt, paprika, curry powder, and pepper in a bowl; add the chicken and marinate at room temperature for 1 hour.

2. Pour the chicken and marinade into the pressure cooker. Lock the lid into place and bring to low pressure; maintain pressure for 10 minutes.

3. Remove the pressure cooker from the heat and quick-release the pressure. Transfer the chicken to a serving platter and keep warm.

4. Mix the cornstarch with the cold water. Stir into the yogurt mixture in the pressure cooker.

5. Return the pressure cooker to heat and bring to a boil over medium-high heat. Boil for 3 minutes or until mixture thickens. Pour sauce over the chicken. Serve immediately.

CHAPTER 7

Turkey

Turkey Broth
68

Mock Bratwurst in Beer
68

Turkey Chili
69

Turkey Drumsticks and
Vegetable Soup
70

Pot Pie–Style Turkey Dinner
71

Turkey Thighs in Fig Sauce
72

Turkey Breast in Yogurt Sauce
72

Herbed Turkey Breast with
Mushroom Gravy
73

Braised Turkey Breast with
Cranberry Chutney
74

Turkey Breast Romano
75

Turkey Gumbo
76

Turkey à la King
77

Turkey in Creamy
Tarragon Sauce
78

Mini Turkey Loaves
79

Turkey Ratatouille
79

Turkey Broth

This method will result in a highly concentrated turkey broth. In most cases, for a cup of regular turkey broth you can mix ½ cup of this broth with ½ cup water.

INGREDIENTS | YIELDS ABOUT 3 CUPS

3 pounds bone-in turkey pieces

1 large onion, peeled and quartered

2 large carrots, scrubbed

1 stalk celery

Salt and freshly ground black pepper, to taste

4 cups water

1. Add the turkey and onion to the pressure cooker. Cut the carrot and celery each into several pieces; add them. Add the salt, pepper, and water.

2. Lock the lid into place and bring to low pressure; maintain pressure for 20 minutes. Remove from the heat and allow pressure to release naturally.

3. Strain, discarding the cooked vegetables. Remove any meat from the bones and save for another use; discard the skin. Cool the broth and refrigerate overnight. Remove and discard the hardened fat.

Mock Bratwurst in Beer

Bavarian seasoning is a blend of Bavarian-style crushed brown mustard seeds, French rosemary, garlic, Dalmatian sage, French thyme, and bay leaves. The Spice House (www.thespicehouse.com) has a salt-free Bavarian Seasoning Blend.

INGREDIENTS | SERVES 6

1 stalk celery, finely chopped

1 1-pound bag baby carrots

1 large onion, peeled and diced

2 cloves garlic, peeled and minced

4 slices bacon, cut into small pieces

1 2½-pound boneless turkey breast

1 2-pound bag sauerkraut, rinsed and drained

1 12-ounce can beer

1 tablespoon Bavarian seasoning

Salt and freshly ground pepper, to taste

6 medium red potatoes, washed and pierced

1. Add the ingredients to the pressure cooker in the order given. Lock the lid in place. Bring to low pressure; maintain pressure for 15 minutes.

2. Remove from the heat and allow pressure to release naturally. Taste for seasoning and adjust if necessary. Serve hot.

Bavarian Seasoning Substitution

You can substitute a tablespoon of stone-ground mustard along with ¼ teaspoon each of rosemary, garlic powder, sage, and thyme. Add a bay leaf (but remember to remove it before you serve the meal). Just before serving, taste for seasoning and adjust if necessary.

Turkey Chili

This dish is perfect for using up your Thanksgiving leftovers. Serve with cornbread or as a topper for baked potatoes and a tossed salad.

INGREDIENTS | SERVES 8

2 tablespoons extra virgin olive oil

3 pounds lean ground turkey

2 large sweet onions, peeled and diced

1 large red bell pepper, seeded and diced

4 cloves garlic, peeled and minced

3 tablespoons chili powder

1½ teaspoons ground cumin

1 teaspoon ground allspice

1 teaspoon ground cinnamon

1 teaspoon ground coriander

1 teaspoon dried oregano

2 14½-ounce cans diced tomatoes

¼ cup chicken broth

1 bay leaf

2 tablespoons cornmeal

Salt and freshly ground black pepper, to taste

1. Bring the oil to temperature in the pressure cooker over medium-high heat. Add the turkey and fry it for 5 minutes, occasionally breaking it apart with a spatula.

2. Stir in the onion and bell pepper; stir-fry with the meat for 3 minutes. Stir in the garlic, chili powder, cumin, allspice, cinnamon, coriander, and oregano.

3. Sauté the spices together with the meat for 2 minutes. Stir in the undrained tomatoes, broth, and bay leaf.

4. Lock the lid into place and bring to high pressure; maintain pressure for 10 minutes. Remove from the heat and allow pressure to release naturally. Remove the lid.

5. Return the pressure cooker to the heat. Stir in the cornmeal and simmer for 15 minutes or until the cornmeal thickens the chili. Remove and discard the bay leaf. Stir in salt and pepper to taste.

Cincinnati-Style Turkey Chili

Stir in a teaspoon of cinnamon when you add the other spices. After you simmer the chili and cornmeal together, stir in 2 tablespoons of semisweet chocolate chips and continue to simmer the chili until the chocolate is melted. Serve over cooked spaghetti and topped with grated Cheddar cheese.

Turkey Drumsticks and Vegetable Soup

Measure the turkey drumsticks to make sure they'll fit in your pressure cooker. It's okay if the end of the bone touches the lid of the cooker, as long as it doesn't block the vent.

INGREDIENTS | SERVES 6

1 tablespoon extra virgin olive oil

1 clove garlic, peeled and minced

2 14½-ounce cans diced tomatoes

6 medium potatoes, peeled and cut into quarters

6 large carrots, peeled and sliced

12 small onions, peeled

2 stalks celery, finely diced

½ ounce dried mushrooms

¼ teaspoon dried oregano

¼ teaspoon dried rosemary

1 bay leaf

2 strips orange zest

Salt and freshly ground black pepper, to taste

2 1¼-pound turkey drumsticks, skin removed

1 10-ounce package frozen green beans, thawed

1 10-ounce package frozen whole kernel corn, thawed

1 10-ounce package frozen baby peas, thawed

Fresh parsley or cilantro

1. Add the oil to the pressure cooker and bring to temperature over medium heat. Add the garlic and sauté for 10 seconds.

2. Stir in the tomatoes, potatoes, carrots, onions, celery, mushrooms, oregano, rosemary, bay leaf, orange zest, salt, and pepper. Stand the two drumsticks meaty side down in the pan.

3. Lock the lid and bring to high pressure; maintain high pressure for 12 minutes.

4. Remove from heat and allow the pressure to drop naturally, and then use the quick-release method for your cooker to release the remaining pressure if needed.

5. Remove the drumsticks, cut the meat from the bone and into bite-size pieces, and return the meat to the pot.

6. Stir in the green beans, corn, and peas; cook over medium heat for 5 minutes. Remove and discard the orange zest and bay leaf. Taste for seasoning and add salt and pepper if needed.

Pot Pie–Style Turkey Dinner

If you prefer, you can thicken this dish with ½ cup cornmeal instead of the butter and flour mixture.

INGREDIENTS | SERVES 8

1 tablespoon extra virgin olive oil

1 clove garlic, peeled and minced

4 cups turkey or chicken broth

6 medium potatoes, peeled and diced

6 large carrots, peeled and sliced

1 large sweet onion, peeled and diced

2 stalks celery, finely diced

½ ounce dried mushrooms

¼ teaspoon dried oregano

¼ teaspoon dried rosemary

1 bay leaf

2 1¼-pound turkey drumsticks, skin removed

2 tablespoons butter

2 tablespoons all-purpose flour

1 10-ounce package frozen green beans, thawed

1 10-ounce package frozen whole kernel corn, thawed

1 10-ounce package frozen baby peas, thawed

Salt and freshly ground black pepper, to taste

8 large buttermilk biscuits

1. Add the oil to the pressure cooker and bring to temperature over medium heat. Add the garlic and sauté for 10 seconds.

2. Stir in the broth, potatoes, carrots, onions, celery, mushrooms, oregano, rosemary, and bay leaf. Stand the two drumsticks meaty side down in the pan, arranging them so they don't block the pressure cooker vent when the lid is in place.

3. Lock the lid and bring to high pressure; maintain pressure for 12 minutes. Remove from the heat and allow the pressure to drop naturally, and then use the quick-release method for your cooker to release the remaining pressure if needed. Remove the drumsticks; cut the meat from the bone and into bite-size pieces and return it to the pot.

4. Mix the flour together with the butter, and then stir in some of the broth from the pan to make a paste. Return the pan to the heat, bring it to a boil over medium-high heat.

5. Stir in the flour mixture; reduce the heat to medium. Maintain a simmer and stir for 5 minutes or until the broth is thickened.

6. Stir in the green beans, corn, and peas; cook over medium heat for 5 minutes or until the vegetables are heated through. Remove and discard the bay leaf. Taste for seasoning and add salt and pepper if needed.

7. To serve, split the buttermilk biscuits in half and place them opened in serving bowls. Spoon the turkey and vegetables over the biscuits. Serve immediately.

Turkey Thighs in Fig Sauce

Balsamic vinegar brings out the flavor of the figs in the sauce for this dish, imparting a tart wine-like flavor. If you have room in the pressure cooker, you can add 4 scrubbed Yukon Gold potatoes and cook them along with the thighs.

INGREDIENTS | SERVES 4

4¾-pound bone-in turkey thighs, skin removed

1 large onion, peeled and quartered

2 large carrots, peeled and sliced

½ stalk celery, finely diced

Salt and freshly ground black pepper, to taste

½ cup balsamic vinegar

2 tablespoons tomato paste

1 cup chicken, turkey, or veal broth

12 dried figs, cut in half

Optional: Lemon zest, grated

Optional: ½ teaspoon fresh rosemary, chopped

1. Add the turkey, onion, carrots, and celery to the pressure cooker. Add balsamic vinegar, tomato paste, and broth to a bowl or measuring cup; whisk to combine and then pour into the pressure cooker. Season with the salt and pepper. Add the figs. Lock the lid into place and bring to high pressure; maintain pressure for 14 minutes. Remove from the heat and allow pressure to release naturally.

2. Remove the lid. Transfer the thighs, carrots, and figs to a serving platter. Tent loosely with aluminum foil and keep warm while you finish the sauce. Strain the pan juices. Discard the onion and celery. Skim and discard fat. Pour strained sauce over the thighs. Serve.

Turkey Breast in Yogurt Sauce

Serve over cooked rice or couscous with a cucumber-yogurt salad. To make the salad, combine plain yogurt, garlic, mint, salt, and ginger. Spritz with lemon juice and add thinly sliced cucumbers.

INGREDIENTS | SERVES 6

1 cup plain yogurt

1 teaspoon ground turmeric

1 teaspoon ground cumin

1 teaspoon yellow mustard seeds

¼ teaspoon salt

½ teaspoon freshly ground black pepper

1 pound boneless turkey breast

1 tablespoon ghee or butter

1 1-pound bag baby peas and pearl onions

1. In a large bowl mix together the yogurt, turmeric, cumin, mustard seeds, salt, and pepper. Cut the turkey into bite-size pieces. Stir into the yogurt mixture. Cover and marinate in the refrigerator for 4 hours.

2. Melt the ghee or butter in the pressure cooker. Add turkey and yogurt mixture. Lock lid into place and bring to low pressure; maintain for 8 minutes. Remove from heat and let pressure release naturally for 5 minutes. Quick-release any remaining pressure.

3. Remove lid and stir in the peas and pearl onions. Return pan to medium heat. Simmer until the vegetables are cooked and the sauce is thickened. Serve.

Herbed Turkey Breast with Mushroom Gravy

If you don't have time to prepare an entire Thanksgiving feast, this recipe will be more than adequate.

INGREDIENTS | SERVES 6

1 tablespoon vegetable oil

3 tablespoons butter

1 large sweet onion, peeled and diced

1 pound fresh mushrooms, sliced

4 cloves garlic, peeled and minced

2 teaspoons Mrs. Dash Garlic and Herb seasoning blend

1 2-pound boneless rolled turkey breast

1¾ cups chicken or turkey broth

½ cup sweet Madeira or Port

1 bay leaf

¼ cup all-purpose flour

Salt and freshly ground black pepper, to taste

1. Bring the oil and 1 tablespoon butter to temperature in the pressure cooker over medium-high heat. Add the onion; sauté for 3 minutes or until transparent.

2. Add the mushrooms; sauté for 3 minutes. Stir in the garlic and herb blend. Push the sautéed vegetables to the sides of the pan and add the turkey breast.

3. Cook the turkey for 3 minutes or until it browns on the bottom; turn the turkey over and fry for another 3 minutes. Use tongs to lift the turkey out of the pressure cooker. Spread the sautéed mixture over the bottom of the pot, and then insert the cooking rack.

4. Nestle the turkey on the rack. Add the broth, Madeira or Port, and bay leaf. Lock the lid into place. Bring to low pressure; maintain low pressure for 25 minutes. Remove from the heat and allow pressure to release naturally.

5. Remove the lid and transfer the turkey to a serving platter. Tent the turkey in aluminum foil and let it rest for at least 10 minutes before you carve it.

6. To make the gravy, remove the rack. Discard the bay leaf. Skim off any excess fat from the top of the broth.

7. In a small bowl or measuring cup, mix the remaining butter together with the flour. Stir in some of the broth to form a paste free of any lumps.

8. Bring the pan juices in the pressure cooker to a boil over medium-high heat. Stir in the flour mixture; lower the temperature to maintain a simmer and stir and cook for 3 minutes or until the gravy is thickened. Taste for seasoning and add salt and pepper if needed. Pour into a gravy boat.

Braised Turkey Breast with Cranberry Chutney

The cranberry juice will add some sweetness to the cooked cranberries. The optional brown sugar is a suggested amount; sweeten the chutney according to your taste.

INGREDIENTS | SERVES 6

2 cups cranberry juice

1 cup whole cranberries

1 large sweet onion, peeled and diced

1 3-pound whole turkey breast

1 teaspoon dried thyme

Salt and freshly ground black pepper, to taste

2 tablespoons butter, melted

1 teaspoon orange zest, grated

1 tablespoon lemon juice

Optional: ¼ cup light brown sugar

Intensified Cranberry Chutney

Reserve about ¼ cup of the diced onion and wait until you stir in the orange zest and lemon juice to add them to the chutney. The onion will cook until it's crisp-tender. Intensify the flavors by adding a generous amount of freshly ground black pepper at the end of the cooking time.

1. Place the rack in the pressure cooker. Add the cranberry juice, cranberries, and onion.

2. Rinse the turkey breast and pat dry with paper towels. Sprinkle the thyme, salt, and pepper over the breast. Place the turkey on the rack.

3. Lock the lid into place and bring to low pressure; maintain pressure for 25 minutes. Remove from the heat and allow pressure to release naturally.

4. Transfer the turkey breast to a broiling rack. Brush the skin with the melted butter. Place under the broiler; broil until the skin is browned and crisp.

5. Transfer the turkey to a serving platter and tent with aluminum foil; let rest for 10 minutes before carving.

6. Drain all but about ¼ cup of the juice from the cranberries and onions. Stir in the orange zest and lemon juice.

7. Return the pressure cooker to the heat and bring contents to a boil. Taste and stir in brown sugar to taste. Maintain a low boil until the mixture is thickened. Transfer to a serving bowl and serve with the turkey.

Turkey Breast Romano

You can substitute chicken breast tenders in this recipe. Serve over pasta along with a salad and garlic bread.

INGREDIENTS | SERVES 8

½ cup all-purpose flour

½ teaspoon salt

½ teaspoon freshly ground black pepper

2 pounds boneless, skinless turkey breast

2 tablespoons olive oil

1 large sweet onion, peeled and diced

4 cloves garlic, peeled and minced

1 tablespoon dried oregano

1 teaspoon dried basil

2 tablespoons tomato paste

½ cup turkey or chicken broth

1 8-ounce can tomato sauce

1 teaspoon balsamic vinegar

2 4-ounce cans sliced mushrooms, drained

1 tablespoon sugar

8 ounces Romano cheese, grated

1. Add the flour, salt, and pepper to a large zip-closure bag; seal and shake to mix. Cut the turkey into bite-size pieces. Add to the bag, seal, and shake to coat the turkey in the flour.

2. Bring the oil to temperature in the pressure cooker over medium-high heat. Add the turkey and onion; fry for 5 minutes or until the turkey begins to brown and the onion is transparent.

3. Stir in the garlic, oregano, basil, and tomato paste; sauté for 2 minutes. Stir in the broth, tomato sauce, vinegar, mushrooms, and sugar.

4. Lock the lid into place and bring to low pressure; maintain low pressure for 12 minutes. Remove from heat and allow pressure to release naturally for 10 minutes.

5. Quick-release any remaining pressure. Stir the cooked turkey and sauce; ladle it over cooked pasta and top with grated Romano cheese.

Turkey Gumbo

Filé powder is made from ground dried sassafras leaves; it helps flavor and thicken the gumbo. For a more robust flavor, add cayenne pepper to taste when you add the black pepper or have hot sauce available at the table.

INGREDIENTS | SERVES 4

2 tablespoons olive or vegetable oil

½ pound smoked andouille sausage or kielbasa

1 pound boneless, skinless turkey breast

1 large sweet onion, peeled and diced

4 cloves garlic, peeled and minced

1½ teaspoons dried thyme

1 teaspoon filé powder

¼ teaspoon dried red pepper flakes

½ teaspoon freshly ground black pepper

¼ teaspoon dried sage

½ cup white wine

3 bay leaves

2 stalks celery, sliced

1 large green bell pepper, seeded and diced

1 10-ounce package frozen sliced okra, thawed

½ cup fresh cilantro, minced

1 14½-ounce can diced tomatoes

1 14-ounce can chicken broth

1. Bring the oil to temperature in the pressure cooker over medium heat. Add the sausage slices.

2. Cut the turkey into bite-size pieces and add to the pressure cooker along with the onion.

3. Stir-fry for 5 minutes or until the turkey begins to brown and the onions are transparent.

4. Stir in the garlic, thyme, filé powder, red pepper flakes, black pepper, and sage.

5. Sauté for a minute and then deglaze the pan with the wine, scraping the bottom of the pressure cooker to loosen anything stuck to the bottom of the pan. Stir in the remaining ingredients.

6. Lock the lid into place and bring to low pressure; maintain pressure for 8 minutes. Remove from the heat and allow pressure to release naturally.

7. Remove the lid. Remove and discard bay leaves. Taste for seasoning and adjust if necessary.

Turkey à la King

Because it's made up of meat, vegetables, and sauce, Turkey à la King is almost a meal in itself.

INGREDIENTS | SERVES 4

3 tablespoons ghee or butter

1 pound skinless, boneless turkey breast

1 small sweet onion, peeled and diced

1 cup frozen peas

1 4-ounce can sliced mushrooms, drained

1 2-ounce jar pimientos, drained and diced

1 14-ounce can chicken broth

¼ cup all-purpose flour

½ cup heavy cream

Optional: ½ cup milk

Salt and freshly ground black pepper, to taste

Leftover Turkey or Chicken

In this recipe, you can substitute 2 or 3 cups of diced cooked turkey or chicken for the skinless, boneless turkey breast. If you do, sauté the onion and stir in the meat with the other ingredients. Reduce the time the dish is cooked under pressure to 2 minutes, and then quick-release the pressure.

1. Bring the ghee or butter to temperature in the pressure cooker over medium heat.

2. Cut the turkey into bite-size pieces and add to the pressure cooker along with the onion.

3. Stir-fry for 5 minutes or until the turkey begins to brown and the onions are transparent. Stir in the peas, mushrooms, pimientos, and broth.

4. Lock the lid into place and bring to low pressure; maintain pressure for 6 minutes. Remove from the heat and allow pressure to release naturally.

5. Remove the lid and return the pressure cooker to medium heat. Whisk the flour into the cream.

6. Once the pan juices in the pressure cooker reach a low boil, whisk in the flour-cream mixture.

7. Stir and cook for 3 minutes or until the mixture thickens and the flour taste is cooked out.

8. If the dish gets too thick, whisk in as much of the optional milk as needed to get it to the desired consistency. Taste for seasoning and add salt and pepper if needed.

Turkey in Creamy Tarragon Sauce

Save some of the white wine to drink with this refined dish. Serve over cooked rice or egg noodles.

INGREDIENTS | SERVES 4

4 slices bacon

1 pound skinless, boneless turkey breast

1 medium sweet onion, peeled and diced

2 cloves garlic, peeled and minced

½ cup dry white wine

2 tablespoons fresh tarragon, minced

1 cup heavy cream

Salt and freshly ground black pepper, to taste

'Tis the Season(ings)

If fresh tarragon isn't available, you can substitute 2 teaspoons of dried tarragon. Or use 2 teaspoons of your favorite seasoning blend, such as Mrs. Dash Onion and Herb Blend, Mrs. Dash Lemon Pepper Seasoning Blend, or Mrs. Dash Garlic and Herb Seasoning Blend. However, if you're using dried herbs, add them at the end of Step 3 instead of in Step 6.

1. Cook the bacon in the pressure cooker over medium heat until crisp. Move the cooked bacon to paper towels and set aside.

2. Cut the turkey into bite-size pieces and add to the pressure cooker along with the onion.

3. Stir-fry for 5 minutes or until the turkey is lightly browned and the onion is transparent. Stir in the garlic and sauté for 30 seconds. Deglaze the pan with the wine.

4. Lock the lid into place and bring to low pressure; maintain low pressure for 8 minutes. Remove from the heat and allow pressure to release naturally.

5. Remove the lid. Use a slotted spoon to transfer the cooked turkey to a serving bowl; keep warm.

6. Return the pressure cooker to medium heat. Stir the fresh tarragon into the pan juices. Bring the pan juices to a simmer. Whisk in the heavy cream; simmer until the cream is heated through.

7. Taste for seasoning and add salt and pepper if desired. Pour the sauce over the cooked turkey. Crumble the bacon over the top of the dish. Serve.

Mini Turkey Loaves

Serve with mashed potatoes and a steamed vegetable. Or use hot or cold in sandwiches.

INGREDIENTS | SERVES 6

1½ pounds lean ground turkey
1 small onion, peeled and diced
1 small stalk celery, minced
1 medium carrot, peeled and grated
½ cup butter cracker crumbs
1 clove garlic, peeled and minced
½ teaspoon dried basil
1 tablespoon mayonnaise
¼ teaspoon salt
¼ teaspoon freshly ground black pepper
1 large egg
3 tablespoons ketchup
Optional: 1 tablespoon light brown sugar

1. Add all ingredients to a large bowl and mix well. Divide the mixture between 2 mini bread loaf pans. Pack down into the pans.

2. Add the rack to the pressure cooker. Pour enough hot water into the pressure cooker to come up to the level of the top of the rack. Place the pans on the rack.

3. Lock the lid into place and bring to low pressure; maintain pressure for 20 minutes. Remove from the heat and allow pressure to release naturally.

4. Remove the lid. Use oven mitts to protect your hands while you lift the pans from the pressure cooker. Serve directly from the pans or transfer to a serving platter.

Turkey Ratatouille

Serve over cooked pasta or potatoes, or with thick slices of buttered French bread.

INGREDIENTS | SERVES 4

1 pound skinless, boneless turkey breast
2 tablespoons olive or vegetable oil
2 medium zucchini, sliced thick
1 medium eggplant, peeled and diced
1 medium sweet onion, peeled and diced
1 medium green bell pepper, seeded and diced
½ pound mushrooms, sliced
1 28-ounce can diced tomatoes
3 tablespoons tomato paste
2 cloves garlic, peeled and minced
2 teaspoons dried basil
¼ teaspoon dried red pepper flakes
Salt and freshly ground black pepper, to taste
Parmigiano-Reggiano cheese, grated

1. Cut the turkey into bite-size pieces. Bring the oil to temperature over medium heat. Add the turkey and fry for several minutes until it begins to brown.

2. Stir in the zucchini, eggplant, onion, bell pepper, mushrooms, undrained diced tomatoes, tomato paste, garlic, basil, and red pepper flakes.

3. Lock the lid into place. Bring to low pressure; maintain the pressure for 5 minutes. Remove from the heat and quick-release the pressure.

4. Taste for seasoning and add salt and pepper, to taste. Serve topped with grated Parmigiano-Reggiano cheese.

CHAPTER 8

Beef

Beef Broth
81

Brown Stock
82

Beef Braised in Beer
83

Grandma's Pot Roast
84

Mock Enchiladas
84

Barbequed Beef
85

Swiss Steak Meal
86

Barbeque Pot Roast
87

Citrus Corned Beef
and Cabbage
88

Onion Steak
89

Shredded Beef Burrito Filling
90

Steak Fajitas
90

Beef Roast Dinner
91

"Corn" Your Own Corned Beef
92

Beef Broth

Unlike chicken or turkey broth, beef broth requires a larger ratio of meat to the amount of bones used to make it. This method makes a concentrated broth. As a general rule, for a cup of regular beef broth you can usually mix ½ cup of this broth with ½ cup water.

INGREDIENTS | YIELD: ABOUT 4 CUPS

1 2-pound bone-in chuck roast

½ pound beef bones

1 large onion, peeled and quartered

2 large carrots, scrubbed

Salt and freshly ground black pepper, to taste

4 cups water

Beef Broth Variations

You can adjust how you season beef broth depending on how you intend to use it. For example, stir in several tablespoons of tomato paste when you add the water if you plan to use it for beef-vegetable soup. Almost any beef dish will benefit from the flavor imparted by several peeled and crushed cloves of garlic.

1. Add the chuck roast, beef bones, and onion to the pressure cooker. Slice the carrot and add to the pressure cooker. Add the salt, pepper, and water. If there is still room in the pressure cooker, add additional water to take the level to the fill line. Lock the lid into place. Bring to high pressure; maintain pressure for 55 minutes. Remove from heat and allow pressure to release naturally.

2. Use a slotted spoon to remove the roast and beef bones. Reserve the roast and the meat removed from the bones for another use; discard the bones.

3. Once the broth has cooled enough to make it easier to handle, strain it; discard the cooked vegetables. Cool and refrigerate the broth overnight. Remove and discard the hardened fat. The resulting concentrated broth can be kept for 1 or 2 days in the refrigerator or frozen for up to 3 months.

Brown Stock

When you add ¼ cup of this concentrated broth to a slow-cooked beef dish, you'll get the same, succulent flavor as if you first seared the meat in a hot skillet before adding it to the slow cooker.

INGREDIENTS | **YIELD: ABOUT 4 CUPS**

2 large carrots, scrubbed

2 stalks celery

1½ pounds bone-in chuck roast

1 pound cracked beef bones

1 large onion, peeled and quartered

Salt and freshly ground black pepper, to taste

4 cups water

1. Preheat oven to 450°F. Cut the carrots and celery into large pieces. Put them along with the meat, bones, and onions into a roasting pan.

2. Season with salt and pepper. Put the pan in the middle part of the oven and, turning the meat and vegetables occasionally, roast for 45 minutes or until evenly browned.

3. Transfer the roasted meat, bones, and vegetables to the pressure cooker. Drain and discard any fat in the roasting pan.

4. Add the water to the roasting pan; scrape any browned bits clinging to the pan and then pour the water into the pressure cooker.

5. If there is still room in the pressure cooker, add additional water to take the level to the fill line.

6. Lock the lid into place and bring the pressure cooker to high pressure; maintain pressure for 55 minutes. Remove from the heat and allow pressure to release naturally.

7. Use a slotted spoon to remove the roast and beef bones. Reserve the roast and the meat removed from the bones for another use; discard the bones.

8. Once the broth has cooled enough to handle, strain it; discard the cooked vegetables. Cool and refrigerate the broth overnight. Remove and discard the hardened fat. The resulting concentrated broth can be kept for 1 or 2 days in the refrigerator or frozen for up to 3 months.

Beef Braised in Beer

You can use a large onion and omit the leek if you wish. Serve with roasted or mashed potatoes and a steamed vegetable.

INGREDIENTS | SERVES 4

2 tablespoons Dijon mustard

Salt and freshly ground black pepper, to taste

1 teaspoon paprika

4 beef minute steaks, tenderized

1 tablespoon olive or vegetable oil

1 12-ounce bottle dark beer

2 tablespoons flour

1 tablespoon tomato paste

1 cup beef broth

1 medium yellow onion, peeled and diced

2 large carrots, peeled and diced

1 small stalk celery, finely diced

1 leek, white part only

Instead of Minute Steaks

You can substitute 6-ounce slices of beef bottom round or flank steak for the minute steaks. If you do, put each slice between two pieces of plastic wrap and pound them into thin slices before you coat them with the mustard mixture.

1. Mix together the mustard, salt, pepper, and paprika. Spread both sides of the meat with the mustard mixture.

2. Bring the oil to temperature in the pressure cooker over medium-high heat. Fry the meat, 2 slices at a time, for 2 minutes on each side. Remove the meat and set aside.

3. Deglaze the pressure cooker with ¼ cup beer, stirring and scraping to loosen any browned bits stuck to the bottom of the pan.

4. Whisk in the flour and the tomato paste. Whisk in the remaining beer. Add the beef back into the pan along with the broth, onion, carrots, and celery. Clean and slice the white part of the leek and add to the pressure cooker.

5. Lock the lid into place and bring to low pressure; maintain the pressure for 15 minutes. Remove from the heat and allow pressure to release naturally.

6. Remove the meat to a serving platter. If desired, use an immersion blender to puree the pan juices. Taste for seasoning and add additional salt and pepper if needed. Pour over the meat. Serve.

Grandma's Pot Roast

Turn this into two meals for four people by making roast beef sandwiches the next day. The meat will be tender and moist if you refrigerate the leftovers in the pan juices.

INGREDIENTS | SERVES 8

1 3-pound boneless chuck roast
1 1-pound bag of baby carrots
2 stalks celery, diced
1 green bell pepper, seeded and diced
1 large yellow onion, peeled and sliced
1 envelope onion soup mix
½ teaspoon black pepper
1 cup water
1 cup tomato juice
2 cloves garlic, peeled and minced
1 tablespoon Worcestershire sauce
1 tablespoon steak sauce

1. Cut the roast into serving-sized portions. Add the carrots, celery, green bell pepper, and onion to the pressure cooker. Place the roast pieces on top of the vegetables and sprinkle with soup mix and black pepper.

2. Add the water, tomato juice, garlic, Worcestershire sauce, and steak sauce to a bowl or measuring cup; mix well and then pour into the pressure cooker.

3. Lock the lid into place and bring to low pressure; maintain pressure for 45 minutes. Remove from the heat and allow pressure to release naturally.

Mock Enchiladas

To make this a one-dish meal, serve this dish over shredded lettuce and topped with chopped green onion, a dollop of sour cream, and some guacamole.

INGREDIENTS | SERVES 8

2 pounds lean ground beef
1 large onion, peeled and diced
1 4½-ounce can chopped chilies
1 12-ounce jar mild enchilada sauce
1 10½-ounce can golden mushroom soup
1 10½-ounce can Cheddar cheese soup
1 10½ ounce can cream of mushroom soup
1 10½-ounce can cream of celery soup
2 cups refried beans
Plain corn tortilla chips, to taste

1. Add the ground beef and diced onion to the pressure cooker. Bring to high pressure and maintain for 5 minutes. Quick-release the pressure and remove the lid. Remove and discard any rendered fat. Stir the ground beef into the onions, breaking the beef apart.

2. Stir in chilies, enchilada sauce, soups, and refried beans. Lock the lid into place and bring to low pressure; maintain for 5 minutes. If you'll be serving the dish immediately, you can quick release the pressure. Otherwise, remove from the heat and allow the pressure to release naturally. Stir 8 ounces or more tortilla chips into the mixture in the pressure cooker. Cover and stir over medium-low heat for 15 minutes or until the tortilla chips are soft.

Barbequed Beef

An English roast tends to pull apart easier, which makes it perfect for beef barbeque sandwiches. You can also serve beef barbeque over your favorite cooked pasta. Top with some grated Cheddar cheese and diced sweet or green onion.

INGREDIENTS | SERVES 8

1 3-pound beef English roast
1 cup water
½ cup red wine
½ cup ketchup
1 tablespoon red wine vinegar
2 teaspoons Worcestershire sauce
2 teaspoons mustard powder
2 tablespoons dried minced onion
1 teaspoon dried minced garlic
1 teaspoon cracked black pepper
1 tablespoon brown sugar
1 teaspoon chili powder
½ teaspoon ground cinnamon
¼ teaspoon ground cloves
¼ teaspoon ground ginger
Pinch ground allspice
Pinch dried pepper flakes, crushed

1. Halve the roast and stack the halves in the pressure cooker. Mix together all the remaining ingredients and pour over the beef.

2. Lock the lid into place and bring to low pressure; maintain pressure for 55 minutes. Remove from the heat and allow pressure to release naturally.

3. Use a slotted spoon to remove the beef from the slow cooker; pull it apart, discarding any fat or gristle. Taste the meat and sauce and adjust seasonings if necessary.

4. To thicken the sauce, return the pressure cooker to the heat. Skim any fat off the surface of the sauce and simmer uncovered while you pull apart the beef. Stir occasionally to prevent the sauce from burning.

Swiss Steak Meal

If you prefer a thick gravy, thicken the pan juices with a roux or cornstarch. Remember that you should never fill a pressure cooker more than two-thirds full. When in doubt about cooking times or other issues, check with the instruction manual that came with your cooker.

INGREDIENTS | SERVES 6

2½ pounds beef round steak, 1-inch thick

1 tablespoon vegetable oil

Salt and freshly ground pepper, to taste

1 medium yellow onion, peeled and diced

2 stalks celery, diced

1 large green pepper, seeded and diced

1 cup tomato juice

1 cup beef broth or water

6 large carrots, peeled

6 medium white potatoes, scrubbed

Optional: 4 teaspoons butter

1. Cut the round steak into 6 serving-size pieces. Add the oil and bring it to temperature over medium heat. Season the meat on both sides with salt and pepper.

2. Add 3 pieces of the meat and fry for 3 minutes on each side to brown them. Move to a platter and repeat with the other 3 pieces of meat.

3. Leave the last 3 pieces of browned meat in the cooker; add the onion, celery, and green pepper on top of them.

4. Lay in the other 3 pieces of meat and pour the tomato juice and broth or water over them. Place the carrots and potatoes on top of the meat.

5. Lock the lid into place; bring to high pressure and maintain the pressure for 17 minutes. Remove from the heat and allow pressure to release naturally.

6. Once pressure has dropped, open the cooker and move the potatoes, carrots, and meat to a serving platter. Cover and keep warm.

7. Skim any fat from the juices remaining in the pan. Set the uncovered cooker over medium heat and simmer the juices for 5 minutes.

8. Whisk in the butter, 1 teaspoon at a time, if desired. Taste for seasoning and add additional salt and pepper if needed.

9. Have the resulting gravy available at the table to pour over the meat. Serve immediately.

Barbeque Pot Roast

Whether you make it with beef or with pork, this barbeque is a delicious part of a casual supper when you serve it on sandwiches along with potato chips and coleslaw.

INGREDIENTS | SERVES 8

½ cup ketchup

½ cup apricot preserves

¼ cup dark brown sugar

¼ cup apple cider white vinegar

½ cup teriyaki or soy sauce

Dry red pepper flakes, crushed, to taste

1 teaspoon dry mustard

¼ teaspoon freshly ground black pepper

1 4-pound boneless chuck roast

1½ cups water for beef

1 large sweet onion, peeled and sliced

1. Add the ketchup, preserves, brown sugar, vinegar, teriyaki or soy sauce, red pepper flakes, mustard, and pepper to a gallon-size plastic freezer bag; close and squeeze to mix. Trim the roast of any fat, cut the meat into 1-inch cubes, and add to the bag. Refrigerate overnight.

2. Add the appropriate amount of water and the cooking rack or steamer basket to a 6-quart or larger pressure cooker. Place half of the sliced onions on the rack or basket. Use a slotted spoon to remove the roast pieces from the sauce and place them on the onions; reserve the sauce. Cover the roast pieces with the remaining onions.

3. Lock the lid in place on the pressure cooker. Place over medium heat and bring to high pressure; maintain for 50 minutes, or 15 minutes per pound (remember: you reduce the weight of the roast when you trim off the fat). Turn off the heat and allow 15 minutes for the pressure to release naturally. Use the quick release to release any remaining pressure, and then carefully remove the lid. Strain the meat, separate it from the onions, and return it to the pan. Puree the onions in a food processor or blender.

4. Pour the reserved sauce into the cooker and use two forks to pull the meat apart and mix it into the sauce. Bring to a simmer over medium heat. Stir in the onion. Skim the sauce for fat. Add ½ cup of the pan juices to the cooker and stir into the meat and sauce. Reduce the heat to low and simmer for 15 minutes, or until the mixture is thick enough to serve on sandwiches.

Citrus Corned Beef and Cabbage

If you want, you can slice 6 medium peeled potatoes and add them when you add the cabbage wedges in Step 4, or you can serve this dish with baked or fried potatoes.

INGREDIENTS | SERVES 6

Nonstick spray

2 medium onions, peeled and sliced

1 3-pound corned beef brisket

1 cup apple juice

¼ cup brown sugar, packed

2 teaspoons orange zest, finely grated

2 teaspoons prepared mustard

6 whole cloves

6 cabbage wedges

If You're Pressed for Space

If there isn't room for the cabbage and the meat, increase the time you maintain the pressure in Step 3 to 55 minutes. Let the pressure release naturally. Wrap the brisket in aluminum foil; keep warm. Add the cabbage to the pressure cooker, lock the lid into place, bring to low pressure, maintain for 8 minutes, quick-release, and proceed with Step 5.

1. Treat the inside of the pressure cooker with nonstick spray. Arrange the onion slices across the bottom of the crock.

2. Trim and discard excess fat from the brisket and place it on top of the onions.

3. Add the apple juice, brown sugar, orange zest, mustard, and cloves to a bowl and stir to mix; pour over the brisket. Lock the lid into place and bring to low pressure; maintain for 45 minutes. Quick-release the pressure and remove the lid.

4. Place the cabbage on top of the brisket. Lock the lid into place and bring to low pressure; maintain pressure for 8 minutes. Quick release the pressure and remove the lid.

5. Move the cabbage and meat to a serving platter, spooning some of the pan juices over the meat. Tent with aluminum foil and let rest for 15 minutes. Carve the brisket by slicing it against the grain. Remove and discard any fat from the additional pan juices and the cloves. Pour the pan juices into a gravy boat to pass at the table.

Onion Steak

Using brown stock saves a step: You don't have to brown the meat. Serve over mashed potatoes.

INGREDIENTS | SERVES 6

1 tablespoon olive or vegetable oil

4 large onions, peeled and sliced

1½ pounds round steak, cut into
6 pieces

4 cloves garlic, peeled and minced

1 tablespoon dried parsley

1 cup Brown Stock (see page 82)

1 teaspoon dried thyme

½ teaspoon dried rosemary

Pinch dried red pepper flakes

Salt and freshly ground black pepper,
to taste

¼ cup milk

2 tablespoons all-purpose flour

Beef Broth Instead of Brown Stock

If you'll be using beef broth instead of brown stock, increase the oil to 2 or 3 tablespoons and bring it to temperature in the pressure cooker. In batches, fry the meat for 3 minutes on each side. Layer the onions with the browned meat and then complete the recipe according to the instructions.

1. Use the oil to coat the bottom of the pressure cooker. In layers, add half of the onions, the meat, and the other half of the onions. Add the garlic, parsley, brown stock, thyme, rosemary, red pepper flakes, salt, and pepper. Lock the lid into place and bring to high pressure; maintain pressure for 14 minutes.

2. Quick-release the pressure and remove the lid. Move the meat to a serving platter; cover and keep warm. Whisk together the milk and flour, and then whisk the milk-flour paste into the onions and broth in the pan. Simmer and stir for 3 minutes or until the onion gravy is thickened and the flour taste is cooked out of the sauce. Pour over the meat or transfer to a gravy boat to pass at the table. Serve.

Shredded Beef Burrito Filling

*For more heat, substitute jalapeño, poblano, panilla, or Anaheim
peppers for the green pepper and use hot enchilada sauce.*

INGREDIENTS | SERVES 6

1 large sweet onion, peeled and diced

1 large green bell pepper, seeded
and diced

1 10-ounce can enchilada sauce

¼ cup water

1 3-pound English roast or beef brisket

1. Add the onion, green pepper, and enchilada sauce to the pressure cooker. Stir in the water. Trim and discard any fat from the roast. Place the roast in the pressure cooker. Lock the lid into place and bring to low pressure; maintain pressure for 50 minutes. Remove from the heat and allow pressure to release naturally.

2. Remove the meat to a cutting board and shred it. Return the shredded beef back into the sauce in the pressure cooker. Return the pan to medium heat; simmer uncovered for a few minutes to bring the meat back up to pressure and thicken the sauce.

Steak Fajitas

*You can serve this meat with the thickened sauce over rice or mashed potatoes. Or, if you
prefer, you can serve the drained meat and vegetables wrapped in a flour tortilla.*

INGREDIENTS | SERVES 4

1 pound round steak

1 small onion, peeled and diced

1 small green bell pepper, seeded
and diced

Salt and freshly ground black pepper,
to taste

2 cups frozen whole kernel corn, thawed

1¼ cups tomato juice

½ teaspoon chili powder

Optional: 1 tablespoon cornstarch

Optional: ¼ cup cold water

1. Trim and discard any fat from the meat. Cut the meat into ½-inch diced pieces and add to the pressure cooker. Stir in the onion, bell pepper, salt, pepper, corn, tomato juice, and chili powder. Lock the lid into place and bring to low pressure; maintain pressure for 12 minutes. Remove from the heat and allow pressure to release naturally for 5 minutes. Quick release any remaining pressure.

2. Optional: To thicken the sauce, in a small bowl or measuring cup whisk the cornstarch together with the cold water. Return the pressure cooker to medium heat and bring to a simmer; whisk in the cornstarch slurry and cook uncovered for 5 minutes Add additional salt and pepper if needed.

Beef Roast Dinner

Serve this roast with a tossed salad and warm buttered dinner rolls. Have sour cream at the table for the potatoes.

INGREDIENTS | SERVES 6

1 tablespoon vegetable oil

1 stalk celery, finely diced

1 1-pound bag baby carrots

1 large onion, peeled and diced

1 3-pound rump roast

Salt and freshly ground black pepper, to taste

Optional: 1 tablespoon Dijon mustard

6 medium Yukon Gold or red potatoes, scrubbed

3 cups beef broth

Optional: Water

1 tablespoon butter

Optional: Fresh parsley

Gravy Alternative

If you prefer gravy with your roast instead of au jus, increase the butter to 2 table-spoons and blend it with 2 tablespoons of all-purpose flour. When the pan juices come to a boil, begin whisking in the butter-flour paste a teaspoon at a time. When it's all added, boil for a minute and then reduce the heat; stir and simmer until the gravy is thickened.

1. Add the oil to the pressure cooker and bring it to temperature over medium-high heat. Add the celery. Grate 6 of the baby carrots and add to the pan. Sauté for 3 minutes.

2. Add the onion, stir it into the celery and carrots, and push to the edges of the pan. Put the meat in the pan, fat side up. Season with salt and pepper.

3. Brown for 5 minutes and then turn the roast fat side down. If desired, spread the mustard over the browned top of the roast. Season with salt and pepper.

4. Spoon some of the sautéed celery, carrots, and onion over the top of the roast. Quarter the potatoes; add potatoes and remaining carrots to the top of the meat.

5. Pour in the broth. Add water, if needed, to bring the liquid level with the ingredients in the pressure cooker; remember not to fill the pressure cooker more than two-thirds full.

6. Lock the lid. Bring the cooker to high pressure; lower the heat to maintain pressure for 1 hour. Turn off the heat and let the pan set for 15 minutes to release the pressure; use the quick-release method to release any remaining pressure.

7. Move the roast, potatoes, and carrots to a serving platter; tent with foil and keep warm.

8. Skim the fat from the pan juices. Bring to a boil over medium-high heat; reduce the heat and simmer for 5 minutes, and then whisk in the butter 1 teaspoon at a time. Pour into a gravy boat to serve with the roast. Garnish the roast platter with fresh parsley if desired.

"Corn" Your Own Corned Beef

The salt used in processing corned beef used to be pieces the size of a kernel of corn. Corned beef got its name because this method of preserving the meat was referred to as corning. This recipe makes enough for 12 sandwiches.

INGREDIENTS | **YIELDS 1 (ABOUT 3-POUND) CORNED BEEF BRISKET**

4 cups water

½ cup kosher salt

¼ cup brown sugar

1 tablespoon saltpeter

1 3-inch cinnamon stick, broken in half

1 tablespoon pickling spice

6 black peppercorns

4 whole cloves

6 whole juniper berries

1 bay leaf, crumbled

1 pound ice

1 3-pound beef brisket, trimmed

1 small onion, peeled and quartered

1 large carrot, peeled and sliced

1 stalk celery, diced

Additional water

Pickling Spice

To make your own pickling spice, combine 1 tablespoon black peppercorns, 1 tablespoon mustard seeds, 1 tablespoon coriander seeds, 1 tablespoon red pepper flakes, 1 tablespoon allspice berries, ½ tablespoon ground mace, 1 3-inch cinnamon stick, 12 bay leaves, 1 tablespoon whole cloves, and ½ tablespoon ground ginger.

1. Add the water, salt, brown sugar, saltpeter, cinnamon stick, pickling spice, peppercorns, cloves, juniper berries, and bay leaf to a 4-quart or larger stockpot.

2. Stir and cook over high heat for 10 minutes or until the salt and sugar have dissolved. Remove from the heat and add the ice. Stir until the ice has melted.

3. When the brine has cooled to 45°F, place the brisket in a 2-gallon zip-closure bag or large covered container. Pour in the brine, making sure brisket is completely submerged in brine. Seal or close the container and place in the refrigerator for 10 days. Turn the meat over in the brine daily, stirring the brine as you do so.

4. At the end of the 10 days, remove the meat from the brine and rinse it well under cool water.

5. Add the brisket to the pressure cooker along with the onion, carrot, and celery. Add enough water to cover the meat.

6. Lock the lid into place and bring to low pressure; maintain pressure for 55 minutes. Remove from the heat and allow pressure to release naturally.

7. If you don't intend to serve the meat until the next day, refrigerate it overnight in the broth.

8. To serve immediately, remove the lid and transfer the meat from the pressure cooker to a serving platter; cover and allow it to rest for 30 minutes. To serve, thinly slice the brisket across the grain.

CHAPTER 9

Pork

Pork Broth
94

Ham Broth
94

German Pork Chops
and Sauerkraut
95

Pork Roast with Root Beer Gravy
95

Barbeque Western Ribs
96

Pork Steak in Fruit Sauce
96

Balsamic Pork Chops with Figs
97

Rosemary Pork Shoulder
with Apples
98

Pork and Beans
99

Apple Harvest Pork
Western Ribs
100

Sausages with Sautéed Onions
and Green Peppers
101

Roast Pork with Cinnamon
Cranberries and Sweet Potatoes
101

Sweet and Sour Pork
102

Ham in Raisin Sauce
103

Pork Loin Dinner
104

Pork Broth

Pork broth is seldom called for in recipes, but it can add layers of flavor when mixed with chicken and ham broth in potato, bean, or vegetable soups. You can also use it as the liquid in your favorite meatball recipe.

INGREDIENTS | YIELDS ABOUT 3½ CUPS

1 3-pound bone-in pork butt roast

1 large onion, peeled and quartered

12 baby carrots

2 stalks celery, cut in half

4 cups water

Pork Roast Dinner

To make concentrated broth and a pork roast dinner at the same time, increase the amount of carrots, decrease the water to 2 cups, and add 4 peeled medium potatoes or sweet potatoes (cut in half) on top. Cook according to the instructions in the recipe. (White potatoes will cloud the broth, but the starch from them will naturally thicken it a little.)

1. Add all ingredients to the pressure cooker. Lock the lid into place and bring to low pressure; maintain pressure for 45 minutes.

2. Remove from heat and allow pressure to release naturally. Remove the lid and check that the roast has reached an internal temperature of 160°F. The pork should be tender and pull away from the bone. If not, lock the lid back into place and cook on low pressure for another 10–15 minutes.

3. Strain; discard the celery and onion. Reserve the pork roast and carrots for another use. Once cooled, cover and refrigerate the broth overnight. Remove and discard the hardened fat. The broth can be kept for 1 or 2 days in the refrigerator, or frozen up to 3 months.

Ham Broth

Using this broth for ham and bean soup improves the soup's flavor in the same way that adding a ham bone to the cooking liquid does. Adding ¼ cup of ham broth for every ¾ cup of chicken broth can give a boost to potato soup, too.

INGREDIENTS | YIELDS ABOUT 3½ CUPS

1 3-pound bone-in ham or 3 pounds ham bones

1 large onion, peeled and quartered

12 baby carrots

2 stalks celery, halved

4 cups water

1. Add all ingredients to the pressure cooker. Lock the lid into place and bring to low pressure; maintain for 45 minutes. Remove from the heat and allow pressure to release naturally. The ham is done if the meat pulls away from the bone.

2. Strain; discard the celery and onion. Reserve any ham removed from the bones and the carrots for another use. Once cooled, cover and refrigerate the broth overnight. Remove and discard any hardened fat. The broth can be kept for 1 or 2 days in the refrigerator or frozen up to 3 months.

German Pork Chops and Sauerkraut

Bavarian seasoning is a mix of a blend of Bavarian-style crushed brown mustard seeds, French rosemary, garlic, Dalmatian sage, French thyme, and bay leaves.

INGREDIENTS | SERVES 4

1 stalk celery, finely chopped

1 1-pound bag baby carrots

1 large onion, peeled and sliced

1 clove garlic, peeled and minced

4 slices bacon, cut into small pieces

4 1-inch-thick bone-in pork loin chops

1 1-pound bag sauerkraut, rinsed and drained

4 medium red potatoes, peeled and quartered

1 12-ounce can beer

2 teaspoons Bavarian seasoning

Salt and freshly ground pepper, to taste

1. Add the ingredients to the pressure cooker in the order given. Lock the lid in place. Bring to high pressure; maintain pressure for 9 minutes.

2. Remove from the heat and allow pressure to release naturally. Taste for seasoning and adjust if necessary. Serve hot.

Pork Roast with Root Beer Gravy

Only use regular (not diet) root beer in this recipe. Soft drinks made with artificial sweeteners cannot withstand the heat of the pressure cooker.

INGREDIENTS | SERVES 6

1 10-ounce can golden cream of mushroom soup

1 12-ounce can root beer

1 1-ounce envelope dry onion soup mix

1 3-pound pork roast

1. Add the soup, root beer, and onion soup mix to the pressure cooker. Stir to mix. Add the pork roast.

2. Lock the lid in place. Bring to low pressure; maintain pressure for 45 minutes. Remove from the heat and allow pressure to release naturally.

3. Transfer the roast to a serving platter; let rest for 5 minutes before slicing.

4. Skim any fat from the gravy in the pressure cooker. Stir to mix and then transfer to a gravy boat or pour over the sliced meat.

Barbeque Western Ribs

At the end of the cooking time, the meat will be tender and falling off of the bones. You can stretch this recipe to 8 servings if you serve barbeque pork sandwiches instead of 4 servings of pork. Add potato chips and coleslaw for a delicious, casual meal.

INGREDIENTS | SERVES 4

1 cup barbeque sauce
½ cup apple jelly
1 3-inch cinnamon stick
6 whole cloves
1 large sweet onion, peeled and diced
½ cup water
3 pounds pork Western ribs

1. Add the barbeque sauce, jelly, cinnamon stick, cloves, onion, and water to the pressure cooker. Stir to mix. Add the ribs, ladling some of the sauce over them. Lock the lid into place and bring to low pressure; maintain pressure for 55 minutes. Remove from heat and allow pressure to release naturally.

2. Remove the meat and bones; cover and keep warm. Skim any fat from the sauce. Remove and discard the cinnamon stick and cloves. Return the pressure cooker to medium-high heat. Cook uncovered for 15 minutes or until the sauce is reduced and coats the back of a spoon.

Pork Steak in Fruit Sauce

Serve this dish over some mashed potatoes and alongside some steam-in-the-bag green beans.

INGREDIENTS | SERVES 6

8 pitted prunes
4 8-ounce pork steaks, trimmed of fat
2 small Granny Smith apples, peeled, cored, and sliced
½ cup dry white wine or apple juice
½ cup heavy cream
Salt and freshly ground pepper, to taste
1 tablespoon red currant jelly
Optional: 1 tablespoon butter

1. Add the prunes, pork steaks, apple slices, wine or apple juice, and cream to the pressure cooker. Salt and pepper to taste. Lock the lid into place and bring to high pressure; maintain pressure for 9 minutes. Quick-release the pressure. Remove the meat and fruit to a serving platter.

2. Leave the pressure cooker on the heat and simmer uncovered for 10 minutes or until the mixture is reduced by half and thickened. Whisk in the red currant jelly. Taste for seasoning and add more salt and pepper if needed. Whisk in the butter a teaspoon at a time if you want a richer, glossier sauce.

Balsamic Pork Chops with Figs

Serve with baked potatoes, a steamed vegetable, and a tossed salad topped with diced apples and toasted walnuts.

INGREDIENTS | **SERVES 4**

4 1-inch-thick bone-in pork loin chops

Salt and freshly ground black pepper, to taste

2 teaspoons butter or ghee

2 teaspoons extra virgin olive oil

2 medium sweet onions, peeled and sliced

4 cloves garlic, peeled and minced

½ teaspoon dried thyme

3 tablespoons balsamic vinegar

2 tablespoons dry white wine

½ cup chicken broth

10 ounces dried figs

Make a Syrupy Sauce

Use a slotted spoon to transfer the pork chops, onions, and figs to a serving platter; cover and keep warm. Return the pressure cooker to medium-high heat. Simmer, uncovered, for 5 minutes or until the pan juices are reduced and coat the back of a spoon. Pour over the pork chops, onions, and figs on the serving platter.

1. Lightly season the pork chops on both sides by sprinkling them with salt and pepper. Add the butter or ghee and oil to the pressure cooker and bring to temperature over medium-high heat. Add 2 pork chops; brown for 3 minutes on each side. Move chops to a plate and repeat with the other 2 chops. Remove those chops to the plate.

2. Add the onions; sauté for 4 minutes or until the onions are transparent. Stir in the garlic; sauté for 30 seconds. Stir in the thyme and balsamic vinegar. Cook uncovered until the vinegar is reduced by half. Stir in the wine and broth. Add the pork chops, spooning some of the onions over the chops. Place the figs on top.

3. Lock the lid into place and bring to high pressure; maintain pressure for 9 minutes. Remove from the heat and quick-release the pressure. Serve immediately.

Rosemary Pork Shoulder with Apples

Using apple juice gives you a sweeter sauce than white wine. Substitute water for the white wine if you want the apples to remain tart. Serve with fried potatoes, a steamed vegetable, and crusty bread or dinner rolls.

INGREDIENTS | SERVES 6

1 3½-pound pork shoulder roast

3 tablespoons Dijon mustard

1 tablespoon olive or vegetable oil

½ cup dry white wine, apple juice, or water

2 tart apples, peeled and quartered

3 cloves garlic, peeled and minced

Salt and freshly ground black pepper, to taste

1 teaspoon dried rosemary

1. Coat all sides of the roast with the mustard. Bring the oil to temperature in the pressure cooker over medium-high heat. Add the pork roast; brown the roast on all sides, reducing the heat if necessary to avoid burning the mustard.

2. Pour the wine, apple juice, or water around the roast. Working around the roast, use the liquid to deglaze the pan, scraping up any browned bits sticking to the bottom of the pan. Add the apples, garlic, salt, pepper, and rosemary.

3. Lock the lid into place and bring to low pressure; maintain pressure for 45 minutes. Remove from heat and allow pressure to release naturally.

4. Remove the lid. Use a meat thermometer to measure whether the roast has reached an internal temperature of 160°F.

5. Remove the roast to a serving platter. Tent and keep warm while you use an immersion blender to puree the pan contents. Slice the roast and pour the pureed juices over the slices. Serve.

Pork and Beans

If the meat or beans are not tender enough, cover and simmer for 15 more minutes, or lock the lid, bring back to high pressure, and cook at high pressure for another 3 minutes.

INGREDIENTS | SERVES 6

2 teaspoons paprika

1 teaspoon garlic powder

¼ teaspoon ground black pepper

½ teaspoon onion powder

⅛ teaspoon cayenne

¼ teaspoon dried oregano

¼ teaspoon dried thyme

2½ pounds pork shoulder, cut into 1½-inch pieces

1½ tablespoons vegetable oil

1 large yellow onion, peeled and diced

6 cups chicken broth or water

2 cups dried white beans, such as great northern or navy

½ pound salt pork or bacon, cut into pieces

1 15-ounce can diced tomatoes

4 cloves garlic, peeled and minced

½ cup packed light brown sugar

2 tablespoons whole grain or Creole mustard

2 teaspoons chili powder

¼ teaspoon salt

1 bay leaf

¼ teaspoon dried thyme

1. Add the paprika, garlic powder, pepper, onion powder, cayenne, oregano, and thyme to a gallon-size plastic bag; shake to mix. Add the pork pieces and shake the bag to season the meat on all sides. Add the oil to the pressure cooker and bring it to temperature over medium-high heat. Add the pork and stir-fry for about 2 minutes per side or until it just begins to brown. Move the meat to a plate and set aside.

2. Add the onions to the cooker; reduce heat to medium and sauté for 2 minutes or until tender. Add the broth or water.

3. Remove any stones or impurities from the beans, and then stir them into the liquid in the cooker, scraping up any browned bits off the bottom of the pot. (This is important because browned bits that remain on the pan bottom could burn during the pressure process, imparting an unpleasant burnt flavor to the final dish.)

4. Lock lid into place on the pressure cooker. Bring to high pressure; maintain for 15 minutes. Turn off the burner; leave pressure cooker in place until it returns to normal pressure. Once the pressure is released, remove the lid to allow excess steam to escape.

5. Add the salt pork, tomatoes, garlic, light brown sugar, mustard, chili powder, salt, bay leaf, thyme, and reserved pork to the cooker; stir to combine. Lock the lid into place; bring the pressure cooker to high pressure and maintain pressure for 15 minutes.

6. Remove from heat and let sit for 10 minutes. Quick-release any remaining pressure and remove the lid. Check for seasoning, and add salt and pepper if needed. Remove and discard the bay leaf. Serve.

Apple Harvest Pork Western Ribs

Cooking the pork in beer with applesauce adds a German influence to these sandwiches. The North Carolina influence comes from the ketchup-based coleslaw served as the condiment on the sandwiches. To continue the comfort-food theme, serve with baked beans and warm German potato salad.

INGREDIENTS | SERVES 12

3 pounds pork Western ribs

1 12-ounce can beer

1 cup unsweetened applesauce

1 large sweet onion, peeled and diced

2 tablespoons brown sugar

½ teaspoon freshly ground black pepper

Salt, to taste

Optional: Orange marmalade or apple jelly

12 hamburger buns

North Carolina–Style Coleslaw

Add ¾ cup cider vinegar, 1 tablespoon ketchup, 1 tablespoon brown sugar, 1 teaspoon salt, ⅛ teaspoon dried red pepper flakes, and ¾ teaspoon freshly ground black pepper to a large bowl. Whisk to mix, and then stir in a 2-pound bag of coleslaw mix. Add hot sauce, to taste.

1. Add the pork to the pressure cooker. Do not trim the fat from the ribs; it's what helps the meat cook up moist enough to shred for sandwiches. A lot of the fat will melt out of the meat as it cooks.

2. Pour the beer over the pork. Add the applesauce, onion, brown sugar, black pepper, and salt. Lock the lid into place and bring to low pressure; maintain pressure for 55 minutes. Remove from heat and allow pressure to release naturally.

3. Remove the lid and use a slotted spoon to move the pork to a cutting board. Remove and discard any fat still on the meat. Use two forks to shred the meat. Skim and discard any fat from the top of the pan juices. Stir the shredded pork back into the sauce. Place the pressure cooker over medium heat and bring to a simmer. Taste for seasoning; stir in orange marmalade or apple jelly a tablespoon at a time if you prefer a sweeter barbeque.

4. Spoon the meat onto hamburger buns. Top the meat with a heaping tablespoon of North Carolina–Style Coleslaw.

Sausages with Sautéed Onions and Green Peppers

For this recipe, you can use your choice of 8 bratwurst, 8 Italian sausages, or 16 breakfast sausage links. Serve in steamed or toasted sandwich rolls.

INGREDIENTS | SERVES 8

8 sausages

1 tablespoon olive oil

1 large green bell pepper, seeded and sliced

1 large red bell pepper, seeded and sliced

1 large orange bell pepper, seeded and sliced

1 large yellow bell pepper, seeded and sliced

2 large sweet onions, peeled and sliced

2 cloves garlic, peeled and minced

½ cup chicken broth

1. Brown sausages in pressure cooker over medium-high heat. Drain and discard any fat. Add the olive oil and bring it to temperature. Add the sliced peppers; sauté for 3 minutes or until they begin to get soft. Add the onion slices; sauté for 3 minutes or until the onions are transparent. Add the garlic; sauté for 30 seconds.

2. Return the sausages to the pressure cooker, pushing them down into the peppers and onions. Pour in the broth. Lock the lid into place and bring to high pressure; maintain pressure for 4 minutes. Quick-release the pressure. Serve.

Roast Pork with Cinnamon Cranberries and Sweet Potatoes

This dish is worthy of a holiday dinner party. Serve with a tossed salad, steamed vegetables, and dinner rolls.

INGREDIENTS | SERVES 6

1 3-pound pork butt roast

Salt and freshly ground pepper, to taste

1 16-ounce can sweetened whole cranberries

1 medium onion, peeled and diced

¼ cup orange marmalade

½ cup orange juice

¼ teaspoon ground cinnamon

⅛ teaspoon ground cloves

3 large sweet potatoes, peeled and quartered

Optional: 1 tablespoon cornstarch

Optional: 2 tablespoons cold water

1. Place the pork, fat side down, in the pressure cooker. Salt and pepper to taste. Combine the cranberries, onion, marmalade, orange juice, cinnamon, and cloves in a large measuring cup; pour over the pork roast.

2. Arrange sweet potatoes around the meat. Lock lid into place and bring to low pressure; maintain for 45 minutes. Remove from heat and allow pressure to release.

3. Transfer meat and sweet potatoes to a serving platter. Cover and keep warm. Skim fat off of the pan juices.

4. Return pressure cooker to medium heat. Combine cornstarch with the water. Whisk into the liquid in the pressure cooker; simmer and stir for 2 minutes.

Sweet and Sour Pork

Serve over cooked rice or Chinese noodles. Have soy sauce and toasted sesame oil available at the table.

INGREDIENTS | SERVES 8

2 pounds pork shoulder

1 tablespoon all-purpose flour

2 tablespoons sesame or peanut oil

1 14-ounce can pineapple chunks

1 tablespoon light brown sugar

⅛ teaspoon mustard powder

½ teaspoon ground ginger

2 tablespoons apple cider vinegar

1 tablespoon low-sodium soy sauce

4 medium carrots, peeled and sliced

1 large red bell pepper, seeded and sliced

½ pound fresh sugar snap peas

2 cups fresh broccoli florets

2 cloves garlic, peeled and thinly sliced

2 large sweet onions, peeled and diced

2 tablespoons cornstarch

2 tablespoons cold water

1 cup bean sprouts

1. Cut the pork into bite-size pieces. Add to a zip-closure bag along with the flour; seal and shake to coat the pork in the flour.

2. Bring the oil to temperature in the pressure cooker over medium-high heat. Fry the pork for 3 minutes or until it begins to brown. Add the pineapple juice and reserve the pineapple chunks; stir and scrape up any bits stuck to the bottom of the pan.

3. Add the sugar, mustard powder, ginger, vinegar, Liquid Aminos or soy sauce, carrots, red bell pepper, and sugar snap peas. Cut the broccoli florets into bite-size pieces and add them to the pressure cooker. Add garlic and ¾ onion. Lock the lid into place and bring to low pressure; maintain pressure for 12 minutes.

4. Quick-release the pressure. Use a slotted spoon to transfer all solids from the pressure cooker to a serving bowl; keep warm.

5. To make the glaze, in a small bowl mix together the cornstarch and water. Stir in some of the pan juices. Put the pressure cooker over medium heat. Bring to a boil and then whisk in the cornstarch mixture.

6. Reduce the heat to maintain a simmer for 3 minutes or until the mixture is thickened and the raw cornstarch taste is cooked out of the glaze. Stir in the bean sprouts, reserved pineapple chunks, and onion. Pour over the cooked pork and vegetables in the serving bowl; stir to combine. Serve.

Ham in Raisin Sauce

The raisins will get soft and cook into the sauce. If you want them to remain firmer, wait to add them until Step 3. Serve with a salad, sweet potatoes, a steamed vegetable, and dinner rolls.

INGREDIENTS | SERVES 8

1 4-pound ready-to-eat ham
1 large sweet onion, peeled and sliced
⅛ teaspoon ground cloves
¼ teaspoon ground ginger
½ teaspoon ground cinnamon
1 14-ounce can pineapple chunks
2 tablespoons brown sugar
½ cup raisins
½ cup apple butter
¼ cup maple syrup
1 tablespoon balsamic vinegar

1. Add the ham and sliced onions to the pressure cooker. Stir together the cloves, ginger, cinnamon, pineapple juice (reserve the pineapple), brown sugar, and raisins. Pour over the ham.

2. Lock the lid into place. Bring to low pressure; maintain pressure for 20 minutes. Remove from the heat and allow pressure to release naturally.

3. Move the ham to a serving platter and keep warm while you finish the sauce.

4. Skim and remove any fat from the pan juices in the pressure cooker. Put the pan over medium heat; simmer to reduce the pan juices to about a cup. Stir in the pineapple chunks, apple butter, maple syrup, and vinegar. Taste for seasoning and adjust if necessary, adding additional maple syrup if you want a sweeter sauce or more vinegar if you need to cut the sweetness. Serve separately to spoon or pour over ham slices.

Pork Loin Dinner

This dish gives you the convenience of cooking everything up in one pot.
Serve this dinner with warm buttered dinner rolls and a tossed salad.

INGREDIENTS | SERVES 4

1 pound boneless pork loin

1 tablespoon vegetable oil

1 small onion, peeled and diced

Salt and freshly ground black pepper, to taste

½ cup white wine or apple juice

1 cup chicken broth

1 rutabaga, peeled and diced

1 large turnip, peeled and diced

4 small Yukon Gold or red potatoes, scrubbed

4 carrots, peeled and diced

1 stalk celery, finely diced

½ cup sliced leeks, white part only

½ teaspoon mild curry powder

¼ teaspoon dried thyme

2 teaspoons dried parsley

3 tablespoons fresh lemon juice

2 Granny Smith or tart green apples, peeled, cored, and diced

Optional: Fresh parsley or thyme sprigs

1. Cut the pork into 1-inch cubes. Add the oil to the pressure cooker and bring to temperature over medium heat. Add the onion; sauté for 3 minutes. Add the pork and lightly season it with salt and pepper. Stir-fry the pork for 5 minutes or until it just begins to brown. Add the wine or apple juice, broth, rutabaga, and turnip. Cut the potatoes into quarters and add them to the pot along with the carrots, celery, leeks, curry powder, thyme, parsley, and lemon juice.

2. Lock the lid into place and bring to high pressure; maintain pressure for 15 minutes. Turn off the heat and allow the pressure to drop naturally.

3. Carefully remove the lid and add the diced apples. Bring to a simmer over medium heat; reduce the heat and simmer covered for 5 minutes or until the apples are tender. Serve rustic style in large bowls, garnished with fresh parsley or thyme if desired.

CHAPTER 10

Ground Meat

Meatloaf
106

Sloppy Joes
107

Hamburger and Cabbage
107

Mushroom Burgers
108

Stuffed Acorn Squash
108

Jambalaya
109

Meatball Subs
110

Stuffed Green Peppers
111

Unstuffed Cabbage
112

South of the Border Meatballs
113

Stuffed Onions
114

Ground Pork and
Eggplant Casserole
115

Meatloaf

Because it's easier to remove it from the pan, this recipe is adjusted for the meatloaf to be cooked in a 2.5-quart pressure fry pan or braiser. Allow an additional 15 minutes under pressure if you're shaping a shorter, taller loaf to fit into a 5-quart pressure cooker.

INGREDIENTS | SERVES 4

½ pound lean ground beef

½ pound lean ground pork

½ teaspoon salt

1½ teaspoons freshly ground black pepper

¾ cup oatmeal

1 tablespoon Worcestershire sauce

2 teaspoons dried parsley

1 medium yellow onion, peeled and finely diced

2 stalks celery, finely diced

2 cloves garlic, peeled and minced

1 small red or green bell pepper, seeded and finely diced

¼ cup ketchup

1 cup water

2 tablespoons tomato paste

Substitutions and Additions

You can substitute an 8-ounce can of tomato sauce for the water and tomato paste. If you prefer, you can omit the salt and add 1 tablespoon of Mrs. Dash Classic Italian Medley Seasoning Blend, Mrs. Dash Extra Spicy Seasoning Blend, or another favorite salt-free seasoning blend to the meatloaf mixture.

1. Add the ground beef, ground pork, salt, pepper, oatmeal, Worcestershire sauce, parsley, onion, celery, garlic, and bell pepper to a large bowl. Mix well.

2. Turn the mixture out onto a large piece of waxed paper or plastic wrap. Shape into a large, somewhat flat oval loaf.

3. Wrap and chill in the freezer for 30 minutes or in the refrigerator for at least 2 hours.

4. Bring a 2.5-quart pressure braiser or fry pan to temperature over medium-high heat. Add the meatloaf and brown for 5 minutes. Turn the loaf.

5. Top the meatloaf with the ketchup. Mix water and tomato paste and pour around the meatloaf.

6. Lock the lid into place and bring to high pressure; maintain pressure for 20 minutes. Remove from the heat and allow pressure to release naturally. Serve sliced, topped with some of the pan sauce if desired.

Sloppy Joes

Serve on hamburger buns with potato chips and coleslaw. Depending on the size of the buns (and individual appetites), this recipe can be stretched to 8 servings.

INGREDIENTS | SERVES 6

1 tablespoon olive oil

1 large sweet onion, peeled and diced

2 cloves garlic, peeled and minced

1½ pounds lean ground beef or ground turkey

½ cup beef broth

¼ cup tomato paste

2 tablespoons light brown sugar

Salt and ground black pepper, to taste

Pinch dried red pepper flakes

½ teaspoon chili powder

1 teaspoon prepared mustard

1 tablespoon Worcestershire sauce

⅛ teaspoon ground cinnamon

Pinch ground cloves

1. Bring the oil to temperature in the pressure cooker over medium-high heat. Add the onion and sauté for 3 minutes. Add the garlic; sauté for 30 seconds.

2. Stir in the remaining ingredients. Lock the lid into place and bring to low pressure; maintain pressure for 10 minutes.

3. Quick-release the pressure and, leaving the pan over the heat, remove the lid. Remove and discard any fat floating on top of the meat mixture.

4. Stir and simmer, breaking apart the cooked ground meat to thicken the sauce. Serve by spooning onto hamburger buns.

Hamburger and Cabbage

Rather than taking the time to make stuffed cabbage rolls, serve this casserole-style dish instead. You can serve it over cooked rice or with toasted cheese sandwiches.

INGREDIENTS | SERVES 6

1½ pounds lean ground beef

1 large sweet onion, peeled and diced

1 14½-ounce can diced tomatoes

1 cup tomato juice

1 tablespoon Mrs. Dash Garlic and Herb Seasoning Blend

3 cups coleslaw mix or shredded cabbage

Salt and freshly ground black pepper, to taste

1. Add the ground beef and diced onion to the pressure cooker. Fry over medium-high heat, breaking apart the hamburger. Drain off any rendered fat and discard.

2. Stir in the undrained tomatoes, tomato juice, seasoning blend, and enough coleslaw mix to bring mixture to the fill line.

3. Lock the lid into place and bring to low pressure; maintain pressure for 8 minutes. Remove from heat and allow pressure to release naturally. Remove the lid. Stir. Check seasoning and add salt and pepper to taste.

Mushroom Burgers

Burgers that substitute Portobello mushrooms for ground beef have become all the rage, and this recipe combines the best of both worlds.

INGREDIENTS | SERVES 4

1 pound lean ground sirloin

1 tablespoon Mrs. Dash Onion and Herb or Garlic and Herb Seasoning Blend

1 10½-ounce can condensed cream of mushroom soup

8 ounces fresh mushrooms, sliced

½ cup milk

1. Mix the ground sirloin with the seasoning blend; shape the meat into four flattened patties.

2. Bring a 2.5-quart pressure braiser or fry pan to temperature over medium-high heat. Add ground sirloin patties; brown for 3 minutes. Turn patties and top with soup. Layer mushrooms over the meat and soup. Pour milk in around the meat. Lock lid into place and bring to low pressure; maintain pressure for 10 minutes.

3. Quick-release the pressure and remove the lid. Transfer the meat to a serving platter and keep warm. Remove and discard any fat. Simmer the pan sauce to thicken it and then pour over the meat.

Stuffed Acorn Squash

The hash browns, peas, and sausage will be easier to mix together if the hash browns and peas are still frozen (but broken apart) and the sausage is at room temperature.

INGREDIENTS | SERVES 2

1 acorn squash

½ cup frozen country-style hash browns

¼ cup frozen peas

½ pound pork sausage

2 teaspoons extra virgin olive oil

Salt and freshly ground black pepper to taste

½ cup water

Optional: 2 poached or fried eggs

1. Cut the squash in half lengthwise and scrape out the seeds. Use a fork to prick the inside of each squash half, being careful not to pierce the skin. Mix hash browns, peas, and sausage. Divide between the squash halves. Drizzle 1 teaspoon oil over each half. Season to taste.

2. Place the rack in the pressure cooker. Pour the water in and carefully place the squash halves on the rack.

3. Lock the lid into place and bring to high temperature; maintain pressure for 12 minutes. Remove from the heat and allow pressure to release naturally. Use tongs and a spatula to move each squash half to serving plates. Top each with an egg if desired. Serve.

Jambalaya

There are as many versions of Jambalaya as there are Southern cooks. Originally created as a dish to use up leftovers, it's a versatile recipe that you can adjust according to your tastes.

INGREDIENTS | SERVES 6

2 tablespoons bacon fat or peanut oil

1 large carrot, peeled and grated

1 stalk celery, finely diced

1 large green bell pepper, seeded and chopped

1 medium yellow onion, peeled and diced

2 green onions, chopped

2 cloves garlic, minced

½ pound pork steak

½ pound boneless, skinless chicken thighs

½ pound smoked sausage, thinly sliced

½ pound cooked ham, diced

1 14½-ounce can diced tomatoes, drained

2 cups chicken broth

½ tablespoon dried parsley

½ teaspoon dried thyme

¼ teaspoon hot sauce, or to taste

2 tablespoons Worcestershire sauce

½ pound shrimp, peeled and deveined

Salt and freshly ground pepper to taste

6 servings cooked long-grain brown rice

Pressure-Cooked Long-Grain Brown Rice

For 6 servings, add 1 cup long-grain brown rice, 2 cups water or broth, 1 tablespoon oil or butter, and 1 teaspoon salt to a pressure cooker over high heat. Lock the lid and bring to low pressure; maintain pressure for 20 minutes. Remove pan from heat and let sit for 10 minutes. Quick-release any remaining pressure, remove lid, and fluff rice.

1. Add the bacon fat or oil to the pressure cooker and bring it to temperature over medium heat.

2. Add the grated carrots, celery, and green bell pepper to the pan; sauté for 3 to 5 minutes or until soft. Add the yellow and green onions and sauté until transparent.

3. Add the garlic and sauté for an additional 30 seconds. Cut the pork and chicken into bite-size pieces. Add to the pressure cooker and stir-fry for 3 minutes.

4. Stir in the smoked sausage and stir-fry for 3 minutes; add the ham and stir-fry for 1 minute.

5. Stir in the tomatoes, broth, parsley, thyme, hot sauce, and Worcestershire sauce. Lock the lid into place and bring to low pressure; maintain pressure for 8 minutes.

6. Quick-release the pressure. If the shrimp are large, halve them; otherwise, add the shrimp to the pot, cover, and cook over medium heat for 3 to 5 minutes or until shrimp are cooked.

7. Taste for seasoning and add salt and pepper if needed. Serve over the rice or stir the rice into the Jambalaya.

Meatball Subs

You can substitute 2 teaspoons dried oregano and 1 teaspoon dried basil for the Italian seasoning blend. Choose the pasta sauce according to what other flavors you want to introduce to the sandwiches: roasted red peppers sauce, mushroom sauce, or traditional marinara sauce.

INGREDIENTS | SERVES 6

1 pound lean ground beef

1 large egg

1 small onion, peeled and diced

½ cup bread crumbs

2 tablespoons Parmigiano-Reggiano or Asiago cheese, freshly grated

1 tablespoon Mrs. Dash Classic Italian Medley Seasoning Blend

1 teaspoon garlic powder

Pinch dried red pepper flakes

Salt and freshly ground black pepper, to taste

1 teaspoon sugar

1 28-ounce jar pasta sauce

6 sub buns

3 tablespoons extra virgin olive oil

1½ cups mozzarella cheese, grated

Meatball Sub Toppers

Peel and slice a large sweet onion; add the slices to the pressure cooker after you pour in the pasta sauce. Add slices of green and red bell peppers. At the end of Step 2, move the cooked onions and peppers to a serving bowl. Pass at the table for those who want to add them to their sandwiches.

1. Add the ground beef, egg, onion, bread crumbs, grated Parmigiano-Reggiano or Asiago cheese, Italian seasoning blend, garlic powder, red pepper flakes, salt, and pepper to a mixing bowl. Combine well. Shape into 12 ping pong ball–size meatballs. Add to the pressure cooker.

2. Stir the sugar into the pasta sauce and pour over the meatballs. Lock the lid into place and bring to low pressure; maintain pressure for 8 minutes. Remove from heat and allow pressure to release naturally. Remove the lid. Skim and discard any fat.

3. Lay the buns flat on a broiling pan. Brush the insides of the buns with the olive oil. Place under the broiler for a few minutes until lightly toasted.

4. Spread 1 tablespoon sauce over the bottom portion of each bun. Halve the meatballs and add 2 meatballs to each bun, cut side down on the bottom portion of the bun.

5. Top with the grated mozzarella cheese. Return to broiler; broil until cheese is melted and bubbly. Pour remaining sauce into a serving bowl.

Stuffed Green Peppers

For a slightly different taste, substitute an equal amount of pasta sauce for the tomato sauce or add a little sugar and some Italian seasoning to the tomato sauce.

INGREDIENTS | SERVES 4

4 medium green bell peppers

1 pound lean ground beef

1 cup cooked rice

2 large eggs

3 cloves garlic, peeled and minced

1 small yellow onion, peeled and diced

Salt and freshly ground black pepper, to taste

Optional: Pinch allspice or nutmeg

½ cup chicken broth

½ cup tomato sauce

1. Cut the tops off the green peppers. Remove and discard the seeds and use a spoon to scrape out and discard some of the white pith inside the peppers. Set aside.

2. Dice any of the green pepper that you can salvage from around the stem and mix well with ground beef, rice, eggs, garlic, onion, salt, pepper, and allspice or nutmeg if using.

3. Evenly divide the meat mixture between the green peppers. Place the rack in the pressure cooker and pour the broth into the cooker.

4. Place the peppers on the rack and pour the tomato sauce over the peppers. Lock the lid into place and bring to low pressure; maintain pressure for 15 minutes.

5. Quick-release the pressure. Remove the peppers to serving plates. Remove the rack and pour the pan juices into a gravy boat to pass at the table.

Unstuffed Cabbage

Use Italian-seasoned tomatoes and cooked orzo pasta instead of the rice to give this dish a Tuscan flair. If you prefer German flavors, add 1 teaspoon caraway seeds and 2 teaspoons brown sugar.

INGREDIENTS | SERVES 6

2 tablespoons extra virgin olive oil

2 stalks celery, diced

3 large carrots, peeled and diced

1 pound lean ground beef

1 medium yellow onion, peeled and diced

1 clove garlic, peeled and minced

½ teaspoon salt

¼ teaspoon freshly ground black pepper

1 teaspoon sugar

1 14½-ounce can diced tomatoes

1½ cups cooked rice

3 cups coleslaw mix or rough-chopped cabbage

1½ cups chicken broth

Optional: ½ cup white wine

1. Bring the oil to temperature over medium heat in the pressure cooker. Add the celery and carrots; sauté for 5 minutes.

2. Add the ground beef and onion; stir-fry until beef is browned and broken apart and onion is transparent. Drain off and discard any excess fat.

3. Add the garlic, salt, pepper, sugar, undrained tomatoes, rice, coleslaw mix or cabbage, and broth; stir into the beef mixture.

4. Use the back of a spoon to press the mixture down evenly in the pan. Add white wine if using, being careful not to exceed the fill line on your pressure cooker.

5. Lock the lid into place and bring to low pressure; maintain for 8 minutes. Remove from heat and allow pressure to release naturally.

6. Uncover and return the pressure cooker to medium heat. Simmer for 15 minutes or until most of the liquid has evaporated.

South of the Border Meatballs

Add extra heat to the sauce by adding more canned chipotles, some Mrs. Dash Extra Spicy Seasoning Blend, or hot sauce. Serve these meatballs with some of the sauce over cooked rice. Top with guacamole and sour cream or serve with an avocado salad.

INGREDIENTS | SERVES 8

1 tablespoon vegetable oil

1 large onion, thinly sliced

3 teaspoons garlic powder

1 tablespoon chili powder

¼ teaspoon dried Mexican oregano

2 canned chipotle chili peppers in adobo sauce

1 14½-ounce can diced tomatoes

1 cup chicken broth

Salt and freshly ground black pepper, to taste

1½ pounds lean ground beef

½ pound ground pork

1 large egg

1 small white onion, peeled and diced

1 tablespoon chili powder

1½ teaspoons garlic powder

10 soda crackers, crumbled

1. Add oil to the pressure cooker and bring to temperature over medium heat. Add the sliced onions; sauté for 3 minutes or until the onions are transparent.

2. Stir in 1½ teaspoons garlic powder, chili powder, oregano, chipotles in adobo sauce, undrained tomatoes, broth, salt, and pepper. Simmer uncovered while you prepare the meatballs.

3. Add the ground beef, ground pork, egg, diced onion, chili powder, 1½ teaspoons garlic powder, and crumbled crackers to a large bowl; use hands to mix. Form into sixteen meatballs.

4. Use an immersion blender to puree the sauce in the pressure cooker. Add the meatballs to the sauce.

5. Lock the lid into place and bring to low pressure; maintain pressure for 12 minutes. Remove from heat and allow pressure to release naturally.

Stuffed Onions

You'll want to nestle the 4 onions beside each other in the bottom of the pressure cooker, so choose the size accordingly. Serve with a salad.

INGREDIENTS | SERVES 4

4 medium onions, peeled

1 pound lean ground beef or lamb

¼ teaspoon ground allspice

¼ teaspoon dried dill

3 tablespoons fresh lemon juice

2 teaspoons dried parsley

Salt and freshly ground black pepper, to taste

1 large egg

1–2 tablespoons all-purpose flour

2 tablespoons extra virgin olive oil

1 cup chicken broth

1. Halve the onions, cutting through the middle (not from bottom to top). Scoop out the onion cores.

2. Chop cores and add to ground beef or lamb, allspice, dill, 2 tablespoons lemon juice, parsley, salt, pepper, and egg; mix well. Fill onion halves with meat mixture. Sprinkle the flour over the top of the meat.

3. Add oil to the pressure cooker and bring to temperature. Add onions to pan, meat side down, and sauté until browned. Turn meat side up. Pour remaining lemon juice and broth around the onions.

4. Lock the lid into place and bring to low pressure; maintain pressure for 8 minutes. Remove from heat and allow pressure to release naturally. Serve.

Egg Drop Soup

Remove and discard any fat from the stuffed onion broth. Add enough additional chicken broth to the pressure cooker to bring it to 2 cups. Bring the broth to a simmer over medium heat. In a small bowl, lightly beat 2 large eggs. Drizzle the eggs into the broth. Simmer until eggs are cooked through. Makes 4 servings of ½ cup each.

Ground Pork and Eggplant Casserole

Ground black pepper contains anticaking agents that can cause stomach upset for some people and can also change the flavor of your dish. That's why dishes always taste better when you grind the pepper yourself. Serve with a tossed salad and toasted garlic bread.

INGREDIENTS | SERVES 8

2 pounds lean ground pork

1 large yellow onion, peeled and diced

1 stalk celery, diced

1 green pepper, seeded and diced

2 medium eggplants, cut into ½-inch dice

4 cloves garlic, peeled and minced

⅛ teaspoon dried thyme, crushed

1 tablespoon freeze-dried parsley

3 tablespoons tomato paste

Optional: 1 teaspoon hot sauce

2 teaspoons Worcestershire sauce

Salt and freshly ground pepper, to taste

1 large egg, beaten

½ cup chicken broth

1. Bring the pressure cooker to temperature over medium-high heat. Add the ground pork, onion, celery, and green pepper to the pressure cooker and stir-fry until the pork is no longer pink, breaking it apart as it cooks.

2. Drain and discard any fat rendered from the meat. Add the eggplant, garlic, thyme, parsley, tomato paste, hot sauce (if using), Worcestershire sauce, salt, pepper, and egg; stir to combine.

3. Pour in the chicken broth. Lock the lid into place and bring to low pressure; maintain pressure for 10 minutes. Remove from heat and allow pressure to release naturally.

CHAPTER 11

Fish and Seafood

Fish Stock
117

Catfish in Creole Sauce
117

Tomato-Stewed Calamari
118

Creamed Crab
118

New England Fish Stew
119

Italian Fish
120

Whitefish Fillets with Vegetables
121

Miso Red Snapper
122

Fish en Papillote
123

Trout in Parsley Sauce
124

Vietnamese-Style Seafood Stew
125

Orange Roughy in
Black Olive Sauce
126

Louisiana Grouper
126

Red Wine–Poached Salmon
127

Fish Stock

If you know how you'll be using the fish stock, you can season it with herbs accordingly. A common seasoning combination is bay leaf, thyme, parsley, and fennel seed.

INGREDIENTS | YIELDS ABOUT 8 CUPS

1 pound fish heads, bones, and trimmings
6 black peppercorns
2 stalks celery, cut to fit in pan
1 carrot, scrubbed and cut in quarters
1 small onion, peeled and quartered
8 cups cold water
Optional: ½ cup dry white wine

1. Add all ingredients to the pressure cooker, only pouring in enough water to take the liquid to the fill line. Bring to a boil over medium-high heat; skim and discard any foam from the surface.

2. Lock the lid into place and bring to low pressure; maintain pressure for 15 minutes. Remove from heat and allow pressure to release naturally.

3. Remove the lid and pour through a fine-mesh strainer, using a spatula to push on the solids in the strainer to release the liquid. Discard the solids. Cool; refrigerate for a day or freeze for up to 3 months.

Catfish in Creole Sauce

Serve over cooked rice. Have hot sauce available at the table for those who want it.

INGREDIENTS | SERVES 4

1½ pounds catfish fillets
1 14½-ounce can diced tomatoes
2 teaspoons dried minced onion
¼ teaspoon onion powder
1 teaspoon dried minced garlic
¼ teaspoon garlic powder
1 teaspoon hot paprika
¼ teaspoon dried tarragon
1 medium green bell pepper, seeded and diced
1 stalk celery, finely diced
¼ teaspoon sugar
½ cup chili sauce
Salt and freshly ground pepper, to taste

1. Rinse the catfish in cold water and pat dry between paper towels. Cut into bite-size pieces.

2. Add all ingredients except fish to the pressure cooker and stir to mix. Gently stir the fillets into the tomato mixture.

3. Lock the lid into place and bring the pressure cooker to low pressure; maintain pressure for 5 minutes. Quick-release the pressure. Remove the lid. Gently stir and then taste for seasoning. Add salt and pepper to taste if needed. Serve.

Tomato-Stewed Calamari

If you have fresh parsley and basil available, omit the dried herbs and stir 1 tablespoon of each into the calamari after you quick-release the pressure.

INGREDIENTS | SERVES 4

2 tablespoons olive oil

1 small carrot, peeled and grated

1 small stalk celery, finely diced

1 small white onion, peeled and diced

3 cloves garlic, peeled and minced

2½ pounds calamari

1 28-ounce can diced tomatoes

½ cup white wine

⅓ cup water

1 teaspoon dried parsley

1 teaspoon dried basil

Salt and freshly ground black pepper, to taste

1. Bring the oil to temperature in the pressure cooker. Add the carrots and celery; sauté for 2 minutes.

2. Stir in the onions; sauté for 3 minutes or until the onions are transparent. Stir in the garlic; sauté for 30 seconds.

3. Clean and wash the calamari; pat dry. Add to the pressure cooker along with the remaining ingredients.

4. Lock the lid into place and bring to low pressure; maintain pressure for 10 minutes. Quick-release pressure. Serve.

Creamed Crab

The moist cooking environment in the pressure cooker allows the flavors to meld without drying out the crabmeat. Serve this rich sauce over cooked rice, egg noodles, or toast along with a large tossed salad.

INGREDIENTS | SERVES 4

4 tablespoons butter

½ stalk celery, finely diced

1 small red onion, peeled and finely diced

1 pound uncooked lump crabmeat

¼ cup chicken broth

½ cup heavy cream

Salt and freshly ground black pepper, to taste

1. Melt the butter in the pressure cooker over medium heat. Add the celery; sauté for 1 minute or until celery begins to soften. Stir in the onion; sauté for 3 minutes. Stir in the crabmeat and broth.

2. Lock the lid into place and bring to low pressure; maintain for 3 minutes. Quick-release the pressure and remove the lid. Carefully stir in the cream. Taste for seasoning and add salt and pepper to taste. Serve.

New England Fish Stew

Fish is a low-fat meat, which lessens the impact of the cream. To make this a special occasion dish, float a pat of butter on top of each portion. Using heavy cream obviously makes this a richer stew, but you can substitute milk if you prefer.

INGREDIENTS | SERVES 4

2 tablespoons butter

1 large onion, peeled and diced

2 stalks celery, diced

4 large carrots, peeled and diced

4 medium potatoes, peeled and cut into ½-inch cubes

1 pound firm-fleshed white fish fillets, cut into ½-inch pieces

2 cups fish stock or clam juice

1 cup cold water

1 bay leaf

½ teaspoon dried thyme

1 cup heavy cream or milk

1 cup fresh or thawed frozen corn kernels

Salt and freshly ground white or black pepper, to taste

Optional: Additional butter

Optional: Fresh parsley

Newer Pressure Cooker Innovation

B/R/K pressure cookers have a continuously adjustable pressure-regulating valve that saves you from constantly having to monitor the pressure level; the valve maintains the pressure you set and also allows you to change that pressure setting at any time during the cooking process.

1. Add the butter to the pressure cooker and bring it to temperature over medium heat. Add the onions; sauté for 3 minutes or until soft.

2. Stir in the celery, carrot, and potatoes; sauté for an additional minute. Add the fish, fish stock or clam juice, water, bay leaf, and thyme.

3. Lock the lid in place and bring the pressure cooker to high pressure; maintain pressure for 4 minutes. Quick-release the pressure.

4. Remove the lid, tilting it away from you to allow any excess steam to escape.

5. Remove and discard the bay leaf. Stir in the cream or milk and corn. Taste for seasoning and add salt and pepper to taste.

6. Simmer until the corn is cooked and the chowder is hot. Transfer to a serving tureen or individual bowls and top with additional butter if desired. Garnish with parsley if desired.

Italian Fish

The pressure cooker rehydrates the dried seasoning and keeps the fish moist. This dish is good served over couscous, orzo, pasta, rice, or steamed cabbage, or alongside polenta.

INGREDIENTS | SERVES 4

4 4-ounce cod fillets

1 14½-ounce can diced tomatoes

¼ teaspoon dried minced onion

¼ teaspoon onion powder

¼ teaspoon dried minced garlic

¼ teaspoon garlic powder

¼ teaspoon dried basil

¼ teaspoon dried parsley

⅛ teaspoon dried oregano

¼ teaspoon sugar

⅛ teaspoon dried lemon granules, crushed

Pinch chili powder

Optional: Pinch dried red pepper flakes

1 tablespoon grated Parmesan cheese

1. Rinse the cod in cold water and pat dry between paper towels.

2. Add the tomatoes and all the remaining ingredients except the fish to the pressure cooker and stir to mix. Arrange the fillets over the tomatoes, folding thin tail ends under to give the fillets even thickness; spoon some of the tomato mixture over the fillets.

3. Lock the lid into place and bring the pressure cooker to low pressure; maintain pressure for 3–5 minutes (depending on the thickness of the fillets). Quick-release the pressure. Serve.

Seasoning Sense

You can enhance flavors without salt by using a variety of complementary seasonings like the combination of dried ingredients and powders used in the Italian Fish recipe. You can mix things up by substituting 1 teaspoon freshly grated lemon zest for the dried lemon granules and garnish the sauce with some fresh minced parsley or basil.

Whitefish Fillets with Vegetables

Omit the nutmeg and turn this steamed meal into a hot fish and vegetable salad by serving it over salad greens.

INGREDIENTS | SERVES 2

1 cup broccoli florets, cut into small pieces

1 large potato, peeled and diced

1 large carrot, peeled and grated

1 small zucchini, grated

4 ounces fresh mushrooms, sliced

¼ teaspoon dried thyme

¼ teaspoon freshly grated lemon zest

½ pound cod, halibut, sole, or other whitefish

½ cup white wine or chicken broth

½ cup fresh lemon juice

1 teaspoon dried parsley

Salt and freshly ground black pepper, to taste

Freshly grated nutmeg

1. Place the steamer basket in the pressure cooker. Add the broccoli florets, potato, carrot, zucchini, and mushroom slices in layers to the basket. Sprinkle the dried thyme and lemon zest over the vegetables.

2. Place the fish fillets over the vegetables. Pour the broth or wine and lemon juice over the fish. Sprinkle the dried parsley, salt, and pepper over the fish and vegetables.

3. Lock the lid in place and bring the pressure cooker to low pressure; maintain the pressure for 5 minutes. Quick-release the pressure. Divide the fish and vegetables between two serving plates. Sprinkle freshly ground nutmeg to taste over each serving.

Whitefish Fillets with Vegetables Salad Dressing

Whisk 1 teaspoon Dijon mustard into ¼ cup strained pan juices and 1 tablespoon fresh lemon juice or white wine vinegar. Slowly whisk in 1–2 tablespoons extra virgin olive oil. Taste for seasoning, adding more oil if the dressing is too tart or more lemon juice or vinegar if it isn't tart enough. Add salt and freshly ground black pepper to taste.

Miso Red Snapper

To prepare this dish, you'll need a glass pie pan that will fit on the rack inside the pressure cooker.

INGREDIENTS | SERVES 4

Water
1 tablespoon red miso paste
1 tablespoon rice wine
2 teaspoons fermented black beans
2 teaspoons sesame oil
1 teaspoon dark soy sauce
½ teaspoon Asian chili paste
Salt
2 pounds red snapper fillets
1 2-inch piece fresh ginger
2 cloves garlic, peeled and minced
4 green onions

1. Insert the rack in the pressure cooker. Pour in enough water to fill the pan to just below the top of the rack.

2. In a small bowl, mix the miso, rice wine, black beans, sesame oil, soy sauce, and chili paste. Lightly sprinkle salt over the fish fillets and then rub them on both sides with the miso mixture.

3. Peel the ginger and cut into matchsticks 1 inch long. Place half of them on the bottom of a glass pie plate. Sprinkle half the minced garlic over the ginger.

4. Halve the green onions lengthwise and then cut them into 2-inch-long pieces; place half of them over the ginger and garlic. Place the fish fillets in the pie plate and sprinkle the remaining ginger, garlic, and onions over the top. Place the pie plate on the rack inside the pressure cooker.

5. Lock the lid into place and bring to high pressure; maintain pressure for 3 minutes. Remove from heat and quick release the pressure. Serve.

Fish en Papillote

You can substitute a scant tablespoon of minced red onion for each shallot called for in a recipe. Serve with a tossed salad and dinner rolls.

INGREDIENTS | SERVES 6

3 pounds whitefish

6 tablespoons butter, softened

¼ cup fresh lemon juice

3 shallots, peeled and minced

2 cloves garlic, peeled and minced

1 tablespoon dried parsley

¼ teaspoon freshly ground white pepper

3 medium potatoes, peeled and cut into matchsticks

3 large carrots, peeled and cut into matchsticks

2 small zucchini, thinly sliced

Salt

Water

1. Thoroughly rinse the fish. Cut away and discard any grayish bands of fat. Cut into 6 portions.

2. In a small bowl, mix together the butter, lemon juice, shallots, garlic, parsley, and white pepper.

3. Cut out 6 pieces of parchment paper to wrap around the fish fillets. Brush the parchment with some of the butter mixture. Lay a fish fillet on each piece of parchment. Equally divide the remaining butter mixture between the fish, brushing it over the tops of the fillets.

4. Layer the potatoes, carrots, and zucchini on top of the fish. Salt each fillet-vegetable packet to taste. Enclose the fish and vegetables in the parchment by wrapping the paper envelope-style over them. Crisscross the packets in the steamer basket for your pressure cooker.

5. Add enough water to the pressure cooker to come up to the bottom of the steamer basket. Lock the lid into place and bring to high pressure; maintain pressure for 5 minutes. Remove from the heat and quick-release the pressure.

6. Remove the steamer basket from the pressure cooker. Using a spatula and tongs, transfer the packets to 6 serving plates. Serve immediately.

Trout in Parsley Sauce

This recipe is a way to use up lettuce that's no longer crisp enough for a salad but isn't totally past its prime. Using the lettuce to steam the fish keeps it firm and adds a bit of extra taste to the poaching liquid.

INGREDIENTS | SERVES 4

4 fresh (½-pound) river trout

Salt, to taste

4 cups torn lettuce leaves

1 teaspoon distilled white or white wine vinegar

½ cup water

½ cup fresh flat-leaf parsley, minced

1 shallot, peeled and minced

2 tablespoons mayonnaise

½ teaspoon fresh lemon juice

¼ teaspoon sugar

Pinch salt

2 tablespoons sliced almonds, toasted

Parsley Sauce Alternatives

Parsley is a versatile herb that will be a worthwhile addition to any garden. For a reduced calorie parsley sauce, you can replace the mayonnaise with water or low-fat yogurt. For a richer sauce, substitute melted butter or extra virgin olive oil for the mayonnaise.

1. Rinse the trout inside and out; pat dry. Sprinkle with salt inside and out. Put 3 cups of the lettuce leaves in the bottom of the pressure cooker. Arrange the trout over the top of the lettuce and top the trout with the remaining lettuce. Stir the vinegar into the water and pour into the pressure cooker.

2. Lock the lid into place and bring to high pressure; maintain pressure for 3 minutes. Remove from the heat and allow pressure to release naturally for 3 minutes. Quick-release any remaining pressure.

3. Remove the lid and use a spatula to move the fish to a serving plate. Peel and discard the skin from the fish. Remove and discard the heads if desired.

4. To make the parsley sauce, mix together the parsley, shallot, mayonnaise, lemon juice, sugar, and salt. Evenly divide between the fish, spreading it over them. Sprinkle the toasted almonds over the top of the sauce. Serve.

Vietnamese-Style Seafood Stew

Vietnamese stew isn't as thick as traditional American stew. The sweetness of the fruit and coconut milk in this version mellows and enhances the spicy richness of the curry spices. Serve in bowls over cooked basmati or jasmine rice.

INGREDIENTS | SERVES 4

2 cloves garlic, peeled and minced

1 small apple, peeled, seeded, and diced

1 banana, peeled and sliced

½ cup raisins

2 tablespoons light brown sugar

¼ teaspoon ground cumin

¼ teaspoon saffron

2 tablespoons curry powder

2 cups chicken broth

2 cups unsweetened coconut milk

2 tablespoons lemon or lime juice

1 teaspoon Worcestershire sauce

¾ cup heavy cream

32 shrimp, peeled and deveined

16 sea scallops

1 pound cod, halibut, snapper, or other firm white fish

1 small red bell pepper, seeded and diced

½ cup cooked chickpeas

¼ cup fresh cilantro, minced

1. Add the garlic, apple, banana, raisins, brown sugar, cumin, saffron, curry powder, broth, coconut milk, lemon or lime juice, and Worcestershire sauce to the pressure cooker; stir to combine. Lock the lid into place and bring to high pressure; maintain pressure for 10 minutes.

2. Remove from the heat and quick-release the pressure. Use an immersion blender to puree. Stir in the cream. Taste for seasoning and add more curry powder if needed.

3. Stir in the shrimp and scallops. Rinse the fish and pat dry; cut into bite-size cubes and add to the pressure cooker along with the bell pepper and chickpeas. Lock the lid in place. Return to the heat and bring to high pressure; maintain pressure for 2 minutes. Remove from the heat and quick-release the pressure.

4. Divide the soup between 4 bowls, ladled over cooked rice if desired. Sprinkle a tablespoon of minced cilantro over each serving.

Orange Roughy in Black Olive Sauce

If fresh dill isn't available, sprinkle ¼ teaspoon dried dill over each fillet when you salt them. Add additional dried dill to taste to the sauce if desired.

INGREDIENTS | SERVES 2

⅜ cup dry white wine
⅜ cup water
2 (8-ounce, 1-inch-thick) orange roughy fillets
Sea salt, to taste
4 thin slices white onion
6 sprigs fresh dill
3 tablespoons butter, melted
4 teaspoons freshly squeezed lime juice
6 Kalamata or black olives, pitted and chopped

1. Pour the wine and water into the pressure cooker. Place the trivet in the cooker. Rinse the fish and pat dry. Lightly sprinkle with salt. Place 2 slices of onion on the trivet and top each onion with a sprig of dill.

2. Place fish over the onion and dill, put a sprig of dill on top of each fillet, and top with the remaining two onion slices. Lock lid into place and bring to high pressure; maintain for 5 minutes. Remove from heat to allow pressure to release naturally for 5 minutes. Quick-release any remaining pressure.

3. To make the sauce, whisk butter, lime juice, and ½ tablespoon cooking liquid from the fish; stir in the olives. Garnish with the remaining dill.

Louisiana Grouper

The grouper is a type of fish that is found all over the world. They use their famously large mouths to swallow their prey whole.

INGREDIENTS | SERVES 4

2 tablespoons peanut or vegetable oil
1 small onion, peeled and diced
1 stalk celery, diced
1 green bell pepper, seeded and diced
1 14½-ounce can diced tomatoes
¼ cup water
1 tablespoon tomato paste
1 teaspoon sugar
Pinch basil
½ teaspoon chili powder
4 grouper fillets
Salt and pepper, to taste

1. Bring the oil to temperature in the pressure cooker over medium-high heat. Add the onion, celery, and green pepper; sauté for 3 minutes. Stir in undrained tomatoes, water, tomato paste, sugar, basil, and chili powder.

2. Rinse the fish and pat dry; cut into bite-size pieces. Sprinkle with salt and pepper, to taste. Gently stir the fish pieces into the sauce in the pressure cooker. Lock the lid into place and bring to high pressure; maintain pressure for 5 minutes. Quick-release the pressure.

Red Wine–Poached Salmon

You can prepare this dish without alcohol by substituting raspberry-apple juice for the red wine.

INGREDIENTS | SERVES 6

1 medium onion, peeled and quartered

2 cloves garlic, peeled and smashed

1 stalk celery, diced

1 bay leaf

½ teaspoon dried thyme

3½ cups water

2 cups dry red wine

2 tablespoons red wine or balsamic vinegar

½ teaspoon salt

½ teaspoon black peppercorns

1 2½-pound center-cut salmon roast

Optional: lemon

1. Add all ingredients except the salmon and lemon to the pressure cooker. Lock the lid into place and bring to high pressure; maintain pressure for 10 minutes. Remove from the heat and allow pressure to release naturally for 15 minutes. Quick-release any remaining pressure.

2. Set the trivet in the pressure cooker. Put the pressure cooker over medium-high heat and bring the wine mixture to a high simmer.

3. Wrap the salmon in cheesecloth, leaving long enough ends to extend about 3 inches. Use two sets of tongs to hold on to the 3-inch cheesecloth extensions and place the salmon on the trivet. Lock the lid into place and bring to high pressure; maintain pressure for 6 minutes. Remove from the heat and allow pressure to release naturally for 20 minutes.

4. Quick-release any remaining pressure. Use tongs to hold on to the 3-inch cheesecloth extensions to lift the salmon roast out of the pressure cooker. Set in a metal colander to allow extra moisture to drain away. When the roast is cool enough to handle, unwrap the cheesecloth. Peel away and discard any skin.

5. Transfer the salmon to a serving platter. Garnish with lemon slices or wedges if desired.

CHAPTER 12

International Flavors

Cuban Black Beans and Rice
129

Grandmother's
Chicken Casserole
130

Chinese Pork Ribs
131

African Lamb Stew
132

Hungarian Goulash
133

Ukrainian Sausage Soup
134

Swedish Meatballs
135

Biryani
136

Borscht
137

Pepper Steak
138

Belgian-Style Chicken
139

Vietnamese Pork Curry
140

Sauerbraten
141

Chicken Tagine
142

Cuban Black Beans and Rice

In Step 2, you can substitute 6 diced slices of bacon for the oil. Fry the bacon until it begins to render its fat and then add and sauté the vegetables in the order given.

INGREDIENTS | SERVES 6

1 cup dried black beans

4 cups water

3 tablespoons olive or vegetable oil

1 medium green bell pepper, seeded and diced

½ stalk celery, finely diced

2 baby carrots, grated

1 medium onion, peeled and diced

2 cloves garlic, peeled and minced

¾ cup medium or long-grain white rice

2 cups chicken broth or water

2 teaspoons paprika

½ teaspoon cumin

¼ teaspoon chili powder

1 bay leaf

Salt and freshly ground black pepper, to taste

1. Rinse the beans and add them to a covered container. Pour in the water, cover, and let the beans soak overnight. Drain.

2. Bring the oil to temperature in the pressure cooker over medium-high heat. Add the green bell pepper, celery, and carrots; sauté for 2 minutes. Add the onion; sauté for 3 minutes or until the onions are soft. Stir in the garlic and sauté for 30 seconds.

3. Stir in the rice and stir-fry until the rice begins to brown. Add the drained beans, 2 cups of broth or water, paprika, cumin, chili powder, and bay leaf.

4. Lock the lid into place and bring to low pressure; maintain pressure for 18 minutes. Remove from the heat and allow pressure to release naturally. Stir, taste for seasoning, and add salt and pepper to taste.

Grandmother's Chicken Casserole

*Serve this French cooking–inspired dish with a tossed salad
and dinner rolls. Carve the chicken at the table.*

INGREDIENTS | SERVES 4

1 medium onion

2 stalks celery, diced

2 medium carrots, peeled and diced

5 cloves garlic, peeled

½ teaspoon extra virgin olive oil

1 3-pound chicken

1 lemon, washed and quartered

Salt and freshly ground black pepper, to taste

1 tablespoon olive or vegetable oil

½ cup dry red wine

¼ cup water

Several sprigs fresh rosemary

1 1-pound bag baby carrots

4 medium red potatoes, washed and quartered

4 shallots, peeled

1 tablespoon brandy

Optional: 1 tablespoon butter

1. Peel the onion and cut in half. Set aside half of the onion and dice the other half.

2. Place the diced onion, celery, carrots, and 3 cloves garlic in a microwave-safe bowl. Stir in the extra virgin olive oil. Cover and microwave on high for 2 minutes. Set aside, leaving the dish covered so the vegetables continue to cook.

3. Wash the chicken inside and out. Pat dry. Cut the reserved onion half in half and insert into the chicken cavity along with the lemon quarters and remaining 2 peeled cloves garlic. Salt and pepper the chicken inside and out. Truss the chicken.

4. Bring the olive or vegetable oil to temperature in the pressure cooker over medium-high heat. Add the chicken and brown on all sides, about 3 minutes per side. Remove and set aside the chicken.

5. Discard any excess oil in the pressure cooker. Stir in the red wine and use it to deglaze the pan, scraping up any browned bits sticking to the pressure cooker.

6. Stir in the water, microwaved vegetables, and rosemary. Add the chicken, breast side down. Lock the lid into place and bring to high pressure; maintain pressure for 20 minutes. Remove from the heat and quick-release the pressure.

7. Remove the chicken to an oven-safe serving platter; tent with aluminum foil and put in a warm oven.

8. Remove and discard the rosemary and excess grease from the cooking liquid. Use an immersion blender to puree the cooking liquid.

Grandmother's Chicken Casserole (*continued*)

9. Add the baby carrots, potatoes, and shallots to the sauce. Return pressure cooker to heat and bring to high pressure; maintain pressure for 6 minutes. Remove from heat and allow pressure to release naturally.

10. Remove the chicken from the oven; discard the aluminum foil tent. Use a slotted spoon to transfer the carrots, potatoes, and shallots to the serving platter.

11. Stir in the brandy and then return the pressure cooker to medium heat. Bring to a simmer; simmer for 3 minutes. If desired, whisk the butter into the sauce 1 teaspoon at a time. Pour into a gravy boat to pass at the table.

Chinese Pork Ribs

Chinese five-spice powder is a blend of ground cinnamon, powdered cassia buds, powdered star anise or anise seed, ground ginger, and ground cloves.

INGREDIENTS | SERVES 6

¾ cup ketchup

½ cup water

¼ cup soy sauce

2 tablespoons balsamic or apple cider vinegar

⅓ cup light brown sugar

2 teaspoons ground ginger

1 teaspoon Chinese five-spice powder

1 teaspoon garlic powder

4 pounds baby back ribs

Optional: Lime wedges, for garnish

Optional: Liquid smoke, to taste

1. Add the ketchup, water, soy sauce, vinegar, brown sugar, ginger, five-spice powder, and garlic powder to the pressure cooker; stir to combine. Cut ribs into single ribs and add to the pressure cooker, submerging in the sauce.

2. Lock the lid into place and bring to low pressure; maintain pressure for 30 minutes. Remove from the heat and allow pressure to release naturally. Transfer the ribs to a serving platter and garnish with lime wedges.

3. Remove and discard any fat from the sauce in the pressure cooker. Add up to 1 tablespoon of liquid smoke, to taste, if desired. If necessary, thicken the sauce by simmering it for several minutes over medium heat. Pour sauce into a gravy boat to pass at the table.

African Lamb Stew

You can make this stew in a 2.5-quart pressure fry pan or in a larger pressure cooker. Serve over cooked rice.

INGREDIENTS | SERVES 6

1 tablespoon olive or vegetable oil
2 pounds boneless lamb shoulder
1 large onion, peeled and diced
2 cloves garlic, peeled and minced
1 cup dried apricots
⅓ cup raisins
½ cup blanched whole almonds
1 tablespoon fresh ginger, minced
½ teaspoon ground cinnamon
¾ cup red wine
¼ cup freshly squeezed orange juice
½ cup fresh mint leaves, packed
Salt and freshly ground black pepper, to taste
Optional: Additional mint leaves for garnish

1. Bring the oil to temperature in the pressure cooker over medium-high heat. Cut the lamb into bite-size pieces.

2. Add the lamb to the pressure cooker in batches and brown each batch for 5 minutes or until well browned. Use a slotted spoon to remove lamb; set aside and keep warm.

3. Add the onion to the pressure cooker; sauté for 3 minutes; Stir in the garlic and sauté for 30 seconds.

4. Halve the apricots and add them to the pressure cooker along with the raisins, almonds, ginger, cinnamon, wine, orange juice, and mint leaves.

5. Lock the lid into place and bring to high pressure; maintain pressure for 20 minutes. Remove from the heat and allow pressure to release naturally.

6. Remove the lid, stir, and taste for seasoning. Add salt and pepper to taste. Garnish with fresh mint leaves if desired.

Hungarian Goulash

Hungarian goulash is often served with prepared spaetzle or hot buttered egg noodles and cucumber salad. Make the cucumber salad in advance of preparing the goulash so that the cucumbers marinate in the dressing while you make the stew.

INGREDIENTS | SERVES 6

1 tablespoon olive or vegetable oil

1 green bell pepper, seeded and diced

4 large potatoes, peeled and diced

3 strips bacon, cut into 1-inch pieces

1 large yellow onion, peeled and diced

2 tablespoons sweet paprika

2½ pounds stewing beef or round steak

1 clove garlic, peeled and minced

Pinch caraway seeds, chopped

2 cups beef broth

1 15-ounce can diced tomatoes

2 tablespoons sour cream, plus more for serving

Salt and freshly ground black pepper, to taste

Cucumber Salad

Thinly slice 2 cucumbers; put slices in a bowl and sprinkle with salt. Let rest for 30 minutes. Drain off excess moisture and add 1 thinly sliced onion; 2 tablespoons vinegar; ¼ cup heavy or sour cream; 2 teaspoons sugar; ⅛ teaspoon sweet paprika; a pinch of dill; and freshly ground black pepper. Mix well, cover, and refrigerate until ready to serve.

1. Add the oil, bell pepper, potatoes, bacon, and onion to the pressure cooker over medium heat; sauté for 10 minutes or until the onion is transparent and the fat is rendering from the bacon.

2. Stir in paprika. Trim the beef of any fat and cut it into ½-inch cubes. Stir the beef into the vegetable mixture along with the garlic and caraway seeds.

3. Stir in the beef broth and tomatoes. Lock the lid into place and bring to low pressure; maintain pressure for 30 minutes.

4. Remove from heat and allow pressure to release naturally. Remove lid and stir 2 tablespoons sour cream into the goulash.

5. Taste for seasoning and add salt, pepper, and additional paprika if needed. Serve with additional sour cream on the side, and over prepared spaetzle or egg noodles if desired.

Ukrainian Sausage Soup

Ukrainian smoked ham sausage is heavily seasoned with garlic. If you use kielbasa or another type of smoked sausage, add the optional garlic to the recipe.

INGREDIENTS | SERVES 8

1½ cups dried red kidney beans

5 cups water

1 tablespoon vegetable oil

2 jalapeño peppers, seeded and diced

1 large onion, peeled and diced

8 ounces kielbasa or Ukrainian smoked ham sausage

1 bay leaf

1 tablespoon chili powder

1 teaspoon dried oregano

½ teaspoon freshly ground black pepper

¼ teaspoon cayenne pepper

Optional: 4 cloves garlic, peeled and minced

3 cups beef broth

1 14½-ounce can diced tomatoes

½ cup tomato sauce

2 tablespoons light brown sugar, packed

Salt, to taste

1. Rinse the kidney beans. Put in a container and add enough water to cover them by at least an inch. Cover and let beans soak overnight.

2. Drain the beans and put in the pressure cooker. Add 5 cups water and the oil. Lock the lid into place and bring to high pressure; maintain pressure for 12 minutes.

3. Remove from heat and allow pressure to release naturally. Drain the beans and set aside.

4. Add the jalapeño and onion to the pressure cooker. Dice the sausage and add to the pressure cooker along with the bay leaf, chili powder, oregano, black pepper, cayenne pepper, and garlic if using.

5. Lock the lid into place and bring to low pressure; maintain the pressure for 2 minutes. Quick-release the pressure.

6. Remove the lid and pour in the broth, tomatoes, tomato sauce, brown sugar, and drained beans.

7. Lock the lid into place and bring to high pressure; maintain pressure for 20 minutes. Remove from the heat and allow pressure to release naturally.

8. Remove and discard the bay leaf. Taste for seasoning and add salt if desired. Serve.

Swedish Meatballs

You can substitute ½ cup (or more to taste) of sour cream for the heavy cream. Serve over egg noodles.

INGREDIENTS | SERVES 4

1 slice whole wheat bread
½ cup milk
1 pound lean ground beef
8 ounces lean ground pork
1 large egg
1 small onion, peeled and minced
1 teaspoon dried dill
Salt and freshly ground black pepper, to taste
4 tablespoons butter
¼ cup all-purpose flour
1½ cups beef broth
1 cup water
½ cup heavy cream or sour cream

1. Add the bread to a large bowl. Pour in the milk and soak the bread until the milk is absorbed.

2. Break up the bread and mix it into the beef, pork, egg, onion, dill, salt, and pepper. Form into 12 meatballs and set aside.

3. Add the butter to the pressure cooker and melt it over medium-high heat; whisk in the flour until it forms a paste. Whisk in the broth and water. Bring to a simmer and then add the meatballs.

4. Lock the lid into place and bring to high pressure; maintain pressure for 10 minutes. Remove from the heat and quick-release the pressure.

5. Carefully stir in the cream. Taste for seasoning and add additional salt and pepper if needed. Serve.

Biryani

This Indian rice dish will serve 2 as a vegetarian main course or 4 as a side dish.

INGREDIENTS | SERVES 4

2 tablespoons vegetable oil

2 teaspoons sweet paprika

2 teaspoons turmeric

2 teaspoons garam masala

Cayenne pepper, to taste

1 medium onion, peeled and sliced

4 ounces fresh mushrooms, sliced

1 small green bell pepper, seeded and diced

1 cup basmati rice

½ cup small cauliflower florets

½ cup diced carrots

2 tablespoons dried apricots, diced

2 tablespoons raisins

2 cups vegetable broth or water

½ cup frozen peas, thawed

Salt, to taste

One-Pot Meal Biryani

Substitute chicken or beef broth for the vegetable broth when you pressure-cook the Biryani. Stir in a cup of diced, cooked chicken or beef when you add the peas. The tantalizing aromas wafting from the kitchen will have everyone anticipating dinner before it's even ready.

1. Bring the oil to temperature in the pressure cooker over low heat. Add the paprika, turmeric, garam masala, and cayenne; sauté for 1 minute.

2. Stir in the onion, mushrooms, and green pepper. Increase the heat to medium and sauté for 3 minutes. Stir in the rice, cauliflower, carrots, apricots, raisins, and broth or water.

3. Lock the lid into place and bring to high pressure; maintain pressure for 7 minutes. Remove from the heat and allow pressure to release naturally for 5 minutes. Quick-release any remaining pressure.

4. Remove the lid and stir in the peas. Cover the pressure cooker (but don't lock the lid into place) and allow to rest for 5 minutes.

5. Uncover and fluff the Biryani with a fork. Taste for seasoning and add salt if desired. Serve.

Borscht

If fresh tomatoes are available, you can substitute about a pound of diced vine-ripened tomatoes for the canned tomatoes.

INGREDIENTS | SERVES 6–8

1½ tablespoons olive oil or ghee

1 clove garlic, peeled and minced

½ pound lamb, cut into ½-inch pieces

1 small yellow onion, peeled and diced

1 pound red beets

1 small head cabbage, cored and chopped

1 14½-ounce can diced tomatoes

7 cups beef broth

¼ cup red wine vinegar

2 bay leaves

1 tablespoon lemon juice

Beet greens

Salt and freshly ground black pepper, to taste

Sour cream

Optional: Fresh dill

Vegetarian Borscht

Omit the lamb and substitute water or vegetable broth for the beef broth. Decrease the first pressure-cooking time to 5 minutes. If desired, add freshly grated orange or lemon zest to taste when you stir in the beet greens.

1. Add the oil or ghee, garlic, and lamb to pressure cooker. Brown the lamb over medium heat, stirring frequently to keep the garlic from burning. Add the onion and sauté until transparent.

2. Peel and dice the beets. Save the beet greens; rinse well and cover them with cold water until needed.

3. Add the beets, cabbage, tomatoes, beef broth, vinegar, bay leaves, and lemon juice to the pressure cooker.

4. Lock the lid into place and bring to low pressure; maintain pressure for 10 minutes. Remove from the heat and quick-release the pressure.

5. Chop the reserved beet greens and stir into the other ingredients in the pressure cooker.

6. Lock the lid into place, return the pan to the heat, and bring to low pressure; maintain pressure for 5 minutes.

7. Remove from heat and allow pressure to release naturally. Taste for seasoning and add salt and pepper to taste.

8. Ladle soup into bowls and garnish each bowl with a heaping tablespoon of sour cream and some fresh dill if using.

Pepper Steak

If you want to be traditional, serve Pepper Steak over cooked rice,
but it's also good over a baked potato or cooked noodles.

INGREDIENTS | SERVES 6

1 tablespoon sesame oil

2 tablespoons peanut or vegetable oil

1 large sweet onion, peeled and sliced

3 cloves garlic, peeled and minced

1 pound beef round steak

½ cup beef broth

1 tablespoon sherry

1 teaspoon light brown sugar

1 teaspoon fresh ginger, grated

Pinch dried red pepper flakes

2 tomatoes

1 large green bell pepper, seeded and sliced

4 green onions, sliced

¼ cup soy sauce

2 tablespoons cold water

2 tablespoons cornstarch

1. Bring the oil to temperature in the pressure cooker over medium-high heat. Add the onion; sauté for 3 minutes. Stir in the garlic; sauté for 30 seconds.

2. Cut the round steak into thin strips. Add to the pressure cooker; stir-fry for 3 minutes. Stir in the broth, sherry, brown sugar, ginger, and pepper flakes.

3. Lock the lid into place and bring to high pressure; maintain pressure for 10 minutes. Quick-release the pressure. Remove the lid.

4. Peel the tomatoes and remove the seeds; cut them into eighths. Add to the pressure cooker along with the bell pepper and green onions.

5. Lock the lid into place and bring to low pressure; maintain pressure for 3 minutes. Quick-release the pressure and remove the lid.

6. In a small bowl or measuring cup, whisk together the soy sauce, water, and cornstarch. Stir the cornstarch mixture into the beef mixture in the pressure cooker.

7. Cook uncovered, stirring gently, for 3 minutes or until the mixture is thickened and bubbly.

Belgian-Style Chicken

Belgium gave us more than just waffles and chocolate. The Belgians are also known for their fried food, including french fries.

INGREDIENTS | SERVES 4

3 stalks celery, cut into thirds

1 medium sweet onion, peeled and quartered

¾ teaspoon dried thyme

1 3-pound chicken

Salt, to taste

8 small carrots, peeled

½ cup chicken broth or water

¼ cup dry white wine

3 tablespoons butter

2 cups coarse dried bread crumbs

Optional: Fresh parsley

1. Place the celery pieces in the bottom of the pressure cooker and top with the onion wedges. Sprinkle with the thyme.

2. Rinse the chicken and pat dry. Season the chicken with salt to taste and place it on top of the onions and celery.

3. Place the carrots around and on top of the chicken. Pour in the broth or water and wine.

4. Lock the lid into place and bring to low pressure; maintain pressure for 25 minutes. Remove from the heat and allow pressure to release naturally for 5 minutes. Quick-release any remaining pressure.

5. Melt the butter in a nonstick skillet over medium heat. Add the bread crumbs and cook uncovered, stirring until toasted to a golden brown. Remove from the heat.

6. Transfer the chicken to a serving platter and cut into sections. Use a slotted spoon to move and arrange the vegetables around the chicken.

7. Skim and discard any fat from the pan juices and then pour the juices over the chicken and vegetables.

8. Sprinkle the toasted bread crumbs over the chicken and vegetables. Garnish with fresh parsley if desired. Serve.

Vietnamese Pork Curry

Pork is one of the most popular meats in Vietnamese dishes. It perfectly picks up the spicy sweetness of this sauce. Serve Vietnamese Pork Curry over cooked rice.

INGREDIENTS | SERVES 6

2 pounds boneless pork steaks

1 tablespoon peanut or vegetable oil

1 medium onion, peeled and diced

3 cloves garlic, peeled and minced

1 large eggplant, peeled and diced

1 jalapeño pepper, seeded and diced

3 carrots, peeled and sliced

2 medium waxy potatoes, peeled and diced

1 tablespoon sugar

1 tablespoon fresh ginger, grated

1 teaspoon curry powder

1 star anise

1 cup chicken broth or water

½ diced tomatoes

¼ cup fish sauce

1 tablespoon cold water

1 tablespoon cornstarch

6 green onions

¼ cup fresh cilantro

1. Trim and discard the fat from the pork steaks; cut steaks into bite-size pieces. Set aside.

2. Bring the oil to temperature in the pressure cooker over medium-high heat. Add the onion; sauté for 3 minutes. Add the garlic; sauté for 30 seconds.

3. Stir in the pork steak, eggplant, jalapeño pepper, carrot, potatoes, sugar, ginger, curry powder, star anise, broth or water, tomato, and fish sauce.

4. Lock the lid into place and bring to high pressure; maintain pressure for 20 minutes. Quick release the pressure. Remove the lid. Remove and discard the star anise.

5. Stir together the water and cornstarch in a small bowl. Whisk into the pork mixture in the pressure cooker.

6. Cook, uncovered, for 5 minutes, stirring until mixture is thickened and bubbly. Stir in the green onion and cilantro. Serve immediately.

Sauerbraten

Sauerbraten is a German dish. (Sauer means sour and braten means roast meat.) In addition to the potatoes in this recipe, it's often also served with cooked cabbage and dumplings or noodles.

INGREDIENTS | SERVES 8

2 tablespoons olive or vegetable oil
1 stalk celery, diced
1 carrot, peeled and grated
2 large onions, peeled and diced
2 cloves garlic, peeled and minced
2 cups beef broth
1 cup sweet red wine
1 teaspoon dried parsley
½ teaspoon dried thyme
½ teaspoon dried marjoram
4 whole cloves
2 bay leaves
1 teaspoon salt
½ teaspoon freshly ground black pepper
1 3-pound beef sirloin roast
8 medium potatoes, peeled and quartered
¼ cup butter, softened
¼ cup tomato sauce
¼ cup all-purpose flour
½ cup sour cream

1. Bring the oil to temperature in the pressure cooker over medium heat. Add the celery and carrot; sauté for 2 minutes.

2. Add the onion; sauté for 5 minutes or until the onion is softened. Stir in the garlic; sauté for 30 seconds.

3. Stir in the broth, wine, parsley, thyme, marjoram, cloves, bay leaves, salt, and pepper. Add the roast.

4. Lock the lid into place and bring to high pressure; maintain pressure for 1 hour. Remove from the heat and quick-release the pressure.

5. Remove the lid and transfer the roast to a serving platter; tent it with aluminum foil and keep warm.

6. Skim and discard the fat from the pan juices, and then strain the juices. Pour 2 cups of the strained juices into the pressure cooker.

7. Add the potatoes to the pressure cooker. Lock the lid in place and bring to high pressure; maintain pressure for 6 minutes.

8. Quick-release the pressure and remove the lid. Use a slotted spoon to transfer the potatoes to the serving platter.

9. In a small bowl, stir together the butter, tomato sauce, and flour. Bring the pan juices to a high simmer and whisk in the flour mixture.

10. Cook and stir for 5 minutes or until the mixture is thickened. Stir in the sour cream. Pour the sauce into a gravy boat to serve with the beef and sauce.

Chicken Tagine

Serve over cooked couscous. To prepare couscous, bring 2¼ cups chicken broth to boil in a saucepan. Stir in 2 cups dried couscous. Cover, remove from the heat, and let stand for 5 minutes. Fluff with a fork. Serve.

INGREDIENTS | SERVES 6

2 tablespoons butter or ghee

1 tablespoon extra virgin olive oil

2 large onions, peeled and diced

2 cloves garlic, peeled and minced

2 teaspoons fresh ginger, grated

1 teaspoon ground cumin

½ teaspoon saffron

2 pounds boneless, skinless chicken breast

2 cups chicken broth

1 lemon

2 tablespoons honey

12 large green olives, pitted

2 tablespoons cornstarch

2 tablespoons cold water

2 tablespoons fresh flat-leaf parsley, minced

Salt and freshly ground black pepper, to taste

1. Bring the butter or ghee and oil to temperature in the pressure cooker over medium heat. Add the onion; sauté for 5 minutes.

2. Stir in the garlic, ginger, cumin, and saffron; sauté for 30 seconds. Cut the chicken into bite-size pieces; add to the pressure cooker and stir-fry for 3 minutes. Stir in the broth, zest from half of the lemon, fresh lemon juice, and honey.

3. Lock the lid into place and bring to high pressure; maintain pressure for 8 minutes. Remove from the heat and quick-release the pressure.

4. Remove the lid; stir in the olives and the zest from the other half of the lemon.

5. In a small bowl, mix together the cornstarch and water, and then whisk it into the chicken mixture in the pressure cooker.

6. Simmer and stir for 3 minutes or until the mixture is thickened and the raw taste is cooked out of the cornstarch. Stir in the parsley. Taste for seasoning, and add salt and pepper if needed.

CHAPTER 13

Soups

Sun-Dried Tomato Soup
144

Chicken-Vegetable Soup
145

Vietnamese Beef Noodle Soup
146

Portuguese Kale Soup
147

Beef-Vegetable Soup
148

Split Pea Soup
149

Lentil Soup
150

Scotch Broth
150

Fresh Tomato Soup
151

Mushroom-Barley Soup
151

Cuban Black Bean Soup
152

Minestrone
153

Greek Meatball Soup
154

Chicken Noodle Soup
155

Turkey Drumsticks
and Vegetable Soup
156

Sun-Dried Tomato Soup

*The dried tomatoes should not be packed in oil. You can substitute 3¾ cups
of peeled, diced fresh tomatoes if you have them on hand. Serve with
toasted cheese sandwiches for a classic comfort food meal.*

INGREDIENTS | SERVES 6

2½ tablespoons unsalted butter

1 stalk celery, finely diced

1 medium carrot, peeled and
finely diced

1 small sweet onion, peeled and diced

1 teaspoon dried basil

½ teaspoon dried marjoram

2 tablespoons unbleached
all-purpose flour

2 14½-ounce cans diced tomatoes

4 whole sun-dried tomatoes

1 teaspoon sugar

⅛ teaspoon baking soda

2½ cups vegetable or chicken broth

Salt and freshly ground black pepper,
to taste

1. Melt the butter in the pressure cooker over medium heat. Add the celery and carrot; sauté for 2 minutes. Stir in the onion, basil, and marjoram; sauté for 3 minutes or until the onion is soft. Add the flour; stir and cook for 2 minutes. Stir in the remaining ingredients.

2. Lock the lid into place. Bring to high pressure; maintain pressure for 8 minutes. Remove from the heat and quick-release the pressure. Remove the lid. Use an immersion blender to puree the soup. If you don't have an immersion blender, you can transfer the soup in batches to a blender or food processor, puree it, and then return it to the pot or a soup tureen. Taste for seasoning and add additional salt and pepper if needed.

Cream of Tomato Soup

For Cream of Tomato Soup, bring a cup of half-and-half or heavy cream to a high simmer and whisk it in after you've pureed the soup. Taste for seasoning and add additional salt and pepper if needed. Serve.

Chicken-Vegetable Soup

Transform Chicken-Vegetable Soup into a tomato-based meal by substituting 2 (14½-ounce) cans of diced tomatoes for the chicken broth.

INGREDIENTS | SERVES 8

7 large carrots

2 stalks celery, finely diced

1 large sweet onion, peeled and diced

8 ounces fresh mushrooms, cleaned and sliced

1 tablespoon extra virgin olive oil

1 teaspoon butter, melted

1 clove garlic, peeled and minced

4 cups chicken broth

6 medium potatoes, peeled and diced

1 tablespoon dried parsley

¼ teaspoon dried oregano

¼ teaspoon dried rosemary

1 bay leaf

2 strips orange zest

Salt and freshly ground black pepper, to taste

8 chicken thighs, skin removed

1 10-ounce package frozen green beans, thawed

1 10-ounce package frozen whole kernel corn, thawed

1 10-ounce package frozen baby peas, thawed

1. Peel the carrots. Dice 6 of the carrots and grate 1. Add the grated carrot, celery, onion, mushrooms, oil, and butter to the pressure cooker. Stir to coat the vegetables in the oil and butter. Lock the lid into place. Bring to low pressure; maintain pressure for 1 minute. Quick-release the pressure and remove the lid.

2. Stir in the garlic. Add the broth, diced carrots, potatoes, parsley, oregano, rosemary, bay leaf, orange zest, salt, pepper, and chicken thighs. Lock the lid into place and bring to high pressure. Remove from the heat and allow pressure to release naturally for 5 minutes. Quick-release any remaining pressure and remove the lid.

3. Use a slotted spoon to remove the thighs, cut the meat from the bone and into bite-size pieces, and return it to the pot. Remove and discard the orange zest and bay leaf. Return the uncovered pressure cooker to medium heat. Stir in the green beans, corn, and peas; cook for 5 minutes or until the vegetables are heated through. Taste for seasoning and add additional salt, pepper, and herbs if needed.

Pot Pie–Style Servings

This soup is also delicious if you use a roux to thicken the broth and serve it pot pie–style: ladled over split buttermilk biscuits. You can buy biscuits in the freezer aisle, but they only take about half an hour to make if you want to fix them from scratch.

Vietnamese Beef Noodle Soup

This is a simplified, Americanized version of pho, substituting brown sugar for the yellow rock sugar found in Asian markets.

INGREDIENTS | SERVES 10

1 3-pound English-cut chuck roast

3 medium yellow onions

1 4-inch piece ginger

5 star anise

6 whole cloves

1 3-inch cinnamon stick

¼ teaspoon salt

2 cups beef broth

Water

1½–2 pounds small dried or fresh banh pho noodles

4 tablespoons fish sauce

1 tablespoon brown sugar

3 or 4 scallions, green part only, cut into thin rings

⅓ cup fresh cilantro, chopped

Freshly ground black pepper

Optional Garnishes for Pho

If desired, have these additional garnishes available at the table: Sprigs of spearmint (hung lui), sprigs of Asian/Thai basil (hung que), thorny cilantro leaves (ngo gai), bean sprouts (about ½ pound), blanched, thinly sliced red hot chilies (such as Thai bird or dragon), or lime wedges.

1. Trim the roast of any fat; cut the meat into bite-size pieces and add to the pressure cooker. Peel and quarter 2 onions. Cut the ginger into 1-inch pieces. Add the onion and ginger to the pressure cooker along with the star anise, cloves, cinnamon stick, salt, broth, and enough water to cover the meat by about 1 inch. Lock the lid into place and bring to low pressure; maintain pressure for an hour. Remove from the heat and allow pressure to release naturally.

2. About ½ hour before serving, peel the remaining onion; cut it into paper-thin slices and soak them in cold water. For dried rice noodles: Cover them with hot water and allow to soak for 15–20 minutes or until softened and opaque white; drain in colander. For fresh rice noodles: Untangle and place in a colander, then rinse briefly with cold water.

3. Remove the meat from the broth with a slotted spoon; shred the meat. Strain the broth through a fine strainer, discarding the spices and onion; return strained broth to the pressure cooker along with the shredded meat. Bring the meat and broth to a boil over medium-high heat. Stir the fish sauce and brown sugar into the broth. (The broth should taste slightly too strong because the noodles and other ingredients are not salted. Therefore, to test for seasoning, you may want to taste the broth and meat with some noodles. If you desire a stronger, saltier flavor, add more fish sauce. Add more brown sugar to make the broth sweeter if desired. If the broth is already too salty, add some additional water to dilute it.)

Vietnamese Beef Noodle Soup (*continued*)

4. Blanch the noodles in stages by adding as many noodles to a strainer as you can submerge in the boiling broth without causing the pressure cooker to boil over. The noodles will collapse and lose their stiffness in about 15–20 seconds. Pull strainer from the broth, letting the excess broth clinging to them drain back into cooker. Empty noodles into bowls, allowing each serving to fill about ⅓ of the bowl, and then ladle hot broth and beef over the noodles. Garnish with onion slices, scallions, and chopped cilantro, and finish with freshly ground black pepper.

Portuguese Kale Soup

Collard greens can be substituted for the kale, but doing so will change the flavor somewhat.

INGREDIENTS | SERVES 6

1 pound kale

1 tablespoon extra virgin olive oil

1 large yellow onion, peeled and thinly sliced

½ pound linguica or kielbasa, sliced

4 large potatoes, peeled and diced

4 cups chicken broth

2 15-ounce cans cannellini beans, rinsed and drained

Salt and freshly ground black pepper, to taste

1. Trim the large ribs from the kale. Slice it into thin strips. Put the kale strips into a bowl of cold water and soak for an hour; drain well.

2. Add the oil, onions, and linguica or kielbasa to the pressure cooker; stir to combine. Place over medium heat; sauté for 5 minutes or until the onions are soft. Add the potatoes, chicken broth, drained kale, and beans. Lock the lid into place and bring to low pressure; maintain pressure for 8 minutes. Remove from the heat and allow pressure to release naturally for 5 minutes. Quick-release any remaining pressure and remove the lid. Taste for seasoning and add salt and pepper to taste.

Beef-Vegetable Soup

*Make Beef-Vegetable Soup a tomato-based dish by substituting
2 15-ounce cans of diced tomatoes for the beef broth.*

INGREDIENTS | SERVES 8

7 large carrots

2 stalks celery, finely diced

1 large sweet onion, peeled and diced

8 ounces fresh mushrooms, cleaned and sliced

1 tablespoon extra virgin olive oil

1 teaspoon butter, melted

1 clove garlic, peeled and minced

4 cups beef broth

6 medium potatoes, peeled and diced

1 tablespoon dried parsley

¼ teaspoon dried oregano

¼ teaspoon dried rosemary

1 bay leaf

Salt and freshly ground black pepper, to taste

1 3-pound chuck roast

1 10-ounce package frozen green beans, thawed

1 10-ounce package frozen whole kernel corn, thawed

1 10-ounce package frozen baby peas, thawed

1. Peel the carrots. Dice 6 of the carrots and grate 1. Add the grated carrot, celery, onion, mushrooms, oil, and butter to the pressure cooker. Stir to coat the vegetables in the oil and butter. Lock the lid into place. Bring to low pressure; maintain pressure for 1 minute. Quick-release the pressure and remove the lid.

2. Stir in the garlic. Add the broth, diced carrots, potatoes, parsley, oregano, rosemary, bay leaf, salt, and pepper. Trim the roast of any fat and cut the meat into bite-size pieces; add to the pressure cooker and stir into the vegetables. Lock the lid into place and bring to high pressure; maintain pressure for 15 minutes. Quick-release the pressure and remove the lid.

3. Remove and discard the bay leaf. Stir in the green beans, corn, and peas; cook for 5 minutes or until the vegetables are heated through. Taste for seasoning and add additional salt, pepper, and herbs if needed.

Tasty Substitutions

Add a bit more flavor to this soup by substituting several strips of bacon cut into bite-size pieces for the oil. The bacon bits themselves will be absorbed into the dish and provide extra crunch and zing. Another alternative is using canned French onion soup in place of some of the beef broth.

Split Pea Soup

This soup tastes even better if you refrigerate it overnight and heat it up to serve the next day. It's hearty enough to stand alone as the main dish. Serve with crusty bread.

INGREDIENTS | SERVES 6

4 strips bacon, diced

1 large sweet onion, peeled and diced

2 large potatoes, peeled and diced

2 large carrots, peeled and sliced

1 cup dried green split peas, rinsed

4 cups chicken broth

2 smoked ham hocks

Optional: 1 10-ounce package frozen peas, thawed

Salt and freshly ground black pepper, to taste

1. Add the bacon to the pressure cooker. Fry it over medium heat until the bacon begins to render its fat. Add the onion; sauté for 3 minutes or until soft. Stir in the diced potatoes; sauté for 3 minutes. Add the carrots, split peas, broth, and ham hocks. Lock the lid into place and bring to low pressure; maintain pressure for 15 minutes. Remove from the heat and allow pressure to release naturally.

2. Remove the lid. Use a slotted spoon to remove the ham hocks; allow to cool until the meat can be removed from the bones. Taste the split peas. If they're not cooked through, lock the lid back into place and cook at low pressure for another 5 minutes; remove from the heat and quick-release the pressure. If the split peas are cooked through and tender, stir the ham removed from the hocks into the soup. If desired, use an immersion blender to puree the soup.

3. Return the soup to medium heat and bring to a simmer. If desired, stir in the peas and cook until they're heated. Taste for seasoning and add salt and pepper if needed.

Lentil Soup

Rather than stirring the spinach into the soup, you can double the amount and serve the soup with spinach salad.

INGREDIENTS | SERVES 6

1 tablespoon olive oil

1 celery stalk, diced

1 large carrot, peeled and diced

1 large yellow onion, peeled and diced

2 cloves of garlic, peeled and minced

1 cup dried brown lentils, rinsed and drained

5 cups chicken broth

Salt and freshly ground black pepper, to taste

Optional: 3 cups baby spinach, washed and dried

⅜ cup Parmigiano-Reggiano cheese, grated

1. Bring the oil to temperature in the pressure cooker over medium heat. Add the celery and carrot; sauté for 2 minutes. Stir in the onion; sauté for 3 minutes or until the onion is transparent. Add the garlic; sauté for 30 seconds.

2. Stir in the lentils and broth. Lock the lid into place and bring to high pressure; maintain pressure for 8 minutes. Remove from the heat and allow pressure to release naturally. Remove the lid and stir the spinach into the soup if using. Return the pressure cooker to medium heat; cook until the spinach is wilted. Taste for seasoning and season with salt and pepper, to taste. Serve in bowls, topping each one with 1 tablespoon of grated Parmigiano-Reggiano cheese.

Scotch Broth

Scotch Broth is not a broth in the traditional sense. Instead, it's the name for a barley soup.

INGREDIENTS | SERVES 4

2 leeks, white part only

4 lamb shoulder chops

⅓ cup pearl barley

1 large carrot, peeled and diced

1 stalk celery, thinly sliced

2 medium potatoes, peeled and diced

6 cups water

Salt and freshly ground black pepper, to taste

Optional: Fresh parsley, minced

Dice the white part of the leeks; rinse well and drain. Add the leeks to the pressure cooker along with the lamb chops, barley, carrot, celery, potatoes, water, salt, and pepper. Lock the lid into place and bring to high pressure; maintain pressure for 9 minutes. Remove from the heat and quick-release the pressure. Remove the lid. Taste for seasoning and add additional salt and pepper if needed. Transfer a lamb chop to each of four bowls and ladle the soup over the meat. Garnish with parsley if desired.

Fresh Tomato Soup

This soup celebrates the simple, yet wondrous, summery taste of fresh vine-ripened tomatoes. You can add sautéed onion or shallots and herbs if you wish. Choose the dairy product that you add to the soup according to your dietary needs—and according to how rich you like your soup.

INGREDIENTS | SERVES 4

8 medium fresh tomatoes

¼ teaspoon sea salt

1 cup water

½ teaspoon baking soda

2 cups milk, half-and-half, or heavy cream

Freshly ground black pepper, to taste

1. Wash, peel, seed, and dice the tomatoes. Add them and any tomato juice you can retain to the pressure cooker. Stir in the salt and water. Lock the lid into place. Place the pressure cooker over medium heat and bring to low pressure; maintain pressure for 2 minutes. Quick release the pressure and remove the lid.

2. Stir the baking soda into the tomato mixture. Once it's stopped bubbling and foaming, stir in your choice of milk, half-and-half, or cream. Cook and stir for several minutes or until the soup is brought to temperature.

Mushroom-Barley Soup

This is a vegetarian soup. If you want the soup to complement a meat entrée, you can substitute chicken or beef broth for the water.

INGREDIENTS | SERVES 6

2 tablespoons butter

1 tablespoon olive or vegetable oil

2 stalks celery, diced

1 large carrot, peeled and diced

1 large sweet onion, peeled, halved, and sliced

2 cloves garlic, peeled and minced

1 portobello mushroom cap, diced

8 ounces fresh mushrooms, cleaned and sliced

1 bay leaf

½ cup pearl barley

6 cups water

Optional: 2 tablespoons vermouth or brandy

Salt and freshly ground black pepper, to taste

1. Melt the butter and bring the oil to temperature in the pressure cooker over medium heat. Add the celery and carrot; sauté for 2 minutes. Add the onion and sauté for 3 minutes or until the onion is soft and transparent. Stir in the garlic and mushrooms; sauté for 5 minutes or until the mushrooms release their moisture and the onion begins to turn golden.

2. Stir in the bay leaf, barley, water, and vermouth or brandy (if using). Lock the lid into place and bring to high pressure; maintain pressure for 20 minutes. Remove from the heat and allow pressure to release naturally.

3. Remove the lid. Remove and discard the bay leaf. Taste for seasoning and add salt and pepper if needed. Serve.

Cuban Black Bean Soup

As with almost any bean dish, you can add diced celery and carrot slices to this soup when you add the onion. In fact, adding some along with another cup of chicken broth will let you increase the servings.

INGREDIENTS | SERVES 8

½ pound bacon, chopped

1 green bell pepper, seeded and diced

1 large yellow onion, peeled and diced

8 ounces smoked sausage

3 cloves garlic, peeled and minced

2 teaspoons paprika

½ teaspoon ground cumin

½ teaspoon chili powder

¼ teaspoon coriander

1 bay leaf

6 cups chicken broth or water

1 smoked ham hock or smoked turkey wing

1 pound dried black beans, soaked overnight, rinsed and drained

⅛ teaspoon cayenne pepper or dried red pepper flakes

½ cup dry sherry

1 tablespoon red wine vinegar

Salt and freshly ground black pepper, to taste

1. Add bacon to the pressure cooker and fry over medium-high heat until the bacon begins to render its fat. Reduce the heat to medium and add the green pepper; sauté for 3 minutes. Stir in the onion. Slice or dice the smoked sausage and stir into the onion; sauté for 3 minutes or until the onion is tender. Stir in the garlic along with the paprika, cumin, chili powder, coriander, bay leaf, broth or water, ham hock or turkey wing, and beans. Lock the lid into place and bring to high pressure; maintain pressure for 30 minutes. Remove from the heat and allow pressure to release naturally, leaving the lid in place for at least 20 minutes. Remove the lid.

2. Remove the ham hock or turkey wing and take the meat off of the bones; return meat to the pot. Remove and discard the bay leaf. Use a potato masher or immersion blender to partially puree the soup. Return the uncovered pan to medium heat and bring to a simmer. Stir in the cayenne pepper or dried red pepper flakes, sherry, and vinegar. Simmer for 20 minutes. Taste for seasoning; add salt and pepper as needed and adjust the herbs, chili powder, and cayenne pepper or red pepper flakes if desired.

Minestrone

Minestrone packs tons of nutrients and is substantial enough to stand on its own as a light meal. Serve with a tossed salad and fresh homemade bread or wholegrain dinner rolls.

INGREDIENTS | SERVES 8

4 strips bacon, diced

1 large onion, peeled and diced

2 cloves garlic, peeled and minced

2 large carrots, peeled and diced

2 leeks, white part only, cleaned and diced

½ head cabbage, cored and rough chopped

2 stalks celery, diced

2 14½-ounce cans diced tomatoes

¼ teaspoon dried rosemary

1 teaspoon dried parsley

¼ teaspoon dried oregano

4½ cups chicken broth

1 2-pound beef shank

Salt and freshly ground black pepper, to taste

½ cup elbow macaroni

½ cup Arborio rice

Salt and freshly ground black pepper, to taste

½ cup Parmigiano-Reggiano cheese, grated

1. Add the bacon to the pressure cooker. Fry over medium heat until it renders its fat. Add the onion and sauté for 3 minutes or until the onion is soft. Stir in the garlic, carrots, leeks, cabbage, celery, undrained tomatoes, rosemary, parsley, oregano, and chicken broth. Add the beef shank and push it down into the vegetables and liquid.

2. Lock the lid into place and bring to low pressure; maintain pressure for 15 minutes. Remove from the heat and quick-release the pressure.

3. Remove the beef shank. When it's cool enough to handle, remove the meat from the bone, cut it into bite-size pieces, and return it to the pan. Stir in the macaroni and rice.

4. Lock the lid into place and bring to low pressure; maintain pressure for 7 minutes. Remove from the heat and quick-release the pressure. Remove the lid.

5. Taste for seasoning and add salt, pepper, and additional herbs if needed. Serve in bowls topped with the grated Parmigiano-Reggiano cheese.

Meatless Minestrone

To turn this delightful winter dish into a vegetarian meal, omit the bacon and substitute a tablespoon of olive or vegetable oil and a tablespoon of unsalted butter or ghee. Omit the beef shank and substitute vegetable broth for the chicken broth. Reduce the servings to 6.

Greek Meatball Soup

This recipe is adapted from a Greek soup (youvarlakia avgolemono). The traditional version doesn't have the vegetables added to the broth, but those vegetables make this soup a one-pot meal. Serve the soup topped with some feta cheese and with crusty bread.

INGREDIENTS | SERVES 6

1 pound lean ground beef

¼ pound ground pork

1 small onion, peeled and minced

1 clove garlic, peeled and minced

6 tablespoons uncooked converted long-grain white rice

1 tablespoon dried parsley

2 teaspoons dried dill or mint

1 teaspoon dried oregano

Salt and freshly ground black pepper, to taste

3 large eggs

6 cups chicken or vegetable broth, or water

1 medium onion, peeled and chopped

1 cup baby carrots, each sliced into thirds

2 large potatoes, peeled and cut into cubes

1 stalk celery, finely chopped

2 tablespoons masa harina (corn flour)

⅓ cup fresh lemon juice

1. In a large bowl, mix the meat, onion, garlic, rice, parsley, dill or mint, oregano, salt, pepper, and 1 of the eggs. Shape into small meatballs and set aside.

2. Add 2 cups of broth or water to the pressure cooker. Add the meatballs, onion, carrots, potatoes, and celery, and then pour in the remaining broth or water to cover the meatballs and vegetables. Lock the lid into place and bring to low pressure; maintain pressure for 10 minutes. Remove from the heat and allow pressure to release naturally. Remove the lid. Use a slotted spoon to move the meatballs to a soup tureen; cover and keep warm.

3. Return the pan to medium heat and bring to a simmer. In a small bowl or measuring cup, beat the two remaining eggs and then whisk in the corn flour. Gradually whisk in the lemon juice. Ladle in about a cup of the hot broth from the pressure cooker, doing so in a slow, steady stream, beating continuously until all of the hot liquid has been incorporated into the egg–corn flour mixture. Stir this mixture into the pressure cooker. Stir and simmer for 5 minutes or until mixture is thickened. Taste for seasoning and adjust if necessary. Pour over the meatballs and serve.

Chicken Noodle Soup

One taste of this dish and you'll never want to eat chicken noodle soup out of a can again!

INGREDIENTS | SERVES 8–10

1 tablespoon butter

1 tablespoon olive or vegetable oil

6 medium carrots, peeled and sliced

3 stalks celery, diced

1 large sweet onion, peeled and diced

4 pounds bone-in chicken thighs and breasts

½ teaspoon sea or kosher salt

1 teaspoon dried parsley

¼ teaspoon dried thyme

2 cups chicken broth

4 cups water

2 cups medium egg noodles

1 cup frozen baby peas, thawed

Freshly ground black pepper, to taste

Homemade Egg Noodle Taste

For richer chicken noodle soup with that homemade egg noodle taste, beat 1 or 2 large eggs in a small bowl. Whisk in some of the chicken broth from the soup (to temper the eggs), and then stir the egg mixture into the soup about 2 minutes before the noodles are cooked through.

1. Melt the butter and bring to temperature with the oil in the pressure cooker over medium heat. Add the carrots and celery; sauté for 2 minutes. Add the onion; sauté for 3 minutes or until the onion is soft. Add the chicken, salt, parsley, thyme, and chicken broth. Lock the lid into place and bring to low temperature; maintain pressure for 20 minutes. Remove from the heat and quick-release the pressure. Remove the lid.

2. Use tongs or a slotted spoon to transfer the chicken pieces to a cutting board. Remove and discard the skin. Once the chicken is cool enough to handle, remove the meat from the bones; shred the meat or cut it into bite-size pieces. Return the chicken to the pressure cooker.

3. Return the pressure cooker to medium heat. Stir in the water; bring to a boil. Add the egg noodles and cook according to package directions. Stir in the thawed peas. Taste for seasoning and add additional salt if needed, and pepper, to taste.

Turkey Drumsticks and Vegetable Soup

Measure the turkey drumsticks to make sure they'll fit in your pressure cooker. It's okay if the end of the bone touches the lid of the cooker, as long as it doesn't block the vent.

INGREDIENTS | SERVES 6

1 tablespoon extra virgin olive oil

1 clove of garlic, peeled and minced

2 14½-ounce cans diced tomatoes

6 medium potatoes, peeled and cut into quarters

6 large carrots, peeled and sliced

12 small onions, peeled

2 stalks celery, finely diced

½ ounce dried mushrooms

¼ teaspoon dried oregano

¼ teaspoon dried rosemary

1 bay leaf

2 strips orange zest

Salt and freshly ground black pepper, to taste

2 1¼-pound turkey drumsticks, skin removed

1 10-ounce package frozen green beans, thawed

1 10-ounce package frozen whole kernel corn, thawed

1 10-ounce package frozen baby peas, thawed

Fresh parsley or cilantro

1. Bring the oil to temperature in the pressure cooker over medium heat. Add the garlic and sauté for 10 seconds. Stir in the tomatoes, potatoes, carrots, onions, celery, mushrooms, oregano, rosemary, bay leaf, orange zest, salt, and pepper. Stand the two drumsticks meaty side down in the pan.

2. Lock the lid into place and bring to high pressure; maintain pressure for 12 minutes. Remove from the heat and allow the pressure to drop naturally for 10 minutes, and then use the quick-release method for your cooker to release the remaining pressure if needed. Remove the drumsticks, cut the meat from the bone and into bite-size pieces, and return it to the pot. Stir in the green beans, corn, and peas; cook over medium heat for 5 minutes. Remove and discard the orange zest and bay leaf. Taste for seasoning and add salt and pepper if needed. Garnish with fresh parsley or cilantro.

Pot Pie Variation

Transform the Turkey Drumsticks and Vegetable Soup recipe into a turkey pot pie–style meal by substituting 4 cups of chicken broth for the tomatoes; thicken the soup with a roux if desired, and serve it over buttermilk biscuits. Experiment with the vegetables and herbs to tailor the recipe to your taste buds.

CHAPTER 14

Stews and Chowders

Quick and Easy Beef Stew
158

African Lamb Stew
158

Herbed Chicken Stew
with Dumplings
159

Green Chicken Chili
160

White Chicken Chili
161

Seafood Chowder
161

Salmon Chowder
162

Corn Chowder
163

Simplified Chicken Stew
163

Old South Chicken Stew
164

Tex-Mex Stew
165

Chicken Chili
166

Chicken in Beer Stew
167

Mushroom Beef Stew
with Dumplings
168

New England Clam Chowder
169

Manhattan Clam Chowder
169

Quick and Easy Beef Stew

This is a quick and easy way to turn leftover roast beef into a hearty stew. Serve with crackers or dinner rolls and you have an easy complete comfort food meal.

INGREDIENTS | SERVES 8

2 cups cooked roast beef, cut into bite-size pieces

1 10¾-ounce can condensed tomato soup

1 10½-ounce can condensed French onion soup

1 tablespoon Worcestershire sauce

2 cups water

1 24-ounce bag frozen vegetables

1 10-ounce box frozen mixed vegetables

1 tablespoon butter

1 tablespoon all-purpose flour

Salt and freshly ground black pepper, to taste

1. Add the roast beef, soups, Worcestershire sauce, water, and frozen vegetables to the pressure cooker. Lock the lid into place and bring to low pressure; maintain pressure for 3 minutes. Remove from heat, quick-release the pressure, and remove the lid.

2. In a small bowl, mix the butter into the flour to make a paste. Ladle ½ cup soup broth into the bowl and whisk into the paste, then pour it into the stew.

3. Place the uncovered pressure cooker over medium-high heat and bring the stew to a boil; boil for 2 minutes, stirring occasionally. Reduce heat and simmer for an additional 2 minutes.

African Lamb Stew

Few things fill the kitchen with a more appetizing aroma than cinnamon simmering in orange juice. Your family will rush to the table for this dish. Serve with couscous.

INGREDIENTS | SERVES 6

1 tablespoon olive or vegetable oil

2 pounds boneless lamb shoulder

1 large onion, peeled and diced

2 cloves garlic, peeled and minced

1 cup dried apricots, quartered

⅓ cup raisins

⅓ cup blanched whole almonds

1 tablespoon fresh ginger, minced

½ teaspoon ground cinnamon

¾ cup red wine

¼ cup fresh orange juice

⅓ cup fresh mint leaves, packed

Salt and freshly ground pepper, to taste

Optional: Fresh mint leaves for garnish

1. Bring the oil to temperature in the pressure cooker over medium-high heat. Trim the lamb of any fat and cut the meat into bite-size pieces. Brown the lamb in 4 batches for 5 minutes each. Set aside browned meat and keep warm.

2. Reduce heat to medium. Add the onion and sauté for 3 minutes. Add the garlic; sauté for 30 seconds. Stir in the lamb. Add apricots, raisins, almonds, ginger, cinnamon, wine, orange juice, and mint leaves.

3. Lock the lid into place and bring to high pressure; maintain pressure for 20 minutes. Remove from heat and allow pressure to release naturally. Remove the lid. Garnish with fresh mint if desired.

Herbed Chicken Stew with Dumplings

Nothing says comfort food like Chicken and Dumplings. You can stretch this recipe to 6 or 8 main dish servings if you serve the stew over another favorite comfort food companion: mashed potatoes.

INGREDIENTS | SERVES 4

¼ cup unbleached all-purpose flour
½ teaspoon salt
¼ teaspoon freshly ground black pepper
8 bone-in chicken thighs, skin removed
2 tablespoons unsalted butter
2 stalks celery, finely diced
1 large onion, peeled and diced
1 teaspoon dried thyme
12 ounces baby carrots, cut in half
2½ cups chicken broth
½ cup dry white wine or water
2 teaspoons dried parsley
1 bay leaf
1 recipe dumplings

Dumpling Batter

To make the dumplings, add 2 cups of unbleached all-purpose flour, 1 tablespoon baking powder, and ½ teaspoon salt to a mixing bowl. Stir to combine, then use a pastry blender or two forks to cut in 5 tablespoons of unsalted butter. Stir in 1 large beaten egg and ¾ cup of buttermilk until the mixture comes together.

1. Add the flour, salt, and pepper to a large zip-closure plastic bag; shake to mix. Trim the chicken of any fat and add to the bag. Seal the bag and shake to coat the chicken in the seasoned flour.

2. Melt the butter in the pressure cooker over medium-high heat. When the butter begins to bubble, add 4 of the chicken thighs; brown for 3 minutes on each side.

3. Transfer chicken to a platter. Add the remaining thighs and brown them in a similar manner; remove to the platter.

4. Add the celery; sauté for 2 minutes. Add the onion and thyme; sauté for 3 minutes or until the onion is softened.

5. Stir in the carrots, broth, wine or water, parsley, and bay leaf. Return the browned chicken thighs (and their juices) to the pressure cooker.

6. Lock the lid into place and bring to high pressure; maintain pressure for 10 minutes. Quick-release the pressure and remove the lid. Remove and discard the bay leaf.

7. Leave the pressure cooker on the heat, adjusting it to maintain a simmer. Drop heaping teaspoons of the dumpling batter into the simmering stew.

8. Cover loosely to allow a small amount of the steam to escape and cook for 10 to 15 minutes or until the dumplings are puffy and cooked through. Serve.

Green Chicken Chili

Serve with cornbread or tortilla chips. Have sour cream, grated Cheddar or jack cheese, and avocado slices or guacamole available at the table.

INGREDIENTS | **SERVES 8**

1 cup dried pinto beans

8 cups water

2 teaspoons vegetable oil

1 tablespoon olive oil

1 medium onion, peeled and diced

1 large carrot, peeled and diced

2 medium red bell peppers, seeded and diced

2 jalapeño peppers, seeded and diced

4 cloves garlic, peeled and minced

4 4-ounce cans chopped green chili peppers

1 chipotle pepper, seeded and diced

3 pounds mixed meaty chicken pieces, skin removed

4 cups chicken broth

2 tablespoons butter

2 tablespoons unbleached all-purpose flour

Salt and freshly ground black pepper, to taste

1. Rinse the beans; soak them in 3 cups of the water overnight. Drain and add the beans, the remaining 5 cups of water, and vegetable oil to the pressure cooker.

2. Lock the lid into place and bring to high pressure; maintain pressure for 15 minutes. Remove from the heat and allow pressure to release naturally. Strain the beans; set aside. Wash and dry the pressure cooker.

3. Bring the olive oil to temperature in the pressure cooker over medium-high heat. Add the onion; sauté for 3 minutes. Stir in the carrot; sauté for 3 minutes.

4. Stir in the red bell and jalapeño peppers; sauté for 5 minutes or until all vegetables are soft.

5. Add the garlic, canned peppers, chipotle peppers, chicken pieces, and chicken broth.

6. Lock the lid into place and bring to high pressure; maintain pressure for 12 minutes. Quick-release the pressure. Remove the chicken pieces to a bowl.

7. When the chicken is cool enough to handle, remove the meat from the bones, cut or tear it into bite-size pieces, and return the meat to the pressure cooker. Stir in the beans.

8. Bring the chili to a boil. Blend the butter together with the flour to make a paste, and then whisk it into the chili.

9. Boil for 1 minute and then reduce heat to maintain a simmer for about 5 minutes or until the chili is thickened. Taste for seasoning and add salt and pepper if desired. Serve.

White Chicken Chili

Serve like you would any other chili, with cornbread or tortilla chips. Have grated cheese and sour cream available for those who wish to use it to top their chili.

INGREDIENTS | SERVES 8

1 tablespoon olive or vegetable oil

1 large white onion, peeled and diced

4 cloves garlic, peeled and minced

2 pounds boneless, skinless chicken breasts

2 teaspoons ground cumin

2 teaspoons dried oregano

¼ teaspoon ground cayenne pepper

1 4-ounce can chopped green chili peppers, undrained

2 14-ounce cans chicken broth

2 16-ounce cans white beans

Hot sauce, to taste

Salt and freshly ground white or black pepper, to taste

1. Bring the oil to temperature in the pressure cooker over medium-high heat. Add the onion; sauté for 3 minutes. Stir in the garlic; sauté for 30 seconds. Cut the chicken into bite-size pieces and add to the pressure cooker along with the cumin, oregano, and cayenne pepper; stir-fry for 1 minute.

2. Stir in the canned chilies and 1 can chicken broth. Lock the lid into place and bring to high pressure; maintain pressure for 6 minutes. Quick-release the pressure and remove the lid. Stir in remaining chicken broth and the beans. Bring to a simmer. Taste for seasoning and add hot sauce, salt, and pepper to taste. Serve.

Seafood Chowder

Clam juice is salty, so if you're using it in this chowder, wait until after you taste for seasoning to add any salt. Serve with a tossed salad and dinner rolls.

INGREDIENTS | SERVES 6

2 tablespoons butter

2 large leeks

4 cups fish broth or clam juice

2 cups water

6 medium russet or Idaho baking potatoes, peeled and diced

1 bay leaf

Salt and freshly ground black pepper, to taste

1 pound scrod or other firm white fish

½ teaspoon dried thyme

½ cup heavy cream

1. Melt the butter in the pressure cooker over medium heat. Cut off the root end of the leeks and discard any bruised outer leaves. Slice the leeks. Add to the pressure cooker and sauté for 2 minutes. Stir in the broth, water, and potatoes. Add the bay leaf, salt, and pepper.

2. Lock lid into place and bring to high pressure; maintain for 4 minutes. Quick-release the pressure and remove the lid. Remove and discard the bay leaf.

3. Cut the fish into bite-size pieces and add to the pressure cooker. Simmer for 3 minutes. Add the thyme and cream. Bring cream to temperature, stirring occasionally.

Salmon Chowder

For a serving variation, place the salmon fillets on top of tossed salad greens and drizzle Green Peppercorn Sauce over the salmon and salad. Garnish with some of the fennel leaves. Have oyster crackers or saltines available for those who wish to add it to their chowder.

INGREDIENTS | SERVES 4

4 teaspoons freshly squeezed lemon juice

4 6-ounce salmon fillets, skin removed

1 tablespoon olive or vegetable oil

1 large leek

1 large fennel bulb

4 medium Yukon Gold potatoes, peeled and diced

1 teaspoon sea salt

4 cups water

1 bay leaf

Optional: Green Peppercorn Sauce

Green Peppercorn Sauce

In a small bowl, whisk together ¾ cup mayonnaise, 1 teaspoon Dijon mustard, 1 teaspoon freshly squeezed lemon juice, 2 tablespoons extra virgin olive oil, and 3 tablespoons of crushed green peppercorns.

1. Sprinkle ½ teaspoon of lemon juice over each side of the salmon fillets. Bring the oil to temperature in the pressure cooker over medium heat.

2. Trim, thinly slice, wash, and drain the leek, patting it dry with a paper towel if necessary.

3. Add the leek to the pressure cooker; sauté for 2 minutes or until it begins to wilt.

4. Quarter the fennel bulb, then thinly slice the quarters. Add the fennel and diced potatoes to the pressure cooker along with the salt, water, and bay leaf.

5. Lock the lid into place and bring to high pressure; maintain pressure for 7 minutes. Quick-release the pressure and remove the lid.

6. Place the salmon fillets in the pressure cooker. Lock the lid back into place and bring to high pressure; maintain pressure for 1 minute. Remove from heat and allow pressure to release naturally.

7. Remove and discard the bay leaf. Use a slotted spoon to lift each salmon fillet into a bowl or, if you wish to serve the salmon separate from the chowder, to a serving plate.

8. Taste the chowder for seasoning and add more salt if needed. Ladle the chowder into bowls. Top the salmon with Green Peppercorn Sauce if desired.

Corn Chowder

*For an extra kick, drain and dice 2 4-ounce cans of green chilies and add
them to the chowder. This dish tastes delicious served with BLTs.*

INGREDIENTS | SERVES 6

2 tablespoons butter

4 large leeks

4 cups chicken broth

2 cups water

6 medium russet or Idaho baking
potatoes, peeled and diced

1 bay leaf

Salt and freshly ground black pepper,
to taste

1½ cups fresh or frozen corn

½ teaspoon dried thyme

Pinch sugar

½ cup heavy cream

1. Melt the butter in the pressure cooker over medium heat. Cut off the root end of the leeks and discard any bruised outer leaves. Slice the leeks. Add to the pressure cooker and sauté for 2 minutes. Stir in the broth, water, and potatoes. Add the bay leaf, salt, and pepper.

2. Lock the lid into place and bring to high pressure; maintain pressure for 4 minutes. Quick release the pressure and remove the lid. Remove and discard the bay leaf.

3. Stir in the corn, thyme, sugar, and cream. Bring to temperature, stirring occasionally

Simplified Chicken Stew

*Serve this stew with warm, buttered dinner rolls or buttermilk biscuits. Use this simple
recipe as a jumping-off point to experiment with your favorite flavors.*

INGREDIENTS | SERVES 4

1 cup baby carrots, cut in half

1 stalk celery, finely diced

1 large onion, peeled and diced

4 large potatoes, peeled and diced

1 teaspoon Mrs. Dash Garlic & Herb or
Original Seasoning Blend

2 tablespoons extra virgin olive oil

2 cups chicken broth

4 bone-in chicken breast halves

Salt and freshly ground black pepper,
to taste

1. Put the carrots, celery, onions, potatoes, seasoning blend, and oil in a pressure cooker. Add broth. Remove and discard the skin from the chicken, then nestle the chicken pieces meat side down on top of the vegetables.

2. Lock the pressure cooker lid and bring to high pressure; maintain pressure for 10 minutes. Remove from heat and quick-release the pressure. Remove the lid, stir, and season to taste.

Old South Chicken Stew

The sugar in this dish offsets the acidity of the tomatoes. The aroma of the bacon fat will transport you back to a time when all Southern cooks kept a container of bacon drippings at the ready.

INGREDIENTS | SERVES 8

3 tablespoons bacon fat

8 chicken thighs

2 cups water

1 28-ounce can diced tomatoes

2 large yellow onions, peeled and sliced

¼ teaspoon sugar

½ cup dry white wine or chicken broth

1 10-ounce package frozen lima beans, thawed

1 10-ounce package frozen whole kernel corn, thawed

1 10-ounce package frozen okra, thawed and sliced

1 cup bread crumbs, toasted

3 tablespoons Worcestershire sauce

Salt and freshly ground black pepper, to taste

Optional: Hot sauce, to taste

1. Bring the bacon fat to temperature in the pressure cooker over medium heat. Add 4 chicken thighs skin-side down and fry them until lightly browned.

2. Remove the fried thighs and fry the remaining thighs. Return the first 4 fried thighs to the pressure cooker and add the water, tomatoes, onions, sugar, and wine or chicken broth.

3. Lock the lid into place and bring to high pressure; maintain pressure for 12 minutes. Quick-release the pressure and remove the lid. Remove the chicken.

4. Once chicken is cool enough to handle, remove the meat from the bones and discard the skin and bones. Shred the chicken meat and set aside.

5. Add the lima beans, corn, and okra to the pot. Bring to a simmer and cook uncovered for 30 minutes.

6. Stir in the shredded chicken, bread crumbs, and Worcestershire sauce. Simmer for 10 minutes, stirring occasionally, to bring the chicken to temperature and thicken the stew.

7. Taste for seasoning and add salt and pepper if needed and hot sauce if desired.

Tex-Mex Stew

As its name implies, Tex-Mex is a fusion of the southwestern flavors of Texas and Mexico. Serve this hearty Tex-Mex Stew over rice along with an avocado salad and cornbread or baked corn chips.

INGREDIENTS | SERVES 8

1 3½-pound English or chuck roast
2 tablespoons olive or vegetable oil
1 7-ounce can green chilies
2 14½-ounce cans diced tomatoes
1 8-ounce can tomato sauce
1 large sweet onion, peeled and diced
1 green bell pepper, seeded and diced
6 cloves garlic, peeled and minced
1 tablespoon ground cumin
1 teaspoon freshly ground black pepper
Cayenne pepper, to taste
2 tablespoons lime juice
2 jalapeño peppers, seeded and diced
Optional: Beef broth or water
1 bunch fresh cilantro, chopped

1. Trim the fat from the roast and cut the meat into 1-inch cubes. Add the oil to the pressure cooker and bring it to temperature over medium-high heat.

2. Add the beef and stir-fry for 8 minutes or until it's well browned. Stir in the chilies, tomatoes, tomato sauce, onion, bell pepper, garlic, cumin, black pepper, cayenne, lime juice, and jalapeño peppers.

3. If needed, add enough beef broth or water to cover the ingredients in the cooker, but remember not to fill the cooker more than two-thirds full.

4. Lock the lid into place and bring to low pressure; maintain pressure for 1 hour. Remove from heat and allow pressure to release naturally. Remove the lid and stir in the cilantro. Serve immediately.

Chicken Chili

Serve this chili with an avocado or tossed salad. Have sour cream and baked corn tortilla chips at the table.

INGREDIENTS | SERVES 4

2 pounds boneless, skinless chicken thighs

2 tablespoons vegetable oil

1 jalapeño pepper, seeded and minced

1 small red bell pepper, seeded and diced

1 small onion, peeled and diced

1 clove garlic, peeled and minced

1 15-ounce can diced tomatoes

1 16-ounce can red kidney beans

1 tablespoon paprika

1 tablespoon tomato paste

1 cup chicken broth

¼ teaspoon dried thyme

¼ teaspoon dried oregano

1 teaspoon chili powder

Salt and freshly ground black pepper, to taste

1. Cut the chicken into bite-size cubes. Add the oil to the pressure cooker and bring it to temperature over medium heat. Add the chicken and stir-fry for 5 minutes.

2. Add the jalapeño and red peppers; stir-fry with the chicken for 2 minutes. Stir in the onion; sauté for 3 minutes or until tender.

3. Stir in the garlic, tomatoes, rinsed and drained kidney beans, paprika, tomato paste, broth, thyme, oregano, chili powder, salt, and pepper.

4. Lock the lid into place and bring to low pressure; maintain pressure for 10 minutes. Remove the pan from the heat and let pressure release naturally for 10 minutes.

5. Quick-release any remaining pressure and remove the lid. Stir the chili and taste for seasoning; add additional salt, pepper, spices, or herbs if needed.

Chicken in Beer Stew

Serve this Cajun-inspired stew over brown rice, cornbread, or mashed potatoes.
Increase the amount of cayenne pepper if you want a zestier, hotter stew.

INGREDIENTS | SERVES 6

1 teaspoon salt
½ tablespoon garlic powder
½ teaspoon cayenne pepper
2 tablespoons unbleached
all-purpose flour
2 pounds boneless, skinless
chicken thighs
2 tablespoons olive or vegetable oil
1 small green bell pepper, seeded
and diced
1 small red bell pepper, seeded
and diced
1 stalk celery, diced
1 medium onion, peeled and diced
1 jalapeño pepper, seeded and diced
2 cloves garlic, peeled and minced
1 bay leaf
1 teaspoon marjoram
1 8-ounce can tomato sauce
1 12-ounce bottle dark beer
½ cup chicken broth
2 teaspoons Worcestershire sauce
1 tablespoon bacon fat or lard
Freshly ground black pepper, to taste

1. Add the salt, garlic powder, cayenne pepper, and flour to a large zip-closure plastic bag; shake the bag to mix the spices into the flour. Trim and discard fat from the thighs and cut into bite-size pieces. Add to the the bag and shake to coat.

2. Bring the oil to temperature in the pressure cooker over medium-high heat. Add the chicken in batches; stir-fry for 3–5 minutes or until browned. Set aside and keep warm.

3. Reduce heat to medium. Add the green bell pepper, red bell pepper, and celery; sauté for 3 minutes. Stir in the onion; sauté for 3 minutes. Add the jalapeño pepper and garlic; sauté for 30 seconds. Stir in the bay leaf, marjoram, tomato sauce, beer, chicken broth, and Worcestershire sauce.

4. Lock the lid into place and bring to low pressure; maintain pressure for 20 minutes. Quick-release the pressure and remove the lid. Remove and discard the bay leaf.

5. While the chicken mixture cooks under pressure, bring the bacon fat or lard to temperature in a cast iron skillet over medium heat. Whisk in the reserved seasoned flour and enough water to make a paste. Cook and stir constantly for 10 minutes.

6. Whisk some of the juices from the pressure cooker into the roux in the skillet to loosen the mixture, and then stir the roux into the mixture in the pressure cooker. Bring the mixture to a simmer; simmer for 3 minutes. Taste for seasoning. Add additional salt and Worcestershire sauce, if needed, and pepper, to taste.

Mushroom Beef Stew with Dumplings

Wait until the stew is fully cooked before adding any salt and pepper; the amount needed will depend on the type of canned mushrooms and soups you use. Serve this stew with buttered dinner rolls and you have an easy comfort-food meal.

INGREDIENTS | SERVES 8

1 3-pound English or chuck roast

2 4-ounce cans sliced mushrooms, drained

1 10¾-ounce can condensed cream of mushroom soup

1 10½-ounce can condensed French onion soup

1 tablespoon Worcestershire sauce

2 cups water

1 24-ounce bag frozen vegetables for stew, thawed

4 cups frozen vegetables, thawed

Quick and Easy Dumplings

Salt and freshly ground black pepper, to taste

Quick and Easy Dumplings

Cut 1 tablespoon shortening or butter into 1½ cups biscuit mix until crumbly. Combine ⅔ cup milk and 1 large beaten egg; add to dry mixture. Stir until just blended. When you cook the dumplings in the stew, small drops of batter will suffice; they expand in the hot liquid.

1. Trim and discard any fat from the roast. Cut into bite-size pieces and add meat, drained mushrooms, soups, Worcestershire sauce, and water to the pressure cooker.

2. Lock the lid into place and bring to low pressure; maintain pressure for 30 minutes. Quick-release the pressure and remove the lid.

3. Stir in the thawed frozen vegetables. Bring to a simmer and then drop tablespoon-size dollops of the Quick and Easy Dumplings batter into the bubbling stew.

4. Lock the lid into place and bring to low pressure; maintain pressure for 5 minutes. Quick-release the pressure and remove the lid.

5. Stir the stew, being careful not to break the dumplings apart. (If dumplings aren't yet puffy and cooked through, loosely cover the pan and let the stew simmer for a few more minutes.) Taste for seasoning and add salt and pepper if needed.

New England Clam Chowder

The clams and their liquid will be salty, so wait until the chowder is cooked to add any salt. Serve with oyster crackers or toasted, buttered sourdough bread.

INGREDIENTS | SERVES 4

4 6½-ounce cans chopped clams

4 slices bacon

1 stalk celery, finely diced

2 large shallots, peeled and minced

1 pound red potatoes, peeled and diced

2½ cups unsalted chicken or vegetable broth

Optional: 1 tablespoon fresh thyme, chopped

1 cup frozen corn, thawed

2 cups milk

1 cup heavy cream

Sea salt and freshly ground black pepper, to taste

1. Drain the clams. Reserve the liquid to add along with the broth. Set the clams aside.

2. Fry bacon over medium-high heat. Crumble. Add celery; sauté for 3 minutes. Add shallots; sauté for 3 minutes. Stir in the potatoes; stir-fry to coat the potatoes in the fat. Stir in clam liquid, broth, and thyme.

3. Lock lid and bring to high pressure; maintain pressure for 5 minutes. Lower the heat to warm and allow pressure to drop naturally for 10 minutes. Quick-release any remaining pressure and remove the lid.

4. Stir in the corn, milk, cream, and reserved clams. Bring to a simmer for 5 minutes.

Manhattan Clam Chowder

The clams and their liquid will be salty, so wait until the chowder is cooked to add any salt. Serve with oyster crackers, dinner rolls, or toasted garlic bread.

INGREDIENTS | SERVES 6

4 6½-ounce cans minced clams

4 slices bacon

2 stalks celery, finely diced

4 large carrots, peeled and finely diced

1 large sweet onion, peeled and diced

1 pound red potatoes, peeled and diced

1 28-ounce can diced tomatoes

2 cups tomato or V-8 juice

1 teaspoon dried parsley

¼ teaspoon dried thyme

⅛ teaspoon dried oregano

½ teaspoon freshly ground black pepper

Sea salt, to taste

1. Drain the clams. Reserve the liquid to add along with the other liquid. Set the clams aside.

2. Fry bacon over medium-high heat. Crumble. Add the celery and carrots; sauté for 3 minutes. Add onion; sauté for 3 minutes. Stir in the potatoes; stir-fry to coat the potatoes in the fat. Stir in clam liquid, undrained tomatoes, juice, parsley, thyme, oregano, and pepper.

3. Lock lid into place and bring to high pressure; maintain for 5 minutes. Lower the heat to warm and allow pressure to drop naturally for 10 minutes. Quick-release remaining pressure and remove the lid. Stir in the reserved clams. Bring to a simmer. Season to taste.

CHAPTER 15

Vegetarian

Vegetable Broth
171

Ratatouille
171

Tomato-Vegetable Broth
172

Mushroom Broth
172

Eggplant Caponata
173

Risotto Primavera
174

Italian Pasta and Bean Soup
175

Mushroom and Barley Soup
176

Vegetable Chili
177

Pasta with Chickpea
and Cabbage Sauce
178

Black Bean and Lentil Chili
179

Meatless Mincemeat
180

Minestrone
181

Vegetable Broth

Vegetable stock, which is also sometimes referred to as vegetable broth, is called for in many vegetarian recipes.

INGREDIENTS | YIELDS 4 CUPS

2 large onions, peeled and halved

2 medium carrots, cleaned and cut into large pieces

3 stalks celery, cut in half

1 whole bulb garlic

10 peppercorns

1 bay leaf

4½ cups water

1. Add the onions, carrots, and celery to the pressure cooker. Break the bulb of garlic into individual cloves; peel the garlic and add to the pressure cooker. Add the peppercorns, bay leaf, and water to completely cover the vegetables. Lock the lid into place and bring to low pressure; maintain pressure for 10 minutes. Remove from the heat and allow pressure to release naturally.

2. Strain the stock through a fine-mesh strainer or through cheesecloth placed in a colander. Store in a covered container in the refrigerator, or freeze until needed.

Ratatouille

Ratatouille is sometimes served over potatoes. This version adds the potatoes to the dish. You can serve this Ratatouille over whole grain pasta or topped with toasted garlic croutons.

INGREDIENTS | SERVES 4

2 tablespoons extra virgin olive oil

2 7-inch zucchini, washed and sliced

1 Japanese eggplant, peeled and sliced

1 small onion, peeled and thinly sliced

1 green bell pepper, seeded and diced

2 medium potatoes, peeled and diced

8 ounces fresh mushrooms, cleaned and sliced

1 28-ounce can diced tomatoes

3 tablespoons tomato paste

3 tablespoons water

2 cloves garlic, peeled and minced

2 teaspoons Mrs. Dash Italian Medley Seasoning Blend

⅛ teaspoon dried red pepper flakes

Salt and fresh black pepper, to taste

Parmigiano-Reggiano cheese, grated

1. Coat the bottom and sides of the pressure cooker with oil. Add the remaining ingredients except cheese in layers in the order given. Lock the lid into place and bring to low pressure; maintain pressure for 6 minutes.

2. Remove from heat and quick-release the pressure. Remove the lid, stir, and taste for seasoning, adjusting if necessary. Serve topped with the grated cheese.

Tomato-Vegetable Broth

You can add some meaty-type richness to any vegetable broth by scraping away and discarding the black gills from two large portobello mushroom caps, dicing the caps, and adding them along with the other vegetables.

INGREDIENTS | YIELDS 4 CUPS

2 large onions, peeled and halved

2 medium carrots, cleaned and cut into large pieces

3 stalks celery, halved

1 whole bulb garlic

4 large tomatoes, quartered

10 peppercorns

1 bay leaf

4 cups water

1. Add the onions, carrots, and celery to the slow cooker. Break the bulb of garlic into individual cloves; peel the garlic and add to the slow cooker.

2. Add the tomatoes, peppercorns, bay leaf, and water. Add additional water if necessary to completely cover the vegetables. Cover and cook on low for 4–8 hours.

3. Strain the stock through a fine-mesh strainer or through cheesecloth placed in a colander. Store in a covered container in the refrigerator or freeze until needed.

Mushroom Broth

This is a good alternative to chicken broth in almost any recipe. You can use button mushrooms or, for a more intense flavor, portobello mushroom caps cleaned of the black gills or wild mushrooms like chanterelles or shiitake.

INGREDIENTS | YIELD 8 CUPS

4 carrots, washed and cut in large pieces

2 large leeks, well cleaned and cut in large pieces

2 large onions, peeled and quartered

1 celery stalk, chopped

5 whole cloves

Pinch dried red pepper flakes

2 cups fresh mushrooms, sliced

8½ cups water

1. Put all ingredients in the pressure cooker. Lock the lid into place and bring to low pressure; maintain pressure for 15 minutes.

2. Remove from the heat and allow pressure to release naturally. Strain for a clear stock. Can be refrigerated for 2 or 3 days or frozen for 3 months.

Eggplant Caponata

This versatile dish can be served hot, at room temperature, or cold. You can use it as a pasta topping, a side dish, or even a sandwich filling if you drain all the liquid.

INGREDIENTS | SERVES 8

¼ cup extra virgin olive oil

¼ cup white wine

2 tablespoons red wine vinegar

1 teaspoon ground cinnamon

1 large eggplant, peeled and diced

1 medium onion, peeled and diced

1 medium green bell pepper, seeded and diced

1 medium red bell pepper, seeded and diced

2 cloves garlic, peeled and minced

1 14½-ounce can diced tomatoes

3 stalks celery, diced

½ cup oil-cured olives, pitted and chopped

½ cup golden raisins

2 tablespoons capers, rinsed and drained

Salt and freshly ground black pepper, to taste

1. Add all ingredients to the pressure cooker. Stir well to mix. Lock the lid into place and bring to low pressure; maintain pressure for 8 minutes.

2. Remove from heat and quick-release the pressure. Remove the lid and stir the contents of the pressure cooker. Taste for seasoning and add salt and pepper, to taste.

Risotto Primavera

Risotto is easy to make, but standing over a stove and waiting for the rice to absorb the broth can be time-consuming. This pressure cooker recipe combines ease and speed for a delicious dish.

INGREDIENTS | SERVES 4

1 tablespoon extra virgin olive oil

1 tablespoon unsalted butter

2 medium carrots, peeled and finely diced

1 stalk celery, finely diced

2 large shallots or 1 small red onion, peeled and diced

1 clove garlic, peeled and minced

½ teaspoon dried basil

1 teaspoon dried parsley

2 cups Arborio rice

½ cup dry white wine or Vermouth

5 cups vegetable or mushroom broth

½ pound asparagus

1 cup peas

1 cup snow peas, shredded

1 cup zucchini, peeled, seeded, and diced

1 cup Fontina cheese, shredded

½ cup Parmigiano-Reggiano or Asiago cheese, grated

1. Bring the oil and butter to temperature in the pressure cooker over medium heat. Add the carrot and celery; sauté for 3 minutes. Add the shallots or red onion; sauté for 3 minutes or until the vegetables are tender. Add the garlic, basil, and parsley; sauté for 30 seconds.

2. Stir in the rice and stir-fry for 4 minutes or until the rice becomes opaque. Add the wine or Vermouth; cook and stir for 3 minutes or until the liquid is absorbed by the rice. Stir in 4½ cups broth.

3. Lock the lid into place and bring to high pressure; maintain pressure for 6 minutes. Quick-release the pressure and remove the lid.

4. Stir in the remaining ½ cup broth. Once the broth is absorbed and the rice is fluffed, adjust heat to maintain a simmer.

5. Clean the asparagus and cut it into 1-inch pieces. Add the asparagus, peas, snow peas, and zucchini. Stir and cook until the vegetables are bright green and cooked through. Stir in the cheese. Serve.

Italian Pasta and Bean Soup

Experiment with the types of grains and beans in this soup.
Smaller pastas and couscous work well for this soup.

INGREDIENTS | SERVES 10

1 pound dried cannellini or white beans

1 tablespoon extra virgin olive oil

4 medium carrots, peeled and diced

2 stalks celery, diced

2 medium onions, peeled and diced

3 cloves garlic, peeled and minced

2 teaspoons Mrs. Dash Italian Medley Seasoning Blend

6 cups water

1 bay leaf

1 teaspoon dried parsley

4 cups vegetable or mushroom broth

1½ cups small macaroni or small shell pasta

Salt and freshly ground black pepper, to taste

Optional: Freshly grated Parmigiano-Reggiano cheese

1. Rinse the cannellini or white beans; soak overnight in enough water to cover them by more than 1 inch. Drain.

2. Bring the oil to temperature in the pressure cooker over medium heat. Add the carrots and celery; sauté for 3 minutes. Add the onion; sauté for 3 minutes or until the vegetables are soft. Add the garlic and a teaspoon of the Italian seasoning blend; sauté for 30 seconds.

3. Add the water, beans, and bay leaf. Lock the lid into place and bring to high pressure; maintain pressure for 35 minutes. Remove from the heat and allow pressure to release naturally for 20 minutes. Quick-release any remaining pressure and remove the lid.

4. Remove and discard the bay leaf. Add the remaining Italian seasoning blend, parsley, and vegetable or mushroom broth. Return to the heat and bring to a boil; stir in the macaroni or shells. Cook pasta to al dente according to package directions. Taste for seasoning and add salt and pepper if needed. Serve topped with grated cheese if desired.

Mushroom and Barley Soup

The barley adds heft to this culinary delight. This is a hearty vegetarian soup perfect for a cold winter night.

INGREDIENTS | SERVES 8

1 tablespoon butter

1 medium onion, peeled and diced

2 medium carrots, peeled and sliced

3 cloves garlic, peeled and minced

1 pound fresh mushrooms, cleaned and sliced

½ teaspoon dried thyme

⅓ cup sherry

¾ cup pearl barley

1 bay leaf

5 cups water or vegetable broth

½ teaspoon freshly ground black pepper

Salt, to taste

2 tablespoons fresh parsley, chopped

1. Melt the butter in the pressure cooker over medium heat. Add the onion; sauté for 3 minutes or until soft. Stir in the carrots, garlic, mushrooms, and thyme. Stir-fry for 5 minutes or until the mushrooms have reduced most of their moisture. Stir in the sherry, barley, bay leaf, and broth. Lock the lid into place and bring to high pressure; maintain pressure for 10 minutes. Remove from heat and allow pressure to release naturally.

2. Remove the lid. Remove and discard the bay leaf. Return to heat if necessary to bring the soup back to temperature. Stir in the pepper, salt, and parsley. Serve immediately.

Vegetable Chili

To make this a tomato-rich chili, substitute a 15-ounce can of tomato puree and 1 cup tomato juice for the vegetable broth. For a spicier chili, add a 16-ounce jar of salsa and 1 cup tomato juice.

INGREDIENTS | **SERVES 8**

2 tablespoons olive or vegetable oil

1 large sweet onion, peeled and diced

3 cloves garlic, peeled and minced

1 15-ounce can pinto beans, rinsed and drained

1 15-ounce can kidney beans, rinsed and drained

1 15-ounce can cannellini or white beans, rinsed and drained

1 large green bell pepper, seeded and diced

2 medium zucchini

1½ cups corn

1 28-ounce can diced tomatoes

2 cups vegetable broth

2 tablespoons chili powder

1 teaspoon cumin

1 teaspoon dried oregano

¼ teaspoon freshly ground black pepper

⅛ teaspoon cayenne pepper

Salt, to taste

8 ounces Monterey jack cheese, grated

1. Bring the oil to temperature in the pressure cooker over medium heat. Add the onion; sauté for 3 minutes or until it begins to soften. Stir in the garlic; sauté for 30 seconds. Stir in the canned beans, green bell pepper, zucchini, corn, tomatoes, broth, chili powder, cumin, oregano, black pepper, and cayenne pepper. Stir to mix.

2. Lock the lid into place and bring to high pressure; maintain pressure for 5 minutes. Remove from the heat and allow pressure to release naturally.

3. Remove the lid, stir, and taste for seasoning. Add salt if desired. Serve topped with grated cheese.

Pasta with Chickpea and Cabbage Sauce

Chickpeas are found all over the world and are the primary ingredient in various Middle Eastern, African, Mexican, and Indian dishes.

INGREDIENTS | SERVES 8

⅔ cup dried chickpeas

6 dried shiitake mushrooms or 8 ounces fresh mushrooms, sliced

2 tablespoons extra virgin olive oil

1 stalk celery, thinly sliced

1 medium red onion, peeled and sliced

1 small head Savoy cabbage, cored and shredded

4 cups water

1 pound rigatoni

Salt and freshly ground black pepper, to taste

Pecorino cheese, grated

1. Rinse the chickpeas. Soak them overnight in enough water to cover them by more than 1 inch.

2. If using dried mushrooms, add them to the soaking liquid for the chickpeas. Drain.

3. Bring the oil to temperature in the pressure cooker. Add the celery; sauté for 2 minutes. Add the onion; sauté for 3 minutes. Stir in the shredded cabbage and sauté until wilted. Add the chickpeas, mushrooms, and water.

4. Lock the lid into place and bring to high pressure; maintain pressure for 20 minutes. Remove from the heat and allow pressure to release naturally while you prepare the pasta according to package directions.

5. Quick-release any remaining pressure and remove the lid. Stir the chickpea sauce and taste for seasoning, adding salt and pepper to taste. If the sauce is too thin, use a fork to mash some of the chickpeas, which will thicken the sauce. Serve over the pasta. Top with grated cheese.

Black Bean and Lentil Chili

If you prefer hotter chili, substitute scotch bonnet or serrano pepper for the jalapeño. You can also use hot chili powder instead of mild, or substitute Mrs. Dash Extra Spicy Seasoning Blend for some of the chili powder. Serve with cornbread.

INGREDIENTS | SERVES 6

2 tablespoons vegetable oil

1 large Spanish onion, peeled and diced

1 jalapeño, seeded and minced

1 clove garlic, peeled and minced

1 cup brown or green lentils

1 15½-ounce can black beans, drained and rinsed

1 cup pearl barley

3 tablespoons chili powder

1 tablespoon sweet paprika

1 teaspoon dried oregano

1 teaspoon ground cumin

1 28-ounce can diced tomatoes

6 cups vegetable broth

Optional: 1 12-ounce can chipotle peppers in adobo sauce

Salt and freshly ground pepper, to taste

1. Bring the oil to temperature in the pressure cooker over medium heat. Add the onion; sauté for 3 minutes. Stir in the jalapeño; sauté for 1 minute.

2. Stir in the garlic; sauté for 30 seconds. Stir in the lentils, black beans, barley, chili powder, paprika, oregano, cumin, undrained tomatoes, and vegetable broth. If using, mince 1 or more chipotle peppers and add them along with some sauce to taste.

3. Lock the lid into place and bring to high pressure; maintain for 10 minutes. Remove from the heat and allow pressure to release naturally for 10 minutes. Quick-release any remaining pressure. Remove the lid. Stir and check that the lentils and barley are tender. If not, lock the lid back into place, return to the heat, and bring to pressure for the estimated time needed. Remove from heat and allow pressure to release naturally.

4. Remove the lid and return the pan to the heat. Bring to a simmer. Taste for seasoning, and add salt and pepper if needed. Simmer until slightly thickened.

Meatless Mincemeat

Serve this mincemeat as a chutney or use as a filling in a mincemeat pie that's succulent enough to be a special occasion meal's main dish.

INGREDIENTS | YIELDS 2 QUARTS

½ cup butter

2 cups light brown sugar, lightly packed

2 cups fresh apple cider

1 medium orange

1 cup raisins

1 cup dried currants

8 ounces dried figs

6 ounces dried apricots

2 medium cooking apples

2 Bosc pears

⅓ cup and ¼ cup brandy, divided

⅓ cup dark rum

1 teaspoon salt

1 teaspoon ground cinnamon

1 teaspoon ground cloves

1 teaspoon ground allspice

1 teaspoon ground nutmeg

Mincemeat Without Alcohol

To make mincemeat without alcohol, replace ⅓ cup of the brandy and the rum with cider. Reduce the amount of brown sugar to 1½ cups. Then, after you've ladled the mincemeat into the jars, top each jar with 2 tablespoons of honey instead of the brandy.

1. Melt the butter in the pressure cooker over medium heat. Stir in the brown sugar and cider. Allow the mixture to simmer while you prepare the fruit for the recipe.

2. Cut the orange into quarters, remove the seeds, and add to a food processor along with the raisins, currants, figs, and apricots; pulse to coarsely chop. Stir into the other ingredients already in the pressure cooker.

3. Peel, core, and seed the apples and pears. Add to the food processor and pulse until finely grated; alternatively, you can feed through the food processor using the grater attachment. Add to the pressure cooker along with ⅓ cup of the brandy, rum, salt, cinnamon, cloves, allspice, and nutmeg.

4. Bring to a simmer; skim off and discard any foam from the top of the mixture. Lock the lid into place and bring to low temperature; maintain pressure for 10 minutes. Remove from the heat and allow pressure to release naturally.

5. Uncover, stir, and check the consistency of the mincemeat. To thicken it, if desired, return the pressure cooker to medium heat and stirring occasionally, continue to cook uncovered for 10–15 minutes or until the mixture is reduced to about 2 quarts. Ladle the mincemeat into two sterilized 1-quart canning jars.

6. Top the mincemeat in each jar with 2 tablespoons of brandy. Screw on the two-piece lids; allow to cool to room temperature. Can be stored in the refrigerator for 1 week or in the freezer for up to 6 months.

Minestrone

Chopping the carrots and green beans into smaller pieces makes them match the size of the other vegetables in this minestrone. If you're using frozen green beans, however, remember to thaw them first.

INGREDIENTS | SERVES 4

1 small onion, peeled and diced

3 cups water

2 medium zucchini, peeled and diced

1 cup baby carrots, chopped

1 cup green beans, chopped

1 15-ounce can cannellini beans, rinsed and drained

2 stalks celery, diced

½ teaspoon dried basil

½ teaspoon dried oregano

Freshly ground black pepper, to taste

1 14½-ounce can diced tomatoes

1 clove garlic, peeled and minced

¼ cup uncooked macaroni

4 teaspoons freshly grated Parmigiano-Reggiano cheese

1. Add all ingredients except the macaroni and cheese to the pressure cooker. Lock the lid into place and bring to low pressure; maintain pressure for 5 minutes. Quick-release the pressure and remove the lid.

2. At this point, you have a choice: You can either cook the macaroni separately according to package directions or you can bring the contents of the pressure cooker to a boil and stir in the uncooked macaroni, adding water or tomato juice as needed until the macaroni is cooked. If you choose the latter option, stir and watch the pot, adding more liquid as needed so that the soup doesn't boil dry.

3. Ladle the minestrone into bowls and sprinkle each serving with 1 teaspoon of the cheese, or more to taste.

Throw in the Leftovers

Minestrone is the perfect way to use leftover vegetables, so feel free to substitute peas, corn, or whatever else is on hand. Add some basil or Italian seasoning, or use vegetable broth, tomato juice, or V-8 juice instead of water. You can even Americanize the recipe by using kidney beans and make it even healthier by using whole wheat macaroni.

CHAPTER 16

Pasta, Legumes, and Grains

Wheat Berry Salad
183

Cranberry-Bean Salad
with Asian Dressing
184

Boston Baked Beans
185

Red Beans and Rice
186

Curried Chicken
and Lentils Salad
187

Chicken and Vegetable Alfredo
188

Sausage with Bow Tie Pasta
189

Fettuccine with
Smoked Salmon Sauce
190

Barley Risotto
190

Warm Chickpea Salad
191

Macaroni and Cheese
192

Quinoa Artichoke Hearts Salad
193

Chicken Tortellini
194

Wheat Berry Salad

Put a teaspoon of Wheat Berry Salad on individual baby romaine hearts sections.

INGREDIENTS | SERVES 12

1½ tablespoons vegetable oil

6¾ cups water

1½ cups wheat berries

1½ teaspoons Dijon mustard

1 teaspoon sugar

1 teaspoon sea salt

½ teaspoon freshly ground black pepper

¼ cup white wine vinegar

½ cup extra virgin olive oil

½ small red onion, peeled and diced

1⅓ cups frozen corn or peas, thawed

1 medium zucchini, peeled, grated, and drained

2 stalks celery, finely diced

1 red bell pepper, seeded and diced

4 green onions, diced

¼ cup sun-dried tomatoes, diced

¼ cup fresh parsley, chopped

Tasty Substitutions

You can add a bit more flavor to this salad by substituting tomato juice or vegetable broth for some of the wheat berries cooking liquid. You can also substitute lemon juice or fruit-infused vinegar for the white wine vinegar. Try substituting a teaspoon or more of Mrs. Dash or other seasoning blend for the fresh parsley.

1. Add the oil, water, and wheat berries to the pressure cooker. Lock the lid into place and bring to high pressure; maintain pressure for 50 minutes. Remove from the heat and quick-release the pressure. Fluff with a fork. If the grains aren't yet as tender as you'd like, simmer and stir the mixture for a few minutes, adding more liquid if necessary. When done to your liking, drain and transfer to a large bowl.

2. Make the dressing by pureeing the mustard, sugar, salt, pepper, vinegar, olive oil, and red onion in a food processor or blender. Start by stirring ½ cup dressing into the cooled wheat berries. Toss the seasoned wheat berries with remaining ingredients. Taste for seasoning; add additional salt, pepper, or dressing if needed. Cover and refrigerate any leftover dressing for up to 3 days.

Cranberry-Bean Salad with Asian Dressing

Serve with your favorite Asian-glazed barbequed entrée or alongside grilled hamburgers or hotdogs.

INGREDIENTS | SERVES 12

1 cup dried pinto, black, or cannellini beans

Water to cover

3 tablespoons sherry vinegar

2 tablespoons fresh lime juice

1½ tablespoons low-sodium soy sauce

1½ teaspoons honey

1½ teaspoons fresh ginger, grated

1 teaspoon Asian chili paste

1 clove garlic, peeled and minced

2 teaspoons vegetable oil

1 cup fresh corn or frozen corn, thawed

8 ounces green beans, cut into ½-inch pieces, steamed, and chilled

1 cup frozen baby peas, thawed

4 stalks celery, thinly sliced

1 red bell pepper, seeded and diced

¾ cup dried cranberries

1 medium red onion, peeled and diced

Salt and freshly ground black pepper, to taste

1. Rinse and drain the beans, then soak them overnight in enough water to cover them by several inches.

2. To make the dressing, add the vinegar, lime juice, soy sauce, honey, ginger, chili paste, and garlic in a bowl; whisk to mix. Cover and refrigerate overnight to allow the flavors to blend.

3. Drain the soaked beans and add them to the pressure cooker along with 3 cups of water and the vegetable oil. Lock the lid into place and bring to high pressure; maintain pressure for 25 minutes. Remove from the heat and allow pressure to release naturally.

4. Drain the beans and transfer them to a large bowl. Stir in half of the dressing; chill.

5. Add the corn, green beans, peas, celery, bell pepper, cranberries, onion, salt, and pepper. Toss, adding more dressing if desired. Serve.

Another Asian Touch

Substitute chilled cooked edamame (soybeans) for the peas. Edamame are Asian soybeans ("edamame" is the Japanese word for them), and they make a great snack food. Buy more than you need for this dish and you can have them on hand to munch on all week long!

Boston Baked Beans

The pressure cooker helps give these beans the flavor that usually comes from slow baking. If you're short on prep time, substitute ¼ cup dried minced onion or onion flakes for the diced onion.

INGREDIENTS | SERVES 8

1 pound dried small white beans

6 cups water

4 slices bacon, diced

2 medium sweet onions, peeled and diced

4 cloves garlic, peeled and minced

3½ cups chicken broth

2 teaspoons dried mustard

¼ teaspoon freshly ground black pepper

¼ cup molasses

½ cup ketchup

¼ brown sugar

1 teaspoon Worcestershire sauce

1 teaspoon cider vinegar

Salt, to taste

Optional: Smoked paprika

1. Wash and drain the dried beans. Soak them overnight in 6 cups water, or enough to cover them by more than 1 inch.

2. Fry the bacon in the pressure cooker over medium-high heat until the bacon begins to render its fat. Lower the heat to medium and add the onion; sauté for 3 minutes or until the onions are soft. Stir in the garlic; sauté for 30 seconds. Add the drained soaked beans, broth, dry mustard, and pepper.

3. Lock the lid into place and bring to low pressure; maintain pressure for 20 minutes. Remove from the heat and allow pressure to release naturally.

4. Remove the lid; the beans should still be somewhat soupy at this point. Stir in the molasses, ketchup, brown sugar, Worcestershire sauce, and vinegar. Stir to mix. Taste and add another ¼ cup of molasses if you prefer a heartier taste. Return the pan to the heat, lock the lid into place, and bring to low pressure; maintain pressure for 5 minutes. Remove from the heat and allow pressure to release naturally.

5. Remove the lid. Stir the beans and taste for seasoning. Add salt to taste and additional Worcestershire sauce if needed. If the beans are still too soupy, return to the heat and simmer them, stirring occasionally, until thickened. Stir in the smoked paprika if using. Serve.

Red Beans and Rice

Soaking beans in water makes them easier for those with sensitive digestive systems to handle.

INGREDIENTS | SERVES 8

1 cup dried red beans

6 cups water

2 teaspoons olive or vegetable oil

2 pounds ham hocks

1 pound smoked sausage, diced

4 stalks celery, finely diced

1 large green bell pepper, seeded and diced

1 medium onion, peeled and diced

3 bay leaves

1 teaspoon freshly ground white pepper

1 teaspoon dried thyme

1 teaspoon garlic powder

¼ teaspoon cayenne pepper

¼ teaspoon freshly ground black pepper

Hot sauce, to taste

Salt, to taste

1. Wash and drain the beans; soak them overnight in 3 cups water.

2. Drain the beans and add them to the pressure cooker along with the remaining 3 cups of water and oil. Lock the lid into place and bring to low pressure; maintain pressure for 15 minutes. Remove from heat and allow pressure to release naturally for 10 minutes. Quick-release any remaining pressure and remove the lid.

3. Add the remaining ingredients except for the hot sauce and salt. Lock the lid into place and bring to high pressure; maintain pressure for 15 minutes. Remove from the heat and allow pressure to release naturally. Remove the lid.

4. Remove and discard the bay leaves. Remove the ham hocks; when cool enough to handle, remove the meat from the bones and stir into the beans. Discard any pork skin, fat, and bones. Taste for seasoning and add salt and hot sauce, to taste.

Curried Chicken and Lentils Salad

This main dish salad gets its salt from the roasted cashews. If you're using unsalted cashews, you may need to add some salt or have it available at the table.

INGREDIENTS | SERVES 6

1 teaspoon vegetable oil

2 pounds boneless, skinless chicken breasts

1 cup dried lentils

2 cups water

2½ teaspoons curry powder

2 small Golden Delicious apples, peeled and diced

1 teaspoon lemon juice

2 cups seedless grapes, cut in half

1 cup roasted cashews

2 stalks celery, diced

½ small red onion, peeled and diced

¾ cup plain yogurt or sour cream

¼ cup mayonnaise

6 cups salad greens

Sweeten the Dressing

Cooking the apples with the lentils cuts some of the heat of the curry powder. The raw apple and grapes in the salad will also sweeten the curry powder taste. But if you still find the taste of the curry powder in the dressing too harsh, you can stir some sugar, honey, or applesauce into the dressing to soften the taste.

1. Bring the oil to temperature in the pressure cooker over medium-high heat. Cut the chicken into bite-size pieces; add to the pressure cooker and stir-fry for 5 minutes or until browned. Stir in the lentils, water, and 1 teaspoon curry powder. Halve one of the apples; peel and dice it and add it to the pressure cooker. Coat the cut side of the other half of the apple with the lemon juice to prevent it from turning brown.

2. Lock the lid into place and bring the pressure cooker to low pressure; maintain pressure for 8 minutes. Remove from the heat and allow pressure to release naturally.

3. Transfer the contents of the pressure cooker to a bowl. Once it's cooled, stir in the remaining diced apple, grapes, cashews, celery, and red onion.

4. To make the dressing, mix together the yogurt or sour cream, mayonnaise, and remaining 1½ teaspoons curry powder.

5. For each serving, place 1 cup salad greens on a plate. Either mix the dressing into the lentil mixture or add the lentil mixture on top of the lettuce and drizzle with the dressing.

Chicken and Vegetable Alfredo

You don't often find this many vegetables in comfort food. In this case, they're needed to offset all that rich, tasty, high-fat content from the butter, cream, and cheese.

INGREDIENTS | SERVES 4

2 tablespoons olive oil

1½ pounds boneless, skinless chicken breasts

1 small onion, peeled and diced

1 red bell pepper, seeded and diced

8 ounces fresh mushrooms, cleaned and sliced

4 cloves garlic, peeled and minced

1 tablespoon dried basil

1 teaspoon dried thyme

⅛ teaspoon freshly ground nutmeg

¼ teaspoon freshly ground black pepper

1 14-ounce can chicken broth

8 ounces sugar snap peas, sliced diagonally

½ cup sliced carrots

1½ cups broccoli florets

1½ cups cauliflower segments

¼ cup Parmigiano-Reggiano cheese, grated

1 stick butter, softened

1 cup heavy cream

8 ounces uncooked linguini

If You Prefer

You can substitute 2 1-pound bags of thawed frozen stir-fry mixed vegetables for the sugar snap peas, carrots, broccoli, and cauliflower called for in the recipe. If you do so, reduce the pressure-maintaining time for the vegetables to 1 minute.

1. Bring the oil to temperature in the pressure cooker over medium heat. Cut the chicken into bite-size pieces and add to the pressure cooker; stir-fry for 5 minutes or until they begin to brown. Add the onion and red bell pepper; sauté for 3 minutes. Add the sliced mushrooms; sauté for 3 minutes or until the mushrooms have released their moisture. Add the garlic, basil, thyme, nutmeg, pepper, and broth. Stir to combine. Lock the lid into place and bring to low pressure; maintain pressure for 3 minutes. Remove from the heat and quick-release the pressure. Remove the lid.

2. Add the sugar snap peas, carrots, broccoli, and cauliflower to the pressure cooker. Return the pressure cooker to the heat, lock the lid into place, and bring to low pressure; maintain pressure for 3 minutes. Remove from the heat and quick-release the pressure.

3. Whip the cheese into the butter and then blend with the cream. Return the pressure cooker to medium heat. Stir in the cream mixture; cook and stir for 3 minutes or until the cream mixture is heated through.

4. Cook the linguini according to package directions. Top the noodles with the sauce and additional grated cheese if desired.

Sausage with Bow Tie Pasta

Serve with a tossed salad and garlic bread.

INGREDIENTS | SERVES 6

1 pound ground sausage

1 tablespoon olive oil

1 large onion, peeled and diced

3 cloves garlic, peeled and minced

3 cups chicken broth

1 cup tomato sauce

2 teaspoons dried parsley

½ teaspoon ground fennel

1 teaspoon dried basil

½ teaspoon sugar

¼ teaspoon freshly ground black pepper

⅛ teaspoon dried red pepper flakes

3 cups bow tie pasta

¼ cup heavy cream

Salt, to taste

½ cup Parmigiano-Reggiano cheese, grated

1. Add the sausage to the pressure cooker over medium-high heat; break the sausage apart as you stir-fry it for 5 minutes or until it is cooked through and has rendered its fat. Drain and discard the fat. Stir in the oil and onion; sauté for 3 minutes or until the onion is soft. Stir in the garlic; sauté for 30 seconds.

2. Stir in the broth, tomato sauce, parsley, fennel, basil, sugar, pepper, red pepper flakes, and pasta. Reduce the heat to medium, lock the lid into place, and bring to low pressure; maintain pressure for 9 minutes. Quick-release the pressure and remove the lid.

3. Stir in the cream. Taste for seasoning and adjust if necessary. Add salt to taste. Transfer to a serving bowl or platter. Top with the cheese. Serve.

Fettuccine with Smoked Salmon Sauce

You can substitute smoked trout, smoked whitefish, or crisp bacon for the smoked salmon.

INGREDIENTS | SERVES 6

¼ cup olive oil

2 cups fettuccine

4 cups chicken broth

½ teaspoon sea salt

¼ teaspoon freshly ground white pepper

1 teaspoon dried thyme

3 tablespoons butter

½ cup sour cream

2 green onions, cleaned and diced

1 pound smoked salmon, in bite-size pieces

⅓ cup Parmigiano-Reggiano cheese, grated

1. Bring the oil to temperature in the pressure cooker over medium heat. Stir in the fettuccine, broth, salt, pepper, and thyme. Lock the lid in place and bring to high pressure; maintain pressure for 8 minutes. Quick-release the pressure and remove the lid.

2. Drain the pasta if necessary. Transfer to a serving bowl. Cut the butter into small chunks and toss with the pasta. Add the sour cream; stir to combine. Add the green onion and smoked salmon; toss to mix. Top with the grated cheese. Serve.

Barley Risotto

If you're not a fan of Parmigiano-Reggiano cheese, you can substitute crumbled blue cheese or grated Cheddar cheese to taste.

INGREDIENTS | SERVES 4

1 tablespoon butter

1 tablespoon olive oil

1 large onion, peeled and diced

1 clove garlic, peeled and minced

1 stalk celery, finely minced

1½ cups pearl barley, well rinsed

⅓ cup dried mushrooms

4 cups chicken or vegetable broth

2¼ cups water

1 cup Parmigiano-Reggiano cheese, grated

2 tablespoons fresh parsley, minced

Salt, to taste

1. Bring the butter and oil to temperature in the pressure cooker over medium heat. Add the onion; sauté for 3 minutes or until the onion is soft. Add the garlic; sauté for 30 seconds. Stir in the celery and barley until the barley is coated with the fat. Add the mushrooms, broth, and water. Lock the lid into place and bring to high pressure; maintain pressure for 18 minutes. Quick-release the pressure and remove the lid.

2. Drain off any excess liquid not absorbed by the barley, leaving just enough to leave the risotto slightly soupy. Reduce heat to low and stir in the cheese and parsley. Taste for seasoning and add salt if needed. Serve.

Warm Chickpea Salad

This recipe is for a side-dish salad. In the summer, you can put the salad in an aluminum baking pan and cook it over indirect heat on a covered grill. Or skip the baking part entirely, chill the salad, and serve it cold.

INGREDIENTS | SERVES 12

1 pound chickpeas

10 cups water

1½ tablespoons vegetable oil

Salt, to taste

4 green onions, sliced

1 medium red onion, peeled and diced

1 small green bell pepper, seeded and diced

1 small red bell pepper, seeded and diced

½ cup fresh parsley, minced

1 large carrot, peeled and grated

¼ cup extra virgin olive oil

2 teaspoons fresh lemon juice

2 teaspoons white wine vinegar

1 tablespoon mayonnaise

1 clove garlic, peeled and minced

⅛ teaspoon freshly ground white pepper

½ teaspoon dried oregano

¼ cup Parmigiano-Reggiano and Romano cheese, grated

1. Rinse and drain the chickpeas. Soak them in 6 cups of water for at least 4 hours or overnight. Drain. Add chickpeas to the pressure cooker along with 4 cups of water and the vegetable oil. Lock the lid in place and bring to high pressure; maintain pressure for 20 minutes. Remove from heat and allow pressure to release naturally. Drain the beans and transfer them to an ovenproof 9" × 13" casserole dish. Sprinkle salt to taste over the beans.

2. Add the green onion, red onion, green and red bell peppers, parsley, and carrot to the casserole and toss with the beans.

3. Preheat the oven to 375°F.

4. To prepare the dressing, add the oil, lemon juice, vinegar, mayonnaise, garlic, pepper, and oregano to a small bowl or measuring cup. Whisk to mix. Pour the dressing over the beans mixture; stir to combine. Sprinkle the cheese over the dressed beans. Bake for 6 minutes. Stir before serving.

Macaroni and Cheese

You can speed up the process by cooking and stirring the cheese into the macaroni over very low heat until it's melted. Then follow the directions in Step 2, except preheat the broiler and brown the breadcrumbs under the broiler.

INGREDIENTS | SERVES 6

1 tablespoon olive or vegetable oil

1 medium sweet onion, peeled and diced

1 clove garlic, peeled and minced

2 cups elbow macaroni

3 cups chicken broth

1 teaspoon salt

⅛ teaspoon freshly ground white pepper

½ cup whole milk

½ cup heavy cream

4 ounces Cheddar cheese, grated

4 ounces mozzarella cheese, grated

4 ounces Colby cheese, grated

¼ cup dried bread crumbs

2 tablespoons butter, melted

1. Bring the oil to temperature in the pressure cooker over medium heat. Add the onion; sauté for 3 minutes or until the onion is soft. Add the garlic; sauté for 30 seconds. Add the macaroni and stir to coat it in the oil. Stir in the broth, salt, and pepper. Lock the lid into place and bring to high pressure; maintain pressure for 6 minutes. Quick release the pressure and remove the lid.

2. Preheat the oven to 350°F. Drain the macaroni. Transfer to a 9" × 13" ovenproof baking dish. Stir in the milk, cream, and cheeses. Mix the bread crumbs together with the melted butter and sprinkle over the top of the macaroni and cheese. Bake for 30 minutes or until the cheeses are melted and the bread crumbs are golden brown. Remove from the oven and let rest for 5 minutes. Serve.

Quinoa Artichoke Hearts Salad

The amount of dressing called for in this recipe is a suggestion and will depend on how strongly the dressing you're using is seasoned. You may wish to use more or less, or use your own homemade vinaigrette.

INGREDIENTS | SERVES 4

1 cup pecans

1 cup uncooked quinoa

2½ cups water

2 cups frozen artichoke hearts

2 cups cherry or grape tomatoes, halved

2 shallots or ½ small red onion, thinly sliced

¼ cup Italian or Caesar salad dressing

2 heads Belgian endive

1. Rough chop the pecans and add them to the pressure cooker over medium heat. Dry roast for several minutes, stirring continuously to prevent the nuts from burning. The pecans are sufficiently toasted when they're fragrant and slightly brown. Transfer to a bowl and set aside to cool.

2. Add the quinoa and water to the pressure cooker. Lock the lid into place and bring to high pressure; maintain pressure for 2 minutes. Remove from the heat and allow pressure to release naturally for 10 minutes. Quick release any remaining pressure. Transfer to a colander; drain and rinse under cold water. Drain well and transfer to a large bowl.

3. While the quinoa is cooking, prepare the artichoke hearts according to package directions and then plunge into cold water to cool and stop the cooking process. When cooled, cut into quarters.

4. Stir the artichoke hearts into the quinoa along with the tomatoes and shallot or red onion. Toss with the salad dressing. At this point, the quinoa mixture can be covered and refrigerated until ready to serve. This allows the flavors to blend. However, if you'll be refrigerating the quinoa mixture for more than 1 hour, leave the cherry or grape tomatoes whole rather than halving them.

5. To prepare the salad, separate the endive leaves. Rinse, drain, and divide them between 4 plates. Top each with one-fourth of the quinoa mixture. Sprinkle ¼ cup of the toasted pecans over the top of each salad.

Chicken Tortellini

You can substitute broccoli florets for the asparagus. Serve with a tossed salad and garlic bread.

INGREDIENTS | SERVES 6

3 slices bacon, diced

¼ cup plus 3 tablespoons butter

4 shallots, peeled and minced

1 tablespoon dried parsley

1½ pounds boneless, skinless chicken breasts

1 small carrot, peeled and finely sliced

1 8-ounce package dried cheese tortellini

1 teaspoon dried tarragon

2 cups chicken broth

1 pound asparagus

2 teaspoons all-purpose flour

¼ cup whole milk

¼ cup heavy cream

½ cup Parmigiano-Reggiano cheese, grated

Salt and freshly ground black pepper, to taste

A Heavier Sauce

You can omit the flour if you use ½ cup of heavy cream for the sauce instead of the combination of milk and cream. This is a good option if you're making the sauce for someone who adheres to a gluten-free diet (make sure you have gluten-free tortellini).

1. Fry the bacon in the pressure cooker over medium heat until it is crisp. Stir in ¼ cup of the butter, shallots, and parsley; sauté for 3 minutes. Cut the chicken into bite-size pieces and add it to the pressure cooker along with the carrot, tortellini, tarragon, and broth. Stir. Lock the lid into place and bring to high pressure; maintain pressure for 6 minutes.

2. Quick release the pressure and remove the lid. Clean and trim the asparagus, cut it into 2-inch pieces, and add it to the pressure cooker. Lock the lid into place and bring to low pressure; maintain pressure for 2 minutes.

3. Quick release the pressure and remove the lid. Combine the remaining 3 tablespoons of butter with the flour and then whisk it into the milk and cream; stir in the cheese. Bring the contents of the pressure cooker to a simmer and slowly stir in the flour mixture. Cook and stir for 3 minutes or until the sauce is thickened and the flour taste is cooked out of the sauce. Taste for seasoning and add salt and pepper to taste. Transfer to a serving bowl or platter. Top with additional cheese if desired.

CHAPTER 17

Rice and Risotto

Shrimp Risotto
196

Rice Pilaf
196

Brown Rice and Vegetables
197

Spanish Chicken and Rice
198

Vegetable Risotto
with Beet Greens
199

Brown Rice Salad
200

Brown Rice with Dried Fruit
201

Chicken Caesar Rice
202

Coconut Rice
203

Confetti Rice
203

Creole Chicken and Rice
204

Hoppin' John
205

Stuffed Head of Cabbage
206

Peppery Brown Rice Risotto
208

Vegetable-Rice Pilaf
209

Shrimp Risotto

Add a vegetable to the Shrimp Risotto by stirring in 1 cup of thawed frozen baby peas when you add the shrimp. A fresh tomato salad goes well with this rich, creamy dish.

INGREDIENTS | SERVES 4

2 tablespoons extra virgin olive oil

1 small onion, peeled and diced

1 teaspoon fennel seeds

3 cloves garlic, peeled and minced

1½ cups Arborio rice

2 tablespoons tomato paste

Pinch saffron threads

¼ cup dry white vermouth

3 cups chicken broth

1 pound medium shrimp, peeled and deveined

Salt and freshly ground black pepper, to taste

1. Bring the oil to temperature in the pressure cooker over medium-high heat. Add the onion and fennel seeds; sauté for 3 minutes or until the onions are softened.

2. Add the garlic, rice, tomato paste, and saffron; stir until the rice is evenly colored. Stir in vermouth and broth.

3. Lock the lid into place and bring to high pressure; maintain pressure for 6 minutes. Quick release the pressure and remove the lid.

4. Stir in the shrimp; simmer for 2 minutes or until the shrimp are pale pink and cooked through.

5. Taste for seasoning and add salt and pepper if needed. Serve immediately.

Rice Pilaf

Make this side dish the perfect complement to a vegetarian meal by substituting vegetable broth for the chicken broth.

INGREDIENTS | SERVES 6–8

1½ tablespoons unsalted butter

1 medium carrot, peeled and grated

1 stalk celery, finely diced

1 medium onion, peeled and diced

2 cups long-grain white rice

¼ teaspoon salt

3 cups chicken broth

1. Melt the butter in the pressure cooker over medium heat. Add the carrot and celery; sauté for 3 minutes.

2. Add the onion; sauté for 3 minutes or until the onion is tender. Add the rice and stir into the vegetables. Add the salt and broth; stir.

3. Lock the lid into place and bring to high pressure; maintain pressure for 3 minutes. Remove from the heat and allow pressure to release naturally for 5 minutes.

4. Quick release any remaining pressure and remove the lid. Fluff the rice with a fork. Serve.

Brown Rice and Vegetables

Add seasoning blend herbs and spices to the rice and water or broth in Step 1. This versatile side dish will go with just about any entrée.

INGREDIENTS | SERVES 8

1 cup brown rice

1½ cups water or chicken broth

1 small turnip, peeled and diced

1 pound banana squash, peeled and diced

½ cup baby carrots, quartered

1 small zucchini, peeled, quartered lengthwise, and sliced

3 stalks Swiss chard, leafy greens chopped and stems diced

1 cup broccoli florets, coarse chopped

⅓ cup water chestnuts, diced

Salt and freshly ground black pepper, to taste

Recipe Versatility

You can use whatever vegetables you have on hand; just dice or slice the vegetable pieces according to the length of time it takes that vegetable to cook. The longer the cooking time, the smaller the dice. For example, butternut squash and carrots are slow cookers, so you should dice those into smaller pieces than onions and celery.

1. Rinse and drain the rice. Bring the rice and water or broth to a boil in the pressure cooker over high heat.

2. Lock the lid into place and adjust heat to bring to low pressure; maintain pressure for 10 minutes.

3. Remove from the heat and allow pressure to release naturally. Remove the lid.

4. Add the turnip, squash, carrots, zucchini, chard, broccoli, and water chestnuts. Stir to mix with the rice.

5. Lock the lid into place, return the pan to the heat, and bring to low pressure; maintain pressure for 1 minute.

6. Remove from the heat and allow pressure to release naturally. Remove the lid.

7. Fluff the rice and vegetables with a fork. Taste for seasoning and add salt and pepper to taste. Serve.

Spanish Chicken and Rice

Adapt the heat level of the Spanish Chicken and Rice recipe by choosing between mild, medium, or hot chili powder, according to your tastes. In addition, you can substitute jalapeño pepper for some or all of the green pepper.

INGREDIENTS | SERVES 4

2 tablespoons extra virgin olive or vegetable oil

1 pound boneless chicken breast, cut into bite-sized pieces

1 large green pepper, seeded and diced

1 teaspoon chili powder

1 teaspoon smoked paprika

¼ teaspoon dried thyme

⅛ teaspoon dried oregano

¼ teaspoon freshly ground black pepper

Pinch cayenne pepper

1 medium white onion, peeled and diced

4 ounces fresh mushrooms, sliced

2 cloves garlic, peeled and minced

2 cups chicken broth

1 cup long-grain rice, uncooked

½ cup black olives, pitted and halved

1. Bring the oil to temperature in the pressure cooker over medium heat. Add the chicken, green pepper, chili powder, paprika, thyme, oregano, black pepper, cayenne, and onion; stir-fry for 5 minutes or until the onion is transparent and the chicken begins to brown.

2. Stir in the mushrooms; sauté for 2 minutes. Add the garlic, broth, rice, and olives.

3. Lock the lid into place and bring to high pressure; maintain pressure for 3 minutes. Remove from the heat and allow the pressure to release naturally for 7 minutes.

4. Quick-release any remaining pressure. Uncover and fluff with a fork. Taste for seasoning and add salt and other seasoning if needed.

Vegetable Risotto with Beet Greens

You can substitute water or vegetable broth for the chicken broth and make this a vegetarian meal.

INGREDIENTS | **SERVES 4**

¼ cup extra virgin olive oil

1 clove garlic, peeled and minced

1 portobello mushroom

1 small Asian eggplant, sliced

1 small zucchini, sliced

1 large red bell pepper, seeded and cut in quarters

1 medium onion, peeled and thickly sliced

Salt and freshly ground black pepper, to taste

¼ cup butter

1 cup Arborio rice

½ cup dry white wine

2 cups chicken broth

2 cups young beet greens, sliced

¼ cup fresh basil, sliced

½ cup Parmigiano-Reggiano cheese, grated

1. Ten minutes before you'll be grilling the vegetables, add the oil and garlic to a small bowl; stir to mix and set aside to infuse the flavor of the garlic into the oil.

2. Preheat the grill or a grill pan over medium-high heat. Remove the stem and black gills from the mushroom cap; slice the cap.

3. Brush all sides of the eggplant slices, zucchini slices, bell pepper quarters, mushroom slices, and onion with the oil.

4. Place vegetables on the grill rack or in the grill pan. Sprinkle with salt and pepper.

5. Turning once, grill the vegetables for several minutes on each side or until softened and slightly charred. Set aside to cool, and then coarsely chop.

6. Bring the remaining garlic-infused oil and 3 tablespoons of the butter to temperature in the pressure cooker over medium heat.

7. Add the rice and stir it to coat it in the oil-butter mixture. Stir in the wine and broth.

8. Lock the lid into place and bring to high pressure; maintain pressure for 7 minutes. Remove from the heat, quick-release the pressure, and remove the lid.

9. Add the chopped grilled vegetables, beet greens, and basil. Cover the pressure cooker (but do not lock the lid into place).

10. Let rest, covered, for 5 minutes or until greens are wilted. Stir in cheese and remaining butter. Taste for seasoning and add additional salt and pepper to taste.

Brown Rice Salad

This is the type of salad that will benefit if you experiment with different flavors. Serve this main-dish salad with honey-mustard dressing over salad greens.

INGREDIENTS | SERVES 6

2 cups long-grain brown rice, rinsed and drained

4½ cups chicken broth

1 whole chicken breast, skin removed

1½ teaspoons salt

3 green onions, finely diced

2 large carrots, peeled and diced

2 stalks celery, sliced

1 small red bell pepper, seeded and diced

3 tablespoons mayonnaise

1 teaspoon Dijon mustard

1 teaspoon honey

2 tablespoons butter, melted

2 tablespoons apple cider vinegar

½ cup extra virgin olive oil

2 hard-boiled eggs, peeled and chopped

Salt and freshly ground white pepper, to taste

2 tablespoons fresh parsley, finely chopped

1. Add the rice, broth, chicken, and salt to the pressure cooker. Lock the lid into place and bring to high pressure; maintain pressure for 12 minutes.

2. Remove from heat, quick-release the pressure, and remove the lid. Transfer the chicken to a cutting board. Fluff the rice with a fork and transfer it to a bowl. Once rice has cooled, toss it with the onions, carrots, celery, and bell pepper.

3. To make the dressing, whisk together the mayonnaise, mustard, honey, melted butter, and vinegar, and then slowly whisk in the olive oil.

4. Fold in the chopped boiled egg. Taste for seasoning and add salt and pepper to taste and more honey if desired.

5. Pour half of the dressing over the rice salad mixture in the bowl. Stir to mix, adding more dressing if desired. Sprinkle the fresh parsley over the salad. Serve.

Brown Rice with Dried Fruit

To dice a large peeled carrot, quarter the carrot lengthwise and then slice the resulting strips into cubes.

INGREDIENTS | SERVES 6

2 tablespoons butter or vegetable oil

2 stalks celery, thinly sliced

2 large carrots, peeled and diced

1 large sweet potato, peeled and diced

1½ cups raw long- or short-grain brown rice, rinsed and drained

⅓ cup pitted prunes, chopped

⅓ cup dried apricots, chopped

½ teaspoon ground cinnamon

2 teaspoons orange zest, grated

3 cups water or chicken broth

1 bay leaf

½ teaspoon salt

1. Melt the butter in the pressure cooker. Add the celery, carrots, sweet potato, and rice. Stir to coat in the butter.

2. Stir in the prunes, apricots, cinnamon, and orange zest. Bring the water or broth to a boil and pour it into the pressure cooker; stir to mix it into the rice mixture. Add the bay leaf and salt.

3. Lock the lid into place and bring to high pressure; maintain pressure for 16 minutes. Remove from the heat and allow pressure to release naturally for 10 minutes.

4. Quick-release any remaining pressure and remove the lid. Use a fork to fluff the rice.

5. Taste to make sure the rice is cooked through. If it isn't, add additional water or broth if needed and simmer or cook under pressure until tender.

6. If the rice is already cooked through, drain off any excess moisture. Remove and discard the bay leaf. Taste for seasoning and adjust if necessary. Transfer to a serving bowl. Serve hot.

Chicken Caesar Rice

You're used to Caesar salads and Caesar wraps, but have you tried Caesar dressing with rice and vegetables? Serve with garlic bread.

INGREDIENTS | SERVES 6

2 tablespoons olive oil

2 pounds boneless, skinless chicken breasts

1 cup long-grain white rice, rinsed and drained

1 14-ounce can chicken broth

½ cup bottled Caesar salad dressing

4 cloves garlic, peeled and minced

1 tablespoon dried Italian herbs blend

1 cup frozen broccoli florets, thawed

1 cup frozen cauliflower pieces, thawed

1 cup frozen sliced carrots, thawed

½ cup pimento-stuffed olives, sliced

½ cup Parmigiano-Reggiano cheese, grated

1. Bring the oil to temperature in the pressure cooker over medium heat. Cut the chicken into bite-size pieces and add to the pressure cooker.

2. Stir-fry for 5 minutes or until lightly browned. Stir in the rice, broth, dressing, garlic, and Italian herb blend.

3. Lock the lid into place and bring to high pressure; maintain pressure for 8 minutes. Quick-release the pressure and remove the lid.

4. Stir the mixture in the pressure cooker. Add the thawed frozen vegetables and green olives to the top of the chicken and rice mixture.

5. Lock the lid back into place and bring to high pressure; maintain pressure for 2 minutes.

6. Remove from the heat and allow pressure to release naturally. Remove the lid. Stir in the cheese, fluffing the rice with a fork. Transfer to a serving bowl. Serve hot.

Coconut Rice

The combination of coconut, currants, and spices transforms this rice into a succulent dish. It is especially good served with a curry entrée.

INGREDIENTS | **SERVES 4**

2 tablespoons butter or vegetable oil

1 cup extra long-grain white rice, rinsed and drained

½ cup unsweetened coconut, flaked or grated

2¼ cups water

¼ cup currants

½ teaspoon ground cinnamon

1 teaspoon anise seeds

⅛ teaspoon ground cloves

½ teaspoon salt

1. Bring the butter or oil to temperature in the pressure cooker over medium heat. Add the rice, stirring well to coat it in the fat.

2. Add the coconut, water, currants, cinnamon, anise seeds, cloves, and salt. Lock the lid into place and bring to high pressure; maintain the pressure for 3 minutes. Turn off the heat and let the pressure drop naturally for 7 minutes.

3. Quick-release any remaining pressure and remove the lid. Fluff the rice with a fork. Drain off any excess moisture. Taste for seasoning and adjust if necessary. Serve.

Confetti Rice

For a healthy, fiber-rich alternative, use brown rice instead of white rice. It's the same thing, except the bran layer and all of its nutrients have not been removed from the brown rice.

INGREDIENTS | **SERVES 6**

3 tablespoons butter

1 small red onion, peeled and diced

2 cloves garlic, peeled and diced

1 cup long-grain white rice, rinsed and drained

3 cups frozen mixed vegetables, thawed

1 14-ounce can chicken broth

¼ cup fresh lemon juice

1 tablespoon ground cumin or herb blend

½ teaspoon salt

½ teaspoon freshly ground black pepper

1. Melt the butter in the pressure cooker over medium heat. Add the onion; sauté for 3 minutes or until soft. Add the garlic; sauté for 30 seconds.

2. Add the rice and stir it to coat it in the butter; sauté until the rice becomes translucent. Add the remaining ingredients. Stir to mix.

3. Lock the lid into place and bring to high pressure; maintain pressure for 7 minutes. Remove from the heat and allow pressure to release naturally. Remove the lid. Fluff the rice with a fork. Taste for seasoning and adjust if necessary.

Creole Chicken and Rice

Serve with cornbread or baked corn tortillas. Have hot sauce at the table for those who wish to add it.

INGREDIENTS | SERVES 6

2 tablespoons vegetable oil

2 pounds boneless, skinless chicken breasts

1 medium white onion, peeled and diced

1 large green bell pepper, seeded and diced

4 cloves garlic, peeled and minced

1 teaspoon dried rosemary, crushed

1 teaspoon dried thyme

1 teaspoon paprika

¼ teaspoon dried red pepper flakes

½ cup white wine

1 28-ounce can diced tomatoes

1 14-ounce can chicken broth

2 cups frozen okra, thawed and sliced

1 cup frozen whole kernel corn, thawed

2 large carrots, peeled and sliced

1 cup long-grain white rice, rinsed and drained

½ cup fresh cilantro, chopped, packed

1 bay leaf

Salt and freshly ground black pepper, to taste

1. Bring the oil to temperature in the pressure cooker. Cut the chicken into bite-size strips.

2. Add chicken along with the onion and green pepper to the oil; sauté for several minutes or until the chicken is slightly browned and the onion is soft.

3. Add the garlic, rosemary, thyme, paprika, and red pepper flakes; sauté for 2 minutes or until the herbs begin to release their aroma.

4. Pour in the wine; deglaze the pan, scraping up any bits stuck to the bottom of the pan.

5. Add the remaining ingredients. Stir to mix. Lock the lid into place and bring to high pressure; maintain pressure for 7 minutes.

6. Remove from the heat and allow pressure to release naturally. Remove the lid. Remove and discard the bay leaf. Fluff the rice with a fork. Taste for seasoning and adjust if necessary. Serve.

Hoppin' John

Hoppin' John is a Southern dish traditionally eaten on New Year's Day. This version is hopped up by adding carrots to make it a one-dish meal.

INGREDIENTS | SERVES 6–8

½ pound thick-cut bacon, diced

1 stalk celery, finely diced

1 1-pound bag baby carrots

1 large onion, peeled and diced

2 15-ounce cans black-eyed peas, rinsed and drained

1 cup long-grain white rice, rinsed and drained

4 cups chicken broth

Salt and freshly ground black pepper, to taste

Beans

You can substitute cooked cowpeas or red lentils for the black-eyed peas. There are more than 200 different types of cowpeas for you to choose from. Red lentils are filling and have more calories than you might expect, so serve yourself a smaller portion than you think you'll eat. You'll be surprised.

1. Fry the bacon in the pressure cooker over medium heat until the fat begins to render out of the bacon. Add the celery; sauté for 2 minutes.

2. Shred 4 baby carrots and add them to the pan with the celery; sauté for another minute. Add the onion and sauté for 3 minutes or until the onions are soft.

3. Dice the remaining baby carrots and add them to the pressure cooker. Stir in the black-eyed peas, rice, and chicken broth.

4. Lock the lid into place and bring to high pressure; maintain pressure for 7 minutes. Remove from the heat and allow pressure to release naturally. Remove lid and stir. Taste for seasoning; add salt and pepper if needed.

Stuffed Head of Cabbage

If you prefer, you can substitute lean ground pork, lamb, chicken, or turkey for the ground beef. Serve with pumpernickel or whole grain country bread.

INGREDIENTS | SERVES 6

1 pound lean ground beef
¼ cup butter
2 large sweet onions, peeled and diced
4 cloves garlic, peeled and minced
1 tablespoon dried parsley
2 tablespoons dried dill
1 teaspoon dried thyme
1 large carrot, peeled and diced
2 stalks celery, diced
1 cup long-grain white rice
2 cups beef or chicken broth, divided
2 14½-ounce cans diced tomatoes, divided
1 teaspoon sugar
2 teaspoons salt, divided
1 teaspoon freshly ground black pepper, divided
1 large head green cabbage
¼ cup olive oil
1 small sweet onion, peeled and sliced
1 small green pepper, seeded and diced
1 tablespoon light brown sugar

2 teaspoons dried oregano

1. Add the ground beef to the pressure cooker. Fry it until cooked through over medium-high heat, breaking it apart as you do so. Drain and discard rendered fat. Transfer the cooked ground beef to a bowl and keep warm.

2. Reduce heat to medium. Melt the butter in the pressure cooker and bring it to temperature.

3. Add the 2 large diced onions; sauté for 3 minutes or until it begins to soften. Add the garlic; sauté for 30 seconds.

4. Mix in the parsley, dill, thyme, carrot, celery, rice, cooked ground beef, 1 cup of the broth, 1 can of the undrained tomatoes, sugar, 1 teaspoon of the salt, and ½ teaspoon of the pepper.

5. Lock the lid into place and bring to high pressure; maintain pressure for 6 minutes.

6. Remove the pressure cooker from heat, quick-release the pressure, and remove the lid. Stir and mix the ground beef-rice mixture.

7. Wash and dry the cabbage. Remove the outer leaves and the core. Use a paring knife to hollow out the cabbage, leaving at least a 2-inch-thick shell.

8. Center the cabbage shell on a 24-inch length of cheesecloth. Spoon the ground beef-rice mixture into the cabbage shell, mounding it over the top of the opening. Pull the cheesecloth up and over the top of the cabbage.

Stuffed Head of Cabbage (*continued*)

9. Add the olive oil to the pressure cooker and bring it to temperature over medium heat.

10. Add the sliced onion and diced green pepper; sauté for 3 minutes or until the onion is soft.

11. Stir in brown sugar, oregano, remaining tomatoes, remaining broth, salt, and pepper. Stir well. Place the steamer basket in the sauce in the pressure cooker.

12. Lift the cabbage by the ends of the cheesecloth and place it in the steamer basket.

13. Lock the lid into place and bring to high pressure; maintain pressure for 10 minutes. Remove the pressure cooker from the heat, quick-release the pressure, and remove the lid.

14. Transfer the cabbage to a serving platter by using tongs to hold the ends of the cheesecloth and a spatula to steady the bottom of the cabbage.

15. Carefully pull the cheesecloth out from the under the cabbage. Cut the cabbage into serving wedges.

16. Remove the steamer basket from the pressure cooker and pour the sauce over the cabbage wedges. Serve.

Peppery Brown Rice Risotto

The white grape juice concentrate gives the rice a touch of sweetness. If you'd rather keep it completely savory, omit the white grape juice concentrate and instead use ¼ cup white wine and 2½ cups water.

INGREDIENTS | SERVES 8

2 medium leeks

1 small fennel bulb

3 tablespoons butter

2 cups short-grain brown rice, rinsed and drained

½ teaspoon salt

2¾ cups water

1 tablespoon frozen white grape juice concentrate

¾ cup Fontina cheese, grated

1½ teaspoons freshly ground or cracked black pepper

1. Cut the leeks into quarters lengthwise, and then slice into ½-inch slices; wash thoroughly, drain, and dry.

2. Clean the fennel. Trim the fronds from the fennel, and chop. Dice the bulb.

3. Melt the butter in the pressure cooker over medium heat. Add the leeks and fennel; sauté for a minute or until the leeks begin to wilt.

4. Add the rice and stir-fry into the leeks until the rice begins to turn golden brown. Stir in the salt, water, and white grape juice concentrate.

5. Lock the lid into place and bring to high pressure; maintain pressure for 20 minutes. Remove from the heat and allow pressure to release naturally for 10 minutes. Quick-release any remaining pressure. Remove the lid.

6. Fluff the rice with a fork. Stir in the cheese, fennel fronds, and pepper. Taste for seasoning and add additional salt if needed. Serve.

Vegetable-Rice Pilaf

Instant pilaf that comes in cardboard boxes at the supermarket is no match for this dish. Serve as a side dish with African-inspired dishes or roast chicken.

INGREDIENTS | SERVES 4

1 tablespoon butter

1 tablespoon vegetable oil

½ small yellow onion, peeled and thinly sliced

2 cloves garlic, peeled and minced

1½-inch piece fresh ginger, peeled and grated

1 serrano pepper, seeded and minced

1½ cups cauliflower florets, quartered

1 cup green beans, cleaned and cut into 1-inch pieces

1 large carrot, peeled and sliced diagonally

1 teaspoon ground cumin

½ teaspoon ground turmeric

¼ teaspoon cardamom seeds

1 teaspoon chili powder

⅛ teaspoon ground cloves

⅛ teaspoon hot paprika

½ teaspoon salt

1 cup long-grain white rice, rinsed and drained

1½ cups water

¼ cup slivered almonds, toasted

1. Melt the butter in the pressure cooker over medium heat. Add the oil and bring to temperature.

2. Add the onion, garlic, ginger, and serrano pepper; sauté for 2 minutes. Stir in the cauliflower, green beans, carrot, cumin, turmeric, cardamom seeds, chili powder, ground cloves, paprika, salt, rice, and water.

3. Lock the lid into place and bring to high pressure; maintain pressure for 6 minutes. Remove from the heat and allow pressure to release naturally for 15 minutes. Quick-release any remaining pressure and remove the lid.

4. Fluff rice with a fork. Transfer to a serving bowl. Top with toasted almonds. Serve.

CHAPTER 18

Stovetop Casseroles

Ham and Potato Casserole
211

Tater Tot Casserole
212

Wild Rice Casserole
212

Spicy Beef Macaroni and Cheese
213

Unstuffed Peppers Casserole
213

Summer Sausage Casserole
214

Paella
215

Ham and Barley Skillet Dinner
216

Ham and Scalloped Potatoes
217

Stuffed Ham Steaks
218

Turkey and Vegetable Casserole
219

Bubble and Squeak
220

Ham and Potato Casserole

This is an assemble-it-on-the-plate casserole. Serve it with warm, buttered dinner rolls. The ham hocks will add a salty back note to the sauce, but have salt and pepper at the table for those who wish to add it.

INGREDIENTS | SERVES 4

4 smoked ham hocks

1 tablespoon gin

1 medium sweet onion, peeled and quartered

2 stalks celery, tops only

1 large carrot, peeled and quartered

1 cup chicken broth

3 cups water

4 large red potatoes, scrubbed and quartered

4 Belgian endives, rinsed, drained, and cut in half lengthwise

¾ cup heavy cream

1. Add the ham hocks, gin, onion, celery tops, carrot, broth, and water to the pressure cooker.

2. Lock the lid into place and bring to low pressure; maintain pressure for 30 minutes. Remove from the heat and allow pressure to release naturally. Remove the lid.

3. Transfer the ham hocks to a serving platter; keep warm. Strain the pan juices. Discard the cooked vegetables.

4. Skim off any fat from the top of the strained juices and discard. Pour the strained, defatted juices back into the pressure cooker.

5. Add the potatoes to the pressure cooker, cut sides down. Lock the lid into place and bring to low pressure; maintain pressure for 7 minutes.

6. Quick-release the pressure and remove the lid. Adjust heat to maintain a low simmer and add the endives.

7. Loosely cover the pan and simmer for 4 minutes to steam the endives. Transfer the endives and potatoes to the serving platter with the ham hocks; keep warm.

8. Stir the cream into the pan juices remaining in the pressure cooker. Bring to a boil over medium-high heat; boil hard for 5 minutes.

9. To assemble, place a ham hock, 4 potato quarters, and 2 endive pieces on each plate. Generously spoon the sauce over the potatoes and endives. Serve.

Tater Tot Casserole

You can add variety by using a herb-seasoned soup or by mixing a tablespoon of your favorite herb seasoning blend in with the soup-milk mixture.

INGREDIENTS | SERVES 8

2 pounds smoked sausage, sliced

1 1-pound bag tater tots

1 1-pound bag broccoli and cauliflower, thawed

1 10¾-ounce can condensed cream of mushroom soup

1 10¾-ounce can condensed cream of chicken soup

1 12-ounce can evaporated milk

1. Treat the inside of the pressure cooker with nonstick spray. Arrange a layer of smoked sausage slices over the bottom of the pressure cooker. Top with a layer of tater tots and a layer of broccoli and cauliflower.

2. In a large measuring cup, mix together the soups and evaporated milk. Pour some of the soup-milk mixture over the layers in the pressure cooker.

3. Layer until all of the smoked sausage, vegetables, and soup-milk mixture have been added to the pressure cooker, ending with a layer of smoked sausage.

4. Lock the lid and bring to low pressure over medium heat; maintain pressure for 10 minutes. Remove from the heat and allow pressure to release naturally. Serve.

Wild Rice Casserole

This side dish casserole goes great with roast turkey or chicken. It's especially good if you mix in some shiitake mushrooms with the fresh button mushrooms.

INGREDIENTS | SERVES 4

2 tablespoons butter

1 small sweet onion, peeled and diced

4 ounces fresh mushrooms, cleaned and sliced

1 cup wild rice, rinsed and drained

½ cup pecans, chopped and toasted

2 teaspoons Mrs. Dash Garlic and Herb Seasoning Blend

2 cups chicken broth

Salt and freshly ground black pepper, to taste

1. Melt the butter in the pressure cooker over medium heat. Stir in the onion and mushrooms; sauté for 5 minutes or until the mushrooms have given off their moisture and begin to brown. Stir in the wild rice, pecans, seasoning blend, and broth.

2. Lock the lid into place and bring to high pressure; maintain pressure for 20 minutes. Remove from the heat and allow pressure to release naturally.

3. Fluff rice with a fork and drain off any excess moisture. Taste for seasoning and add salt and pepper if needed.

Spicy Beef Macaroni and Cheese

Serve this Southwestern-inspired dish with an avocado salad and baked tortilla chips.

INGREDIENTS | SERVES 6

1 pound lean ground beef
1 tablespoon olive or vegetable oil
1 small yellow onion, peeled and diced
1 jalapeño pepper, seeded and minced
2 cloves garlic, peeled and minced
2 cups bottled salsa
1 3-ounce can tomato paste
2 tablespoons chili powder
3 cups uncooked penne or ziti pasta
Water
8 ounces sharp Cheddar cheese, grated

1. Fry ground beef in the pressure cooker over medium-high heat. Drain off and discard fat. Stir in the oil, onion, and jalapeño; sauté for 3 minutes. Stir in the garlic and sauté for 30 seconds. Stir in the salsa, tomato paste, chili powder, and pasta. Pour in enough water to cover all of the ingredients.

2. Lock the lid into place and bring to low pressure; maintain pressure for 6 minutes. Remove from heat and allow pressure to release naturally. Remove lid and drain off any excess moisture. Stir in the cheese. Cover the pressure cooker for 3 minutes. Stir again.

Unstuffed Peppers Casserole

You can use a can of whole tomatoes instead of diced if you prefer. Just crush or cut up the tomatoes when you add them to the casserole.

INGREDIENTS | SERVES 4

1 pound ground beef
1 tablespoon olive or vegetable oil
1 medium onion, peeled and chopped
2 large green bell peppers, seeded and diced
2½ cups herb-seasoned bread crumbs
1 8-ounce can whole kernel corn, drained
1 14½-ounce can diced tomatoes
½ cup beef broth
1 tablespoon butter, melted

1. Fry ground beef in the pressure cooker over medium-high heat. Drain and discard fat. Stir in the oil, onion, and green bell pepper. Sprinkle 1½ cups bread crumbs over the mixture.

2. Layer corn and tomatoes over the bread crumbs. Layer the tomatoes over the corn. Drizzle with the beef broth. Lock lid into place and bring to high pressure; maintain for 3 minutes. Remove from heat, quick-release the pressure, and remove the lid.

3. Preheat oven to 400°F. In a small bowl, mix remaining bread crumbs with melted butter. Transfer contents of the pressure cooker to a casserole dish treated with nonstick spray and sprinkle buttered breadcrumbs over the top. Bake for 10 minutes. Remove from the oven and let rest for 10 minutes.

Summer Sausage Casserole

The cream cheese and cream in this recipe serve as a quick and easy substitute for using canned condensed soup.

INGREDIENTS | SERVES 6

1 tablespoon butter

1 stalk celery, finely diced

2 baby carrots, grated

1 small onion, peeled and diced

1½ pounds summer or smoked sausage, diced

1 8-ounce can mushroom stems and pieces, drained

3 cups uncooked penne or ziti pasta

Water

1 8-ounce package cream cheese, cubed

¼ cup heavy cream

1 cup frozen baby peas, thawed

Salt and freshly ground black pepper, to taste

1. Melt the butter and bring it to temperature over medium heat. Add the celery and carrot; sauté for 2 minutes.

2. Add the onion; sauté for 3 minutes or until the onion is tender. Stir in the sausage and mushrooms; sauté for 2 minutes. Stir the pasta into the other ingredients in the pressure cooker.

3. Pour in enough water to cover all of the ingredients. Lock the lid into place and bring to low pressure; maintain pressure for 6 minutes.

4. Remove from heat and allow pressure to release naturally. Remove the lid. Drain off and discard any excess moisture.

5. Add the cream cheese and cream to a microwave-safe bowl. Heat on high for 30 seconds or long enough to soften the cream cheese so that it can be whisked into the cream.

6. Add the cream cheese mixture to the pressure cooker and stir into the pasta mixture along with the baby peas.

7. Cover the pressure cooker for 3 minutes to allow time to warm the peas. Taste for seasoning and add if needed. Serve.

Paella

You can stretch this recipe to 8 servings if you serve it with homemade bread. You can also increase the servings by adding sliced red and yellow bell pepper when you add the green bell pepper and stirring in a cup of green beans when you add the peas.

INGREDIENTS | SERVES 6

6 slices bacon, diced

¼ cup olive oil

2 large yellow onions, sliced

4 cloves garlic, peeled and minced

1¾ cups long-grain white rice

1 pound boneless, skinless chicken thighs

1 pound boneless, skinless chicken breasts

5 cups chicken broth

6 tablespoons tomato paste

½ cup bottled clam juice

3 tablespoons fresh lemon juice

2 tablespoons sherry

1 tablespoon light brown sugar

2 tablespoons dried parsley

1 teaspoon salt

Pinch saffron threads

½ teaspoon sweet paprika

¼ teaspoon red pepper flakes, crushed

2 teaspoons dried oregano

2 bay leaves

1 small green bell pepper, seeded and sliced

½ pound sea scallops

½ pound uncooked, cleaned shrimp

1 cup frozen peas, thawed

1 cup black olives, pitted and sliced

6 lemon slices

1. Add the bacon to the pressure cooker and fry it over medium-high heat until crisp. Add the oil and bring it to temperature.

2. Stir in the onions; sauté for 3 minutes or until the onion begins to soften. Add the garlic; sauté for 30 seconds. Stir in the rice, sautéing it until the rice is coated in the oil and translucent.

3. Cut the chicken thighs and breasts into bite-size pieces. Add to the pressure cooker, stirring it into the contents of the pan along with the broth, tomato paste, clam juice, lemon juice, sherry, brown sugar, parsley, salt, saffron, paprika, pepper flakes, oregano, and bay leaves.

4. Lock the lid into place and bring to high pressure; maintain pressure for 8 minutes. Remove from heat, quick-release the pressure, and remove the lid.

5. Stir in the bell pepper, scallops, and shrimp. Return to heat, lock the lid into place, and bring to low pressure; maintain pressure for 3 minutes. Remove from the heat, quick-release the pressure, and remove the lid. Remove and discard the bay leaves.

6. Stir in the peas and olives. Taste for seasoning and adjust if necessary. Serve garnished with lemon slices.

Ham and Barley Skillet Dinner

You can substitute brown rice for the pearl barley. Follow the same cooking instructions given in Step 2, but leave the lid ajar over the rice for 20 minutes instead of 10.

INGREDIENTS | SERVES 8

4 tablespoons butter

1 cup pearl barley, rinsed and drained

1 teaspoon salt

4 cups water or chicken broth

1 tablespoon oil

2 teaspoons fresh ginger, peeled and grated

2 cloves garlic, peeled and minced

1 large green bell pepper, seeded and diced

1 large red bell pepper, seeded and diced

1 stalk celery, sliced

1 5-ounce can sliced water chestnuts, drained

8 ounces fresh mushrooms, cleaned and sliced

8 green onions, chopped and whites and greens separated

½ pound bean sprouts, rinsed and well drained

1 pound cooked ham, diced

1 tablespoon toasted sesame oil

Soy sauce, to taste

1. Melt the butter in the pressure cooker over medium-high heat. Stir in the barley and salt. Add the water.

2. Lock the lid into place and bring to high pressure; maintain pressure for 4 minutes. Reduce to low pressure; maintain low pressure for 20 minutes.

3. Remove from heat and allow pressure to release naturally for 10 minutes. Quick-release any remaining pressure.

4. Unlock the lid, but leave the pressure cooker covered with the lid slightly ajar for 10 minutes.

5. If necessary, drain or place the pan over low heat for a few minutes to remove any excess moisture.

6. Bring the oil to temperature in a large, deep nonstick skillet or wok over medium-high heat. Add the ginger and garlic; sauté for 30 seconds.

7. Add the peppers, celery, water chestnuts, mushrooms, and the whites of the green onions; sauté an additional 2 minutes, stirring frequently.

8. Stir in the bean sprouts, barley, and ham; stir-fry for 3 minutes or until the ingredients are hot and most of the liquid given off by the vegetables has evaporated.

9. Stir in the scallion greens. Stir in the toasted sesame oil. Taste for seasoning and add soy sauce to taste.

Ham and Scalloped Potatoes

You can easily increase the number of servings to 8 by adding a thinly sliced sweet onion and a sliced bell pepper to the potatoes.

INGREDIENTS | SERVES 6

1 cup chicken broth

6 medium potatoes, peeled and cut into ½-inch slices

¼ teaspoon salt

⅛ teaspoon freshly ground white or black pepper

1 tablespoon fresh chives, chopped

½ cup milk

2 tablespoons butter, softened

2 tablespoons all-purpose flour

½ cup sour cream

1 pound cooked ham, diced

4 ounces medium or sharp Cheddar cheese, grated

Optional: Sweet paprika

Cheese-Lover's Scalloped Potatoes

To make this dish even cheesier, melt 4 ounces of cubed cream cheese into the sauce before you add the sour cream and increase the amount of Cheddar cheese used to top the scalloped potatoes to 8 ounces. If desired, sprinkle 2 tablespoons or more grated Parmigiano-Reggiano cheese over the Cheddar cheese.

1. Add the broth, potatoes, salt, pepper, and chives to the pressure cooker. Lock the lid into place and bring to high pressure; maintain pressure for 5 minutes.

2. Remove the pressure cooker from the heat, quick-release the pressure, and remove the lid.

3. Treat a 9" × 13" ovenproof casserole dish with nonstick spray. Use a slotted spoon to transfer the potatoes to the casserole dish. Preheat the oven to 350°F.

4. Place the uncovered pressure cooker over medium-high heat. Stir the milk into any broth left in the pressure cooker and bring to a boil.

5. Add the butter and flour to a small bowl; mash into a paste, then stir in 1–2 tablespoons boiling liquid from the pressure cooker.

6. Whisk the butter-flour mixture into the liquid in the pressure cooker; boil and stir for a minute and then continue to cook and stir until the mixture begins to thicken.

7. Remove from heat and stir in the sour cream. Pour over the potatoes in the casserole dish.

8. Evenly sprinkle the ham over the potatoes. Top with cheese. If desired, evenly sprinkle paprika to taste over the cheese.

9. Bake for 15 minutes or until the cheese is melted and bubbly.

Stuffed Ham Steaks

The instant potato flakes serve as a thickener for the stuffing. Because the veggies are already in with the ham steaks, you can serve Stuffed Ham Steaks with a tossed salad and have a complete lunch. For dinner, consider adding a sweet potato dish and biscuits or warm homemade bread.

INGREDIENTS | SERVES 4

1½ cups fresh spinach or collard greens, chopped

1 medium onion, peeled and diced

1 stalk celery, finely diced

Pinch dry red pepper flakes, crushed

⅓ cup instant mashed potato flakes

2 1-inch-thick ham steaks

1 cup chicken broth

½ cup water

1 large red or green bell pepper, seeded and diced

2 tablespoons butter, softened

2 tablespoons all-purpose flour

1. Add the spinach or collard greens, onion, celery, red pepper and potato flakes to a bowl and mix together.

2. If necessary, trim ham steaks so they'll fit onto the rack of the pressure cooker.

3. Pour the broth and water into pressure cooker. Add the diced bell pepper. Place one ham steak on rack.

4. Spread the spinach or collard greens mixture evenly over the ham steak. Place the other ham steak on top of the mixture. Place the rack in the pressure cooker.

5. Lock the lid into place and bring to high pressure; maintain pressure for 5 minutes.

6. Remove from heat and allow pressure to release naturally. Remove lid. Transfer ham to a heated serving platter and keep warm.

7. Add enough water or broth to the pressure cooker to bring the remaining pan juices to 1 cup.

8. Place the pressure cooker over medium-high heat and bring the pan juices and cooked bell pepper mixture to a boil.

9. Mash the butter and flour into a paste, then thin it with some of the boiling pan juices. Whisk the thinned butter-flour mixture into the pan and boil for 1 minute.

10. Reduce heat and simmer and stir until the mixture thickens into a gravy. Pour over the stuffed ham steaks. Cut into 4 portions and serve.

Turkey and Vegetable Casserole

The meat, potatoes, and vegetables are already in this casserole. It's good served over or alongside buttermilk biscuits. Add a tossed salad if you wish.

INGREDIENTS | SERVES 6

1 tablespoon extra virgin olive oil

1 clove garlic, peeled and minced

4 cups chicken broth

6 medium potatoes, peeled and diced

6 large carrots, peeled and sliced

1 large sweet onion, peeled and diced

2 stalks celery, finely diced

½ ounce dried mushrooms

¼ teaspoon dried oregano

¼ teaspoon dried rosemary

1 bay leaf

2 strips orange zest

Salt and freshly ground black pepper, to taste

2 1¼-pound turkey drumsticks, skin removed

1 10-ounce package frozen green beans, thawed

1 10-ounce package frozen whole kernel corn, thawed

1 10-ounce package frozen baby peas, thawed

1. Add the oil to the pressure cooker and bring to temperature over medium heat. Add the garlic and sauté for 10 seconds.

2. Stir in the broth, potatoes, carrots, onions, celery, mushrooms, oregano, rosemary, bay leaf, orange zest, salt, and pepper. Stand the two drumsticks meaty side down in the pan.

3. Lock the lid and bring to high pressure; maintain pressure for 12 minutes. Remove from heat and allow pressure to drop naturally.

4. Remove the drumsticks, cut the meat from the bone and into bite-size pieces, and return it to the pot.

5. Stir in the green beans, corn, and peas; cook over medium heat for 5 minutes. Remove and discard the orange zest and bay leaf. Taste for seasoning and add salt and pepper if needed.

Bubble and Squeak

Adding some ham and bacon to this traditional British dish makes it a complete meal, even if you choose to serve it without a salad. For variety, you can add some chopped celery and grated carrots, too.

INGREDIENTS | SERVES 6

6 slices bacon, cut into pieces

1 medium yellow onion, peeled and diced

1 zucchini, grated

3 large potatoes, scrubbed and diced

8 ounces cooked ham, diced

1 small head cabbage, cored and chopped

Salt and freshly ground black pepper, to taste

1. Add the bacon pieces to the pressure cooker; fry until just beginning to crisp over medium-high heat.

2. Reduce heat to medium and add the onion; sauté for 3 minutes or until the onion is softened. Add the zucchini and potatoes and stir into the onion and bacon.

3. Lock the lid into place and bring to low pressure; maintain pressure for 3 minutes. Remove from heat, quick-release the pressure, and remove the lid.

4. Mash the potatoes into the bacon and onions. Spread the ham over the potato mixture, then spread the cabbage over the ham.

5. Lock the lid into place and bring to high pressure; maintain pressure for 3 minutes. Remove from the heat and allow pressure to release naturally. Remove the lid.

6. If necessary, place the pan over low heat until any excess moisture from the cabbage and zucchini evaporates. Add salt and pepper, to taste. To serve, invert onto a serving plate.

CHAPTER 19

Foods Worth the Extra Effort

Duck in Orange Sauce
222

Mediterranean Braised
Lamb Shanks
223

Mushroom-Stuffed Veal Roast
224

Cassoulet
226

Greek Meatballs in Tomato
Sauce
227

Beef Bourguignon
228

Coq au Vin
229

Osso Buco
230

Braciole
232

Stuffed Round Steak
233

Pork Loin with Cornbread and
Cranberry-Pecan Stuffing
234

Duck in Orange Sauce

*Save the rest of the white wine to serve with the meal. Serve over
cooked brown rice along with steamed asparagus or broccoli.*

INGREDIENTS | SERVES 4

4 duck leg-thigh sections

½ tablespoon duck fat or vegetable oil

1 stalk celery, diced

1 large carrot, peeled and grated

2 large shallots, peeled and minced

3 cloves garlic, peeled and minced

¼ cup triple sec or Grand Marnier

½ cup dry white wine

⅛ teaspoon dried thyme

1 teaspoon dried parsley

Optional: ⅛ teaspoon sage

Zest and juice of 1 orange

2 tablespoons white wine or
sherry vinegar

Salt and freshly ground black pepper,
to taste

1. Rinse the duck legs, blot dry, and place in the pressure cooker skin side down. Fry over medium-high heat for about 7 minutes on each side. Remove and keep warm.

2. Remove and discard all but 1 tablespoon of fat rendered from the duck. Reduce heat to medium and add the celery and carrots; sauté for 2 minutes. Add the shallots; sauté for 2 minutes or until they begin to soften. Stir in the garlic and sauté for 30 seconds.

3. Add the triple sec or Grand Marnier, white wine, thyme, parsley, and sage if using. Add one quarter of the orange zest. Return the browned duck legs to the pressure cooker. Lock the lid into place and bring to high pressure; maintain pressure for 45 minutes.

4. Quick-release the pressure, remove the lid, and transfer the duck legs to a serving platter; keep warm. Use an immersion blender to puree the vegetables and juices remaining in the pressure cooker. Stir in the remaining orange zest, orange juice, and half the vinegar. Taste for seasoning and add remaining vinegar if desired, and salt and pepper if needed. Pour the sauce over the duck legs. Serve.

Mediterranean Braised Lamb Shanks

Serve with a tossed salad, baked potatoes, and dinner rolls. Enjoy with a glass of red wine.

INGREDIENTS | SERVES 4

¼ cup all-purpose flour

¼ teaspoon sea salt

¼ teaspoon freshly ground black pepper

4 ¾-pound lamb shanks

1 tablespoon olive oil

1 large carrot, peeled and diced

1 medium onion, peeled and diced

2 cloves garlic, peeled and minced

1 tablespoon herbes de Provence

1 14½-ounce can diced tomatoes

½ cup dry white wine

½ cup veal or chicken broth

1 bay leaf

1 12-ounce jar pimiento-stuffed olives, drained

1 8-ounce package frozen artichokes, thawed

1. Add the flour, salt, and pepper to a large zip-closure plastic bag. Shake to mix. Add the lamb shanks to the bag, seal the bag, and shake to coat them in the flour. Bring the oil to temperature in the pressure cooker over medium-high heat.

2. Remove 2 lamb shanks, shaking off any excess flour, and add to the pressure cooker. Fry for 10 minutes, turning until they're browned on all sides. Transfer to a platter and keep warm. Repeat with the remaining lamb.

3. Add the carrot to the oil in the pressure cooker; sauté for 1 minute. Add the onion and sauté for 3 minutes or until the onion begins to soften. Stir in the garlic; sauté for 30 seconds. Stir in the herbes de Provence, undrained tomatoes, wine, broth, and bay leaf.

4. Return lamb and juices to the pressure cooker. Lock the lid in place and bring to high pressure; maintain pressure for 25 minutes. Remove from heat and allow pressure to release naturally for 10 minutes. Quick release remaining pressure and remove the lid.

5. Transfer the lamb shanks to an ovenproof platter and tent loosely with aluminum foil. Place in a warm (200°F) oven.

6. Place the pressure cooker over medium heat and bring the pan juices to a simmer. Stir in the olives and artichokes. Simmer, stirring occasionally, for 15 minutes.

7. Taste the sauce for seasoning and add salt and pepper if needed. Remove the platter with the lamb shanks from the oven, remove the foil, and pour the sauce over the lamb shanks. Serve.

Mushroom-Stuffed Veal Roast

You can just as easily substitute a butterflied pork roast for the veal. Serve with a salad, baked potatoes, steamed vegetable, and dinner rolls.

INGREDIENTS | SERVES 6

8 ounces fresh button mushrooms

4 ounces fresh shiitake mushrooms

2 tablespoons olive oil, divided

½ tablespoon unsalted butter

2 large shallots, peeled and minced

1 clove garlic, peeled and minced

1 tablespoon Mrs. Dash Original Blend, divided

5 tablespoons all-purpose flour

½ teaspoon sea salt

½ teaspoon freshly ground black pepper

1½ cups veal or chicken broth, divided

1 3½-pound boneless veal shoulder roast, butterflied

4 ounces prosciutto, thinly sliced

1 large carrot, peeled and grated

1 stalk celery, finely diced

1 small onion, peeled and diced

1 clove garlic, peeled and minced

¼ cup dry white wine

Prosciutto

Prosciutto is dry-cured spiced Italian ham. There are many different types of prosciutto, but all of them are made through the same basic process. The meat is sliced off of the rear haunches, trimmed of fat, salted, air cured, greased with lard, and cured for as long as two years.

1. Clean and slice the button mushrooms. Clean the shiitake mushrooms, remove and discard the stems, and slice the caps. Add 1 tablespoon oil and the butter to the pressure cooker and bring to temperature over medium-high heat.

2. Add the mushrooms; sauté for 3 minutes or until they begin to soften. Stir in the shallots, garlic, and 2 teaspoons seasoning blend. Sauté for another 10 minutes or until the mushrooms have given off most of their moisture.

3. Add 3 tablespoons flour, half the salt, and all of the pepper to a bowl; stir to mix and set aside. Add the remaining flour to a 2-cup measuring cup; gradually whisk in 1 cup broth. Set aside.

4. Place the veal roast cut side up on a flat working surface. Arrange the prosciutto over the cut side of the roast, overlapping the edges opposite the center of the roast by several inches. Spread all but ¼ cup of the sautéed mushroom mixture over the prosciutto up to where the prosciutto overlaps the edges of the roast.

5. Fold the overlapped edges over the mushroom mixture and then roll the prosciutto-mushroom layers to the center of the roast. Pull the edges of the roast up and over the prosciutto-mushroom roll and secure at 1-inch intervals with butcher's twine. Dust all sides of the roast with the seasoned flour.

6. Add the remaining oil to the pressure cooker and bring it to temperature over medium-high heat. Add the roast and brown it for about 5 minutes on each side. Transfer the roast to a platter.

Mushroom-Stuffed Veal Roast (*continued*)

7. Add the carrot and celery to the pressure cooker; sauté for 2 minutes. Stir in the onion and sauté for 3 minutes or until the onion and other vegetables are softened. Add the garlic; sauté for 30 seconds. Stir in the remaining ½ cup broth and the wine. Place the rack in the pressure cooker and place the roast on the rack. Lock the lid into place and bring to high pressure; maintain pressure for 10 minutes for each pound, or 35 minutes if using a 3½-pound roast. Remove the pressure cooker from the heat, quick-release the pressure, and remove the lid.

8. Transfer the roast to a serving platter and tent loosely with aluminum foil; let rest for at least 10 minutes before slicing.

9. Use an immersion blender to puree the pan juices and vegetables in the pressure cooker. Return the pan to medium-high heat and bring to a boil. Whisk in the broth-flour mixture and boil for 1 minute.

10. Reduce heat and simmer for 5 minutes or until thickened. Slice the roast into ½-inch slices and either pour the thickened pan juices over the slices or serve with the sauce on the side.

Cassoulet

Cassoulet is a simple dish that perfectly melds the flavors of succulent meats and beans. Serve over or with thick slices of toasted French bread.

INGREDIENTS | SERVES 8

1 pound dried white beans, rinsed and drained

6 cups cold water

5 cups chicken broth

2 tablespoons olive or vegetable oil

4 whole cloves

1 small white or yellow onion, peeled

2 bay leaves

2 teaspoons dried parsley

½ teaspoon dried thyme

2 large whole bone-in chicken breasts

4 slices bacon, diced

1 large sweet onion, peeled and diced

1 clove garlic, peeled and minced

1 8-ounce package brown-and-serve sausage links

1 14½-ounce can diced tomatoes

Optional: Dry white wine, or additional broth or water

1. Soak the beans overnight in the water; drain. Add the beans, chicken broth, and 1 tablespoon oil to the pressure cooker. Place over medium-high heat and bring to a boil.

2. Push the cloves into the onion and add it to the pressure cooker along with the bay leaves, parsley, and thyme. Lock the lid into place and bring to high pressure; maintain pressure for 10 minutes. Remove from the heat and allow pressure to release naturally while you prepare the other ingredients.

3. Quarter each chicken breast. Rub each chicken breast piece with the remaining oil.

4. Remove the lid from the pressure cooker and transfer the beans and broth to a bowl. Cover and keep warm.

5. Wipe out the pressure cooker. Return it to medium-high heat and add the bacon. Fry the bacon until it begins to brown. Add 4 chicken breast quarters. Brown for 5 minutes. Transfer the chicken and cooked bacon to the bowl with the beans. Repeat with the remaining 4 chicken breast pieces.

6. Add the onion; sauté for 3 minutes. Add the garlic; sauté for 30 seconds. Carefully transfer the beans, broth, and browned chicken pieces to the pressure cooker. Add the sausage links and tomatoes. If necessary, add enough white wine, broth, or water to cover the ingredients in the pressure cooker completely.

Cassoulet (*continued*)

7. Lock the lid into place and bring to high pressure; maintain pressure for 10 minutes. Remove from heat and allow pressure to release naturally. Remove the lid. Remove and discard the onion studded with cloves and the bay leaves. Transfer the sausage links to a soup tureen. Remove the chicken meat from the bones and add that to the tureen; discard the skin and bones. Mash some of the beans into the pan juices to thicken the sauce and then pour into the tureen. Carefully stir to mix. Taste for seasoning and add salt and pepper if needed.

Greek Meatballs in Tomato Sauce

You can serve the meatballs and sauce over pasta, beans, or a combination of both. Serve with pita and a salad tossed with a lemon and extra virgin olive oil vinaigrette and topped with some feta cheese.

INGREDIENTS | SERVES 8

1½ pounds lean ground beef or lamb

1 cup uncooked rice

1 small yellow onion, peeled and finely chopped

3 cloves garlic, peeled and minced

2 teaspoons dried parsley

½ tablespoon dried oregano

1 egg

All-purpose flour

2 cups tomato juice or tomato-vegetable juice

1 14½-ounce can diced tomatoes

Optional: Water

2 tablespoons extra virgin olive oil

Salt and freshly ground black pepper, to taste

1. Make the meatballs by mixing the ground beef or lamb together with the rice, onion, garlic, parsley, oregano, and egg; shape into small meatballs and roll each one in flour.

2. Add the tomato or tomato-vegetable juice and diced tomatoes to the pressure cooker. Carefully add the meatballs. If necessary, pour in enough water to completely cover the meatballs, making sure not to take the liquid above the fill line. Add the oil.

3. Lock the lid into place and bring to low pressure; maintain pressure for 10 minutes. Remove from heat and allow pressure to release naturally for 10 minutes. Quick-release any remaining pressure and remove the lid. Salt and pepper to taste.

Beef Bourguignon

This is a classic French recipe that probably originated as a way to tenderize tough cuts of meat. Serve over buttered noodles or mashed potatoes with a salad and a steamed vegetable.

INGREDIENTS | SERVES 8

8 slices bacon, diced

1 3-pound boneless English or chuck roast

Salt and freshly ground black pepper, to taste

1 large yellow onion, peeled and diced

2 tablespoons tomato paste

3 cloves garlic, peeled and minced

½ teaspoon thyme

1 bay leaf

4 cups Burgundy wine

1 large yellow onion, peeled and thinly sliced

½ cup plus 2 tablespoons butter

16 ounces fresh mushrooms, sliced

2 cups water

½ cup all-purpose flour

1. Fry bacon over medium heat until it renders its fat; remove bacon and set aside. Trim roast of fat and cut into bite-size pieces; add beef pieces to the pressure cooker, sprinkle with salt and pepper to taste, stir-fry for 5 minutes. Add diced onion and sauté for 3 minutes. Add the tomato paste, garlic, and thyme; stir to coat the meat. Add the bay leaf and stir in enough of the Burgundy to cover the meat in the pan completely, being careful not to exceed the fill line in the pressure cooker. Lock the lid into place and bring to low pressure; maintain pressure for 45 minutes. Remove from heat and allow pressure to release naturally.

2. Add onion and 2 tablespoons butter to a microwave-safe bowl. Cover and microwave on high for 2 minutes. Add mushrooms; cover and microwave on high for 1 minute. Stir, cover and microwave on high in 30-second increments until mushrooms are sautéed and onion is transparent.

3. Quick-release any remaining pressure in the pressure cooker and remove the lid. Stir in the mushroom-onion mixture into the pan. Lock the lid into place and bring to low pressure; maintain pressure for 5 minutes.

4. Meanwhile, mix remaining ½ cup butter with the flour to form a paste; whisk in some pan liquid to thin the paste. Strain out lumps. Whisk the butter-flour mixture into; boil for 1 minute. Reduce the heat and simmer uncovered, cooking and stirring for 5 minutes or until the pan juices have been reduced and a gravy results.

5. Quick-release the pressure and remove the lid. Stir in remaining Burgundy and water. Increase heat to medium-high and bring the contents to a boil.

Coq au Vin

Traditional Coq Au Vin is made with an old rooster, slowly cooked in wine to tenderize the meat. This updated version is simpler but just as good, especially if you use the cognac to add to the authentic flavors of the dish. Serve it over cooked noodles or boiled potatoes.

INGREDIENTS | SERVES 8

6 slices smoked bacon, diced

1 tablespoon olive or vegetable oil

2 pounds boneless, skinless chicken thighs

2 pounds boneless, skinless chicken breasts

1 large carrot, peeled and grated

2 stalks celery, sliced

1 1-pound bag pearl onions, thawed

2 cloves garlic, peeled and minced

8 ounces button mushrooms, cleaned and sliced

½ teaspoon dried thyme

2 teaspoons dried parsley

2 cups dry red wine

¼ cup cognac

2 tablespoons cornstarch

3 tablespoons cold water

Salt and freshly ground black pepper, to taste

1. Add the bacon to the pressure cooker and fry it over medium-high heat until crisp. Use a slotted spoon to transfer the cooked bacon to a bowl. Add the oil to the pressure cooker and bring to temperature.

2. Cut the chicken into bite-size pieces. Brown in batches in the bacon fat and oil in the pressure cooker, transferring it to the bowl with the bacon once it's lightly browned.

3. Add the carrot and celery to the pressure cooker; sauté for 2 minutes. Add the onions; sauté for 3 minutes or until they begin to brown. Add the garlic, mushrooms, thyme, and parsley; sauté for 5 minutes or until the mushrooms have released their moisture.

4. Stir in the wine and cognac. Lock the lid into place and bring to low pressure; maintain pressure for 10 minutes. Remove from heat, quick-release the pressure, and remove the lid.

5. In a bowl, whisk the cornstarch into the water. Return the pressure cooker to medium heat. Bring to a simmer and whisk in the cornstarch slurry.

6. Simmer for 3 minutes or until the sauce is thick and glossy and the cornstarch flavor has cooked out of the sauce. Taste for seasoning and add salt and pepper if needed. Serve.

Osso Buco

This Osso Buco recipe is a hybrid, combining today's tradition of adding tomatoes and the nineteenth-century Milanese practice of using allspice and cinnamon. Americans often prefer eating it with a baked potato, steamed vegetable, and tossed salad.

INGREDIENTS | **SERVES 8**

1 cup all-purpose flour

Salt and freshly ground black pepper, to taste

8 veal shanks, cross-cut 1½-inches thick

3 tablespoons extra virgin olive oil

3 tablespoons unsalted butter

1 celery stalk, diced

2 carrots, diced

1 medium onion, peeled and diced

1 head garlic, cut horizontally through the middle

1 14½-ounce can low-sodium beef broth

1 28-ounce can diced tomatoes

¼ teaspoon cinnamon

⅛ teaspoon allspice

2 bay leaves

1 bottle dry white wine

¼ cup fresh flat-leaf parsley, stems removed and chopped

Zest of 1 lemon

Zest of ½ orange

1. Add the flour to a large plastic bag and season with a generous amount of salt and pepper; add the veal shanks to the bag and shake to coat them. Bring the oil to temperature in the pressure cooker over medium heat. Add the butter and swirl it around the pan to melt. Remove 4 veal shanks from the plastic bag, tap off any excess flour, and add them to the pan. Use tongs to turn the shanks until all sides are a rich brown caramel color. Remove the browned veal shanks to a side plate. Repeat with the remaining 4 veal shanks.

2. Add the celery and carrots to the pressure cooker; sauté for 3 minutes. Stir in the onion; sauté for 10 minutes or until the vegetables start to get some color and develop an intense aroma. Add the veal shanks back to the pan. Add the garlic to the pan.

3. Stir in the broth, tomatoes, cinnamon, allspice, and bay leaves. Lock the lid into place and bring to low pressure; maintain pressure for 20 minutes. Quick-release the pressure and remove the lid. Skim off and discard any fat from the top of the pan juices.

4. Pour the wine into a separate pan over medium heat; simmer for 20 minutes or until the wine is reduced by half. If necessary, remove and reserve enough of the pan juices to allow adding all of the wine to the pressure cooker. Lock the lid into place and bring to low pressure; maintain pressure for 20 minutes.

Osso Buco (*continued*)

5. Quick-release the pressure and remove the lid. If necessary, leave the pan over medium heat and simmer until the veal is tender and nearly falling off the bone. Remove and discard the bay leaves.

6. Transfer the meat to a serving platter; cover and keep warm. Return any reserved pan juices to the pan. Increase the heat and bring to a boil. Skim off and discard any fat.

7. Cook for 20 minutes or until the sauce has thickened and coats the back of a spoon. Stir in the parsley and and lemon and orange zests. Taste for seasoning and add additional salt, pepper, cinnamon, and/or allspice if needed. Simmer for another 5 minutes, then pour over the meat and serve immediately with Gremolata if desired.

Gremolata

Add a generous dollop of Gremolata to each serving of Osso Buco. To make the Gremolata, combine ¼ cup chopped fresh flat-leaf parsley, the zest of 1 lemon, 2 minced cloves of garlic, ¼ teaspoon minced dried rosemary, a pinch of salt, and freshly ground black pepper in a bowl.

Braciole

The stuffing in the Braciole already adds substance to this dish, but you can serve it with cooked pasta or garlic bread, too, if you wish. Add a salad and a steamed vegetable for a complete meal.

INGREDIENTS | SERVES 4

4 tablespoons extra virgin olive oil

2 pounds flank steak

Salt and freshly ground black pepper, to taste

3 cloves garlic, peeled and minced

1 cup bread crumbs

1 medium carrot, peeled and grated

½ stalk celery, minced

1 small yellow onion, peeled and minced

1 teaspoon dried oregano

¼ teaspoon dried rosemary

¼ teaspoon dried thyme

2 teaspoons dried parsley

2 ounces freshly grated Parmigiano-Reggiano

2 large eggs

1 teaspoon sugar

1 25-ounce jar pasta sauce

¼ cup tomato juice or beef broth

Optional: Fresh parsley

Optional: Additional freshly grated Parmigiano-Reggiano

1. Rub 2 tablespoons oil over both sides of the steak. Put the steak between 2 pieces of plastic wrap; use a tenderizer utensil to pound the meat out until it's ¼-inch thick. Remove the top piece of plastic wrap and season the meat with salt and pepper. Sprinkle the garlic over the meat, and then rub it into the meat

2. Add the bread crumbs, carrot, celery, onion, oregano, rosemary, thyme, parsley, Parmigiano-Reggiano, and eggs to a bowl; mix well. Use your hands to shape the mixture into a log and place it in the center of the meat.

3. Roll up the steak like a jellyroll so that when you later slice the meat, the slices will be against the grain of the meat; tie with butcher's twine. Cut in half so that the meat will fit the bottom of the pressure cooker.

4. Bring the remaining 2 tablespoons oil to temperature over medium heat in the pressure cooker. Add the meat rolls; brown them for 5 minutes on each side.

5. Stir the sugar into the pasta sauce, and then pour it over the meat. Add the tomato juice or broth. Lock the lid into place and bring to low pressure; maintain pressure for 40 minutes. Remove from the heat and allow pressure to release naturally. Remove the lid.

6. Transfer the meat to a serving platter and tent with aluminum foil. If you want a thicker sauce, return the pressure cooker to medium heat and bring the sauce to a simmer. Simmer while the meat rests for 10 minutes and the sauce thickens. Remove the foil, carve the meat, and spoon the sauce over the meat. Garnish with fresh parsley and serve topped with additional freshly grated Parmigiano-Reggiano if desired.

Stuffed Round Steak

To serve with potatoes, scrub 4 medium potatoes and prick each potato several times with a fork or knife. Add them to the pressure cooker when you add the pasta sauce.

INGREDIENTS | SERVES 4

3 tablespoons extra virgin olive oil

2 pounds round steak

Salt and freshly ground black pepper, to taste

3 cloves garlic, peeled and minced

4 hard-boiled eggs, peeled and sliced

4 large carrots, peeled and grated

1 small yellow onion, peeled and minced

1 cup zucchini, grated and squeezed dry

2 ounces freshly grated Parmigiano-Reggiano

1 25-ounce jar pasta sauce

1 teaspoon sugar

¼ cup tomato juice or beef broth

1. Rub 2 tablespoons oil over both sides of the round steak. Put the steak between 2 pieces of plastic wrap; use a rolling pin, mallet, or the flat surface of a meat tenderizer utensil to pound the meat out flatter. Remove the top piece of plastic wrap and season the meat with salt and pepper. Sprinkle the garlic over the meat, and then rub it into the meat.

2. Down the center of the meat, evenly arrange the egg slices, carrots, onion, zucchini, and half of the Parmigiano-Reggiano. Roll up the steak like a jellyroll and tie with butcher's twine. Cut in half if necessary to fit the meat roll in the bottom of the pressure cooker. Rub the remaining oil over the meat roll.

3. Bring the pressure cooker to temperature over medium-high heat. Add the meat and sear it on all sides. Lower the temperature to medium and pour the pasta sauce over the meat.

4. Add the sugar and tomato juice or broth. Lock the lid into place and bring to low pressure; maintain pressure for 40 minutes. Remove from heat and allow pressure to release naturally.

5. Remove the cover. Transfer the meat to a serving platter. Slice the meat. Pour the sauce over the meat slices and sprinkle the remaining Parmigiano-Reggiano over the meat and pasta sauce. Serve.

Pork Loin with Cornbread and Cranberry-Pecan Stuffing

To make apple-walnut stuffing, omit the dried cranberries, apple juice, and pecans. Peel, core, and grate an apple. Substitute chopped walnuts for the pecans. If the moisture from the grated apple isn't sufficient, add apple juice or water as needed.

INGREDIENTS | SERVES 4

2 tablespoons dried cranberries

2 tablespoons apple juice

2 strips bacon, diced

1 small stalk celery, finely diced

1 small onion, peeled and diced

1 cup cornbread stuffing mix

2 tablespoons pecans, toasted and chopped

1 large egg, beaten

Pinch nutmeg, freshly grated

4 1-inch-thick pork chops

Salt and freshly ground black pepper, to taste

1 tablespoon olive or vegetable oil

1 tablespoon butter

½ cup chicken broth

1. Put the dried cranberries and apple juice in a microwave-safe bowl. Cover and microwave on high for 1 minute to soften the cranberries. Set aside.

2. Fry the bacon in the pressure cooker over medium-high heat until it begins to render its fat. Add the celery; sauté for 2 minutes. Add the onion; sauté for 3 minutes. Pour the contents of the pressure cooker into a bowl.

3. Use a paper towel to blot up some of the excess bacon fat. Mix in the cranberries and apple juice, cornbread stuffing mix, pecans, egg, nutmeg, salt, and pepper. The cornbread stuffing mixture should be moist, but not wet. If some of the stuffing mix is still dry, add apple juice or water a teaspoon at a time until moistened.

4. Trim and discard any excess fat from the pork chops. Cut a pocket into each one, slicing from the outside edge to the bone. Fill each pork chop with a fourth of the stuffing mixture. Press to close. Season each side of the pork chops with salt and pepper.

5. Bring the oil and butter to temperature over medium heat in the pressure cooker. Add the pork chops and brown well on both sides. Pour the broth into the bottom of the pan.

6. Lock the lid into place and bring to high pressure; maintain pressure for 15 minutes. Remove the pressure cooker from the heat, quick-release the pressure, and remove the lid. Serve.

CHAPTER 20

Side Dishes

Curried Yams and Potatoes
236

Herb-Roasted Potatoes
237

Buttered Beets
237

Tie-Dyed Baby Carrots
238

German Red Cabbage
239

Braised Lima Beans with Bacon
240

Polenta
240

Warm Broccoli Caesar Salad
241

Corn on the Cob
241

Broccoli in Lemon-Butter Sauce
242

Asparagus with
Olive Oil Dressing
242

Thai Sweet Potatoes
243

Zesty Mashed Root Vegetable
244

Sautéed Garlic Mashed Potatoes
245

Curried Yams and Potatoes

Growing your own potatoes is easy, especially if you live in a cooler climate. Purchase seed potatoes from your local gardening store, and use organic fertilizers to keep them healthy.

INGREDIENTS | SERVES 8

1 tablespoon ghee or butter

1 small onion, peeled and finely diced

2 tablespoons curry paste

3 cloves garlic, peeled and minced

4 large yams, peeled and diced

1 large potato, peeled and diced

¼ cup applesauce

¼ cup water

1 cup frozen baby peas, thawed

Optional: Plain yogurt

Optional: Mango Chutney (page 17)

Optional: 1 cucumber, peeled and sliced

1. Melt the ghee or butter in the pressure cooker and bring to temperature over medium-high heat. Add the onion; sauté for 3 minutes.

2. Stir in the curry paste and garlic; sauté for 2 minutes. Stir in the diced yams and potatoes; sauté for several minutes or until the pan is sticky and the mixture is about to burn. Stir in the applesauce and water.

3. Lock the lid into place and bring to low pressure; maintain pressure for 5 minutes. Remove from the heat and allow pressure to release naturally.

4. Remove the lid. Stir and slightly mash the potato mixture. Add the peas. Stir into the potatoes. Cover and let rest for a few minutes to bring the peas to temperature.

5. If desired, serve with a dollop of plain yogurt and Mango Chutney over each serving and garnish with cucumber slices.

Herb-Roasted Potatoes

You can adjust the herb or seasoning blend according to how you've flavored your meat entrée.

INGREDIENTS | SERVES 8

2 tablespoons olive oil

1 medium onion, peeled and diced

8 large red potatoes, scrubbed and quartered

¼ cup water

1 teaspoon Italian herb blend or Mrs. Dash Classic Italian Medley Seasoning Blend

Salt and freshly ground black pepper, to taste

1. Bring the oil to temperature over medium heat in the pressure cooker. Add the onion; sauté for 3 minutes or until the onion is softened.

2. Add the potatoes, cut side down. Fry uncovered for 5 minutes or until the potatoes begin to brown. Pour in the water. Sprinkle the herb blend over the potatoes. Season with salt and pepper.

3. Lock the lid into place and bring to high pressure; maintain pressure for 5 minutes. Remove from the heat and allow pressure to release naturally. Remove the lid. Serve.

Buttered Beets

This down-on-the-farm comfort food side dish goes well with just about any entrée.

INGREDIENTS | SERVES 8

4 large golden or red beets

1 cup water

Butter, to taste

Salt and freshly ground black pepper, to taste

The Night Before Buttered Beets

You can fix the unpeeled beets ahead of time. Cool them, put them in a zip-closure bag, and refrigerate. When you're ready to use them, peel and slice the beets, then microwave covered at 70 percent power for 3 minutes or until heated through.

1. Scrub the beets and trim both ends. Place the beets on the rack in the pressure cooker. Pour in the water.

2. Lock the lid into place and bring to high pressure; maintain pressure for 25 minutes.

3. Remove the pressure cooker from the heat, quick-release the pressure, and remove the lid. Transfer the beets to a cutting board. Test for doneness. If beets aren't cooked, simmer or cook, covered, in the microwave for a few extra minutes.

4. When the beets are cool enough to handle, use a paring knife to remove the peel. Slice the beets. Reheat the beets and melt butter to taste over the heated beets. Season with salt and pepper to taste.

Tie-Dyed Baby Carrots

The name of this recipe comes from the beautiful mottled color the beets give to the carrots.

INGREDIENTS | SERVES 8

8 small red beets

1 1-pound bag peeled baby carrots

¼ cup water

Butter, to taste

Salt and freshly ground black pepper, to taste

Cooked Beets and Carrot Salad

Toss chilled leftover beets and carrots with honey-mustard salad dressing or your favorite vinaigrette. Stir in some finely diced shallot or red onion and minced fresh parsley, and top with toasted walnuts and feta cheese.

1. Scrub and peel the beets and trim the ends; quarter the beets. Add the baby carrots to the pressure cooker and put the beets on top. Pour in the water.

2. Lock the lid into place and bring to high pressure; maintain pressure for 8 minutes.

3. Remove the pressure cooker from heat, quick-release the pressure, and remove the lid.

4. Test the beets and carrots to determine whether or not they're cooked through.

5. If they're not yet tender, return the pan to medium heat. Add more water if necessary, and bring to a simmer. Simmer loosely covered until the vegetables are tender.

6. Once they're cooked through, drain off any excess moisture and transfer to a serving bowl. Top with butter, salt, and pepper to taste.

German Red Cabbage

Red wine will help preserve the color of the cabbage. Serve with smoked pork chops or other pork entrées.

INGREDIENTS | SERVES 8

4 slices bacon, diced
2 Granny Smith apples
1 medium onion, peeled and diced
½ cup Merlot, sweet red wine, or apple juice
⅓ cup light brown sugar, packed
3 tablespoons red wine vinegar
1 2½-pound red cabbage
Salt and freshly ground black pepper, to taste

1. Add the bacon to the pressure cooker; fry over medium-high heat until crisp. Use a slotted spoon to remove the bacon to paper towels; set aside.

2. Peel the apples, remove the cores, and slice them. Reduce the heat to medium and add the apples and onion. Sauté for 3 minutes or until the onion is soft. Stir in the wine, brown sugar, and vinegar.

3. Wash the cabbage and remove and discard the outer leaves. Quarter the cabbage. Remove and discard the core. Slice the quarters into thin strips.

4. Gradually add to the pressure cooker, at first filling the pressure cooker to the top and loosely covering until the cabbage wilts, freeing up more space in the pan.

5. Stir in enough of the remaining cabbage to bring the pressure cooker to the fill line.

6. Lock the lid into place and bring to high pressure; maintain pressure for 8 minutes.

7. Remove the pressure cooker from the heat, quick-release the pressure, and remove the lid. Stir and then use a slotted spoon to transfer the cabbage to a serving bowl. Stir in the reserved crisp bacon. Season with salt and pepper to taste.

Braised Lima Beans with Bacon

For a tomato-based dish, add 1 or 2 peeled and diced plum tomatoes (and their juice) when you add the lima beans and add an additional ¼ teaspoon of freshly ground black pepper.

INGREDIENTS | SERVES 4

4 slices bacon, diced
1 small onion, peeled and diced
1 clove garlic, peeled and minced
1 1-pound bag frozen lima beans
¼ cup water
¼ teaspoon freshly ground black pepper
2 tablespoons fresh parsley, minced

1. Add the bacon to the pressure cooker and fry over medium-high heat until almost crisp. Add the onion and sauté for 3 minutes or until soft.

2. Stir in the garlic; sauté for 30 seconds. Stir in the lima beans, water, and pepper.

3. Lock the lid into place and bring to high pressure; maintain pressure for 10 minutes. Remove the pressure cooker from the heat and allow the pressure to release naturally for 10 minutes.

4. Quick-release any remaining pressure and remove the lid. Stir in the parsley. Transfer to a serving bowl and serve.

Polenta

Polenta works as a hot cereal or a side dish. Substitute broth for some or all of the water if you'll be serving it as a side dish.

INGREDIENTS | SERVES 6

1 cup yellow cornmeal
4 cups cold water
½ teaspoon salt
1 tablespoon butter

1. In a bowl or measuring cup, mix together the cornmeal, 1 cup cold water, and salt. Set aside.

2. Bring the remaining 3 cups water to a boil in the pressure cooker over medium heat. Stir in the moistened cornmeal mixture and the butter. Continue to cook and stir until the mixture comes to a low boil or begins to bubble.

3. Lock the lid into place and bring to low pressure; maintain pressure for 10 minutes.

4. Remove the pressure cooker from heat, quick-release the pressure, and remove the lid. Stir and taste for seasoning; add additional salt if needed. Serve warm.

Warm Broccoli Caesar Salad

This salad is the perfect accompaniment for grilled chicken breasts. Serve over torn romaine leaves if desired.

INGREDIENTS | SERVES 6

4 cups broccoli florets
¼ teaspoon salt
1 cup water
2 large hard-boiled eggs
2 cloves garlic, peeled and sliced
2 canned anchovies, rinsed and drained
1 tablespoon fresh lemon juice
¼ teaspoon Dijon mustard
2 tablespoons mayonnaise
2 tablespoons Parmigiano-Reggiano cheese, freshly grated
¼ cup extra virgin olive oil
Additional salt, to taste
Freshly ground black pepper, to taste

1. Put the broccoli in the pressure cooker along with the salt and water. Lock the lid into place and bring to low pressure; maintain pressure for 2 minutes.

2. Remove the pressure cooker from heat, quick-release the pressure, and remove the lid. Drain and transfer the broccoli to a serving bowl.

3. Chop the egg whites and add to the serving bowl with the broccoli. Add the egg yolks to a blender or food processor along with the garlic, anchovies, lemon juice, mustard, mayonnaise, and cheese; process until smooth.

4. Gradually drizzle in the olive oil and process until oil is completely incorporated into the dressing. Pour the dressing over the broccoli and chopped egg whites. Stir to mix. Season with salt and pepper to taste. Serve.

Corn on the Cob

If you're cutting fat from your diet or watching your calories, you'll love this dish! Corn served this way tastes delicious without any butter or salt.

INGREDIENTS | SERVES 4

4 ears fresh sweet corn, shucked
½ cup water
1 lime, quartered
Freshly ground black pepper, to taste

1. Place the rack in the pressure cooker and place the corn on the rack. Pour in the water.

2. Lock the lid into place and bring to low pressure; maintain pressure for 3 minutes. Remove the pressure cooker from heat, quick-release the pressure, and remove the lid.

3. Transfer the corn to 4 serving plates. Have diners squeeze a wedge of lime juice over the corn and grind black pepper to taste over each ear of corn.

Broccoli in Lemon-Butter Sauce

Make this moderately simple dish healthier by substituting extra virgin olive oil for the butter.

INGREDIENTS | SERVES 6

4 cups broccoli florets

¼ teaspoon salt

1 cup water

4 tablespoons butter, melted

1 tablespoon fresh lemon juice

¼ teaspoon Dijon mustard

Lemon-Butter and Broccoli Pasta

For 8 side-dish servings, cook a 1-pound package of angel hair pasta, adding 1 or 2 crushed cloves of garlic to the pasta cooking water. Discard the garlic. Mix pasta and broccoli. Double the amount of lemon-butter sauce and pour it over pasta and broccoli; toss to mix. Top with freshly grated Parmigiano-Reggiano or Asiago cheese.

1. Put the broccoli, salt, and water in the pressure cooker. Lock the lid into place and bring to low pressure; maintain pressure for 2 minutes.

2. Remove the pressure cooker from the heat, quick-release the pressure, and remove the lid. Drain and transfer the broccoli to a serving bowl.

3. While the broccoli cooks, whisk together the butter, lemon juice, and mustard. Pour over the cooked broccoli and toss to mix.

Asparagus with Olive Oil Dressing

Replace the salt with your favorite seasoned salt or herb blend. Asparagus is especially good in the spring, and the simpler the recipe, the better the dish.

INGREDIENTS | SERVES 4

1½ pounds fresh asparagus

½ cup water

2 tablespoons shallot or red onion, minced

1 tablespoon fresh lemon juice

3 tablespoons extra virgin olive oil

Salt and freshly ground white or black pepper, to taste

1. Clean asparagus and snap off the ends. If necessary, peel the stems. Lay flat in the pressure cooker and add water. Lock lid into place and bring to high pressure; maintain for 3 minutes. Remove from heat and allow pressure to release naturally for 2 minutes.

2. In a small bowl or measuring cup, whisk together the shallot or onion, lemon juice, oil, salt, and pepper.

3. Quick release any remaining pressure and remove the lid. Drain the asparagus and transfer to a serving platter. Pour the dressing over the asparagus. Serve.

Thai Sweet Potatoes

This dish is a soup that can be served over rice noodles and topped with a cooked egg to make it a complete meal. For more spice, use Thai red curry paste instead of green curry paste.

INGREDIENTS | **SERVES 6**

2 tablespoons peanut or vegetable oil
1 red bell pepper, seeded and sliced
1 yellow bell pepper, seeded and sliced
1 orange bell pepper, seeded and sliced
1 large onion, peeled and sliced
2 cloves garlic, peeled and minced
1 tablespoon Thai green curry paste
3 large sweet potatoes, peeled and diced
1 14-ounce can unsweetened coconut milk
¼ cup water
1 teaspoon fresh lemon or lime juice
1½ cups snow peas or green beans
1½ tablespoons fresh cilantro, minced

1. Bring the oil to temperature over medium heat. Add the bell pepper slices; sauté for 2 minutes.

2. Add the onion slices; sauté for 3 minutes or until the vegetables are soft. Add the garlic and curry paste; sauté for 1 minute.

3. Stir in the sweet potatoes, coconut milk, water, and lemon or lime juice. Lock the lid into place and bring to high pressure; maintain pressure for 3 minutes.

4. Remove the pressure cooker from heat, quick-release the pressure, and remove the lid. Taste for seasoning, adding more curry paste if desired.

5. Cut the snow peas or green beans into 1-inch segments. Stir into the sweet potato mixture in the pressure cooker.

6. Return the pressure cooker to medium heat and bring to a simmer. Maintain the simmer for 3 minutes or until the vegetables are cooked to tender-crisp. Stir in the cilantro. Serve.

Zesty Mashed Root Vegetable

Serve as a substitute for mashed potatoes. The carrots add a touch of sweetness. The horseradish in this dish makes it especially good with roast beef.

INGREDIENTS | SERVES 8

1 cup water

2 pounds potatoes, peeled and diced

½ pound carrots, peeled and diced

1½ pounds white turnips, peeled and diced

1 teaspoon salt

4 tablespoons butter

1 cup heavy cream

2 teaspoons prepared horseradish

Freshly ground black pepper, to taste

Mashing the Vegetables

Run the cooked vegetables through a food mill or mash with a hand-held potato mashers. For this recipe, the high fat content of the heated cream and butter will let you use a handheld or a stand mixer to mash the vegetables if you do so in short bursts at a low setting. A food processor is not recommended.

1. Add the water, potatoes, carrots, turnips, and salt to the pressure cooker in that order.

2. Lock the lid into place and bring to high pressure; maintain pressure for 7 minutes. Remove from the heat and allow pressure to release naturally for 10 minutes.

3. Quick-release any remaining pressure and remove the lid. Drain the vegetables and put them in a large serving bowl. Set aside and keep warm.

4. Wipe out the pressure cooker. Melt the butter and add ⅔ cup of the cream. Heat to low simmer over medium heat.

5. Mash the vegetables, stirring in the heated butter-cream mixture. Gradually add the remaining ⅓ cup cream if needed.

6. Stir in 1 teaspoon horseradish; taste for seasoning and add additional salt and the remaining horseradish if needed. Season to taste with pepper. Serve.

Sautéed Garlic Mashed Potatoes

The touch of garlic in this mashed potatoes dish will complement just about any meat dish. You can serve it with fried pork chops, roast beef, steak, or grilled Italian-seasoned chicken breast. To round out the meal, add a tossed salad and a steamed vegetable.

INGREDIENTS | SERVES 6

6 medium potatoes, peeled and quartered

2 cups water

½ teaspoon salt

2 tablespoons butter

3 cloves garlic, peeled and minced

¼ cup sour cream

Freshly ground white or black pepper, to taste

Roasted Garlic Mashed Potatoes

Place 6 unpeeled cloves of garlic on a piece of heavy-duty aluminum foil. Toss them in 1 tablespoon of olive oil. Wrap the ends of the foil up and around the garlic, sealing the packet. Bake at 350°F for 45 minutes. When cool enough to handle, squeeze each clove directly into mashed potatoes rather than sautéing them in the butter.

1. Add the potatoes, water, and salt to the pressure cooker. Lock the lid into place and bring to high pressure; maintain pressure for 7 minutes.

2. While the potatoes cook, melt the butter in a small skillet over medium heat. Add the garlic; sauté for 2 minutes, being careful not to burn the garlic. Stir the garlic-infused butter into the sour cream.

3. Remove the pressure cooker from the heat, quick-release the pressure, and remove the lid. Drain the potatoes.

4. Return the potatoes to the pressure cooker and put it over low heat for 1–2 minutes to evaporate any residual moisture.

5. Mash the potatoes. Stir in the sour cream mixture and pepper. Taste for seasoning and add more salt if needed. Transfer to a bowl and serve.

CHAPTER 21

Out-of-the-Ordinary Vegetables

Celery with Lemon Butter Sauce
247

Parsnip Pudding
247

Swiss Chard and Vegetables
in Parmesan Sauce
248

Stewed Green Tomatoes
249

Bavarian Kale
249

Fennel Cooked in White Wine
250

Mashed Turnips
250

Braised Beet Greens
251

Turnip and Carrot Puree
251

Seasoned Baby Turnips
252

Creamed Radishes
252

Turnip Greens in Olive Oil
253

Mashed Rutabagas and Parsnips
253

Celery with Lemon Butter Sauce

Serve as you would any vegetable dish. The mild flavor will make a convert of any vegetable hater in your family.

INGREDIENTS | SERVES 4

2 bunches celery

1 cup chicken broth

3 tablespoons butter

1 tablespoon fresh lemon juice

Optional: 2 teaspoons capers, rinsed and chopped

Optional: 1 tablespoon fresh parsley, chopped

1. Quarter the celery stalks. Add celery, broth, and 1 tablespoon butter to the pressure cooker. Lock the lid into place and bring to high pressure; maintain for 5 minutes. Reduce to low pressure and maintain for 5 minutes. Remove from heat and allow pressure to release naturally for 5 minutes. Quick-release remaining pressure and remove the lid. Transfer the cooked celery to a serving platter; keep warm.

2. Reserve ½ cup of the liquid in the pressure cooker. Return to heat and bring to a boil over medium-high heat. Boil until reduced by half. Stir in the lemon juice. Whisk in remaining butter a teaspoon at a time. Remove from heat. Stir in capers and parsley if using. Pour over the celery.

Parsnip Pudding

This dish requires a three-step preparation process: first, cooking the parsnips in the pressure cooker; second, pureeing the parsnips and assembling the pudding; and three, baking the pudding.

INGREDIENTS | SERVES 4

½ cup water

2 pounds parsnips, peeled and quartered

½ teaspoon salt

½ cup bread crumbs

¼ cup milk

¼ cup heavy cream

2 large eggs

2 tablespoons butter

Freshly grated nutmeg, to taste

1. Preheat the oven to 350°F. Add the rack to the pressure cooker and pour in water. Place parsnips on the rack and sprinkle with salt. Lock the lid into place and bring to high pressure; maintain for 4 minutes. Remove the pressure cooker from heat, quick-release the pressure, and remove the lid.

2. Drain and transfer the parsnips to a food processor. Add the bread crumbs, milk, cream, and eggs. Puree.

3. Use 1 tablespoon butter to grease a large ovenproof casserole dish. Pour in the pudding mixture. Dot the top of the pudding with remaining butter and grate nutmeg over the top. Bake for 1 hour.

Swiss Chard and Vegetables in Parmesan Sauce

Serve with Italian-seasoned grilled chicken breast or veal cutlets. This rich side dish also goes well with something as simple as leftover roast turkey or chicken.

INGREDIENTS | **SERVES 8**

½ cup water
1 pound Swiss chard
1 onion, peeled and sliced
3 stalks celery, diced
2 carrots, sliced on the diagonal
1 pound Brussels sprouts
1 zucchini
1 cauliflower
4 tablespoons butter
4 cloves garlic, peeled and minced
½ cup Parmigiano-Reggiano cheese, grated
⅛ teaspoon dried red pepper flakes, crushed
½ cup light or heavy cream

1. Add the water to the pressure cooker.

2. Wash and drain the chard. Remove and discard the tough stems. Tear the chard into bite-size pieces. Set aside.

3. Layer the onion, celery, carrots, and chard into the pressure cooker. Wash and drain Brussels sprouts. Remove and discard the outer leaves. Cut in half and add on top of the chard. Slice the zucchini and put on top of the Brussels sprouts. Divide the cauliflower into large florets and add on top of the zucchini.

4. Lock the lid into place and bring to high pressure; maintain pressure for 3 minutes. Remove the pressure cooker from the heat, quick-release the pressure, and remove the lid. Drain the vegetables and transfer them to a serving bowl.

5. Melt the butter in the pressure cooker over medium heat. Stir in the garlic and sauté for 30 seconds to 1 minute, being careful not to let the garlic burn. Stir in the cheese and pepper flakes. Slowly whisk in the cream.

6. Continue to cook and stir until the sauce is smooth and bubbling. Pour over the vegetables. Toss to coat the vegetables. Serve.

Stewed Green Tomatoes

*This dish is another way to use up the green tomatoes that
remain in your garden at the end of the growing season.*

INGREDIENTS | SERVES 4

2 tablespoons butter

2 tablespoons onion, minced

4 large green tomatoes, sliced

¼ cup water

½ teaspoon sugar

½ teaspoon salt

¼ teaspoon paprika

½ teaspoon curry powder

2 slices white bread

1 tablespoon fresh parsley, chopped

1. Melt the butter in the pressure cooker over medium heat. Add the onion and sauté for 2 minutes. Add the tomatoes, water, sugar, salt, paprika, and curry powder. Stir to mix.

2. Lock the lid into place and bring to low pressure; maintain pressure for 8 minutes. Remove from the heat and allow pressure to release naturally.

3. Process bread in a food processor to make bread crumbs.

4. Remove lid from pressure cooker. Return to medium heat and bring to a simmer. Stir in bread crumbs. Simmer and stir until thickened. Top with parsley.

Bavarian Kale

*This dish provides all the starch and vegetable dish for a meal. Kale is
a leafy green vegetable that is both colorful and nutritious.*

INGREDIENTS | SERVES 4

2 cups water

½ teaspoon salt

2 bunches kale, washed and drained

2 tablespoons olive or vegetable oil

1 small onion, peeled and diced

1 clove garlic, minced

1½ cups chicken broth

4 medium potatoes, peeled and diced

1 stalk celery, diced

Sour cream, for garnish

1. Bring water to a boil in the pressure cooker. Stir in the salt. Cut the kale leaves into ½-inch-wide strips. Blanch kale for 1 minute, drain, and set aside.

2. Bring oil to temperature in the pressure cooker over medium heat. Add the onion; sauté for 5 minutes. Add the garlic; sauté for 30 seconds. Add the broth, potatoes, celery, and blanched kale. Lock the lid into place and bring to high pressure; maintain pressure for 6 minutes. Remove from the heat and allow pressure to release naturally. Remove the lid.

3. Stir, slightly mashing the potatoes into the mixture. Garnish each serving with a dollop of sour cream.

Fennel Cooked in White Wine

After the fennel has simmered uncovered in Step 2, use a slotted spoon to transfer it to a food processor. Pulse until smooth, adding some of the cooking liquid if necessary. The light anise flavor of fennel makes it a perfect companion for roast pork.

INGREDIENTS | SERVES 4

4 fennel bulbs
1 tablespoon butter
1 tablespoon olive oil
1 small onion, peeled and diced
1 cup white wine
Salt and freshly ground black pepper, to taste

1. Cut off the tops and bottoms of the fennel bulbs and remove the two outer leaves. Thoroughly rinse the bulbs under cold running water. Dice the bulbs. Set aside.

2. Bring the butter and oil to temperature in the pressure cooker over medium heat. Add the onion; sauté for 3 minutes. Stir in the diced fennel; sauté for 3 minutes. Stir in the wine. Lock the lid into place and bring to low pressure; maintain for 8 minutes.

3. Quick-release the pressure and remove the lid. Simmer until the fennel is cooked through and soft and the alcohol is cooked out of the wine. Add salt and pepper, to taste. Serve.

Mashed Turnips

Serve this low-carb dish in place of mashed potatoes. Choose the broth to best complement the entrée.

INGREDIENTS | SERVES 4

4 medium turnips, peeled and diced
1 small onion, peeled and diced
½ cup beef or chicken broth
¼ cup sour cream
Salt and freshly ground black pepper, to taste

1. Add the turnips, onion, and broth to the pressure cooker. Lock the lid into place and bring to high pressure; maintain pressure for 5 minutes. Remove from the heat and allow pressure to release naturally for 10 minutes.

2. Drain the turnips or use a slotted spoon to transfer them to a serving bowl. Use a hand-held mixer or immersion blender to puree the turnips, adding some of the broth from the pressure cooker if necessary.

3. Stir in the sour cream. Taste for seasoning and add salt and pepper, to taste.

Braised Beet Greens

Young, fresh greens will cook quicker than older, tougher ones. Adjust cooking time accordingly.

INGREDIENTS | SERVES 4

1 tablespoon olive oil

1 large shallot or small red onion, peeled and minced

1 pound beet greens

Salt and freshly ground black pepper, to taste

¼ cup chicken broth or water

Optional: White wine or an infused vinegar

1. Bring the oil to temperature in the pressure cooker over medium heat. Add the shallot or onion; sauté for 3 minutes. Add the beet greens. Sprinkle with salt and pepper. Stir the greens to coat them in the oil. Once they're slightly wilted, add the broth or water, making sure not to exceed the fill line in your pressure cooker.

2. Lock the lid into place and bring to low pressure; maintain pressure for 1–3 minutes. Quick-release the pressure and remove the lid. Simmer and stir for a minute or until the remaining moisture in the pan evaporates. Taste for seasoning and add more salt and pepper if needed. Serve warm, with a splash of vinegar if desired.

Turnip and Carrot Puree

This is a good side dish to serve with leftover turkey. The nutmeg will put you in the mood for some leftover pumpkin pie or eggnog.

INGREDIENTS | SERVES 6

3 large turnips, peeled and quartered

4 large carrots, peeled and cut into 2-inch pieces

2 cups water

1 teaspoon salt

2 tablespoons extra virgin olive oil

½ teaspoon nutmeg, freshly grated

2 tablespoons sour cream

1. Put the turnips, carrots, water, and salt in the pressure cooker. Lock the lid into place and bring to high pressure; maintain pressure for 8 minutes. Remove the pressure cooker from the heat, quick-release the pressure, and remove the lid.

2. Drain the vegetables. Return them to the pressure cooker and put it over low heat for a minute or two to evaporate any residual moisture. Mash the vegetables together with the oil, nutmeg, and sour cream. Taste for seasoning and add additional salt if needed. Serve.

Seasoned Baby Turnips

The allspice in this dish makes it go well with Chinese barbequed ribs, but it will work well with just about any meat entrée.

INGREDIENTS | SERVES 4

½ cup water
4 baby turnips, peeled and quartered
½ teaspoon salt
3 tablespoons butter
1 small onion, peeled and sliced
½ teaspoon sugar
¼ teaspoon freshly ground black pepper
¼ teaspoon ground allspice
2 tablespoons fresh lemon juice
Optional: 1 tablespoon fresh parsley, minced

1. Place the rack in the pressure cooker. Pour in the water. Place the turnips on the rack and sprinkle with salt.

2. Lock the lid into place and bring to low pressure; maintain for 8 minutes. Remove pressure cooker from heat, quick-release the pressure, and remove the lid.

3. Transfer the turnips to a serving bowl; set aside. Remove the rack and discard remaining water. Wipe out the pressure cooker; add the butter and melt over medium heat. Add the onion; sauté for 3 minutes. Stir in the sugar, pepper, allspice, and lemon juice. Whisk and cook until the sugar is dissolved. Add the turnips and toss to coat. Top with parsley if desired.

Creamed Radishes

Braised radishes are another easy side dish. Just cover your radishes in enough water to cover them, add some butter, sugar, salt, and pepper, and bring to a boil. Simmer for 10–12 minutes or until radishes are tender.

INGREDIENTS | SERVES 4

24 large red radishes rinsed and drained
2 tablespoons butter
2 tablespoons all-purpose flour
1 cup chicken broth or water
⅓ cup heavy cream
Salt and freshly ground white or black pepper, to taste

1. Cut off tops of radishes leaving about 1 inch of the stem. Half lengthwise. Melt the butter in the pressure cooker over medium heat. When it begins to foam, whisk in the flour, broth or water. Stir in the radishes.

2. Lock the lid into place and bring to low pressure; maintain for 5 minutes. Remove from heat and allow pressure to release naturally for 5 minutes. Quick-release any remaining pressure and remove the lid.

3. Transfer the radishes to a serving bowl. Return the pressure cooker to medium heat and bring to a boil. Whisk in the cream; boil and stir for 2 minutes. Pour over the radishes. Season to taste.

Turnip Greens in Olive Oil

Try using 1 shallot in place of the garlic to give the turnips a different flavor. Serve in place of a salad or as a vegetable side dish.

INGREDIENTS | SERVES 4

10 cups turnip greens, shredded
½ cup chicken broth or water
1 clove garlic, peeled and crushed
½ teaspoon salt
4 teaspoons extra virgin olive oil
Freshly ground black pepper, to taste
½ cup pecans, pine nuts, or pistachios, toasted

1. Rinse and drain the turnip greens. Add to the pressure cooker along with the broth or water, garlic, and salt.

2. Lock the lid into place and bring to low pressure; maintain pressure for 3 minutes. Remove from heat and allow pressure to release naturally for 5 minutes. Quick-release any remaining pressure and remove the lid.

3. Drain the turnip greens and transfer to a serving bowl. Toss with the oil. Add the pepper. Taste for seasoning and add additional salt if needed. Stir in the toasted nuts. Serve.

Mashed Rutabagas and Parsnips

Unlike many mashed root vegetable dishes where you can substitute milk for the cream or sour cream, this dish needs the added fat to offset the strong flavors of the vegetables.

INGREDIENTS | SERVES 4

1 ¾-pound rutabaga, peeled, quartered, and sliced
2 parsnips, peeled and sliced
2 tablespoons butter
¼ teaspoon salt
¼ water
¼ cup heavy cream
¼ cup sour cream
Nutmeg, freshly grated

1. Add the rutabaga, parsnips, butter, salt, and water to the pressure cooker. Lock the lid into place and bring to low pressure; maintain pressure for 8 minutes.

2. Remove from heat and allow pressure to release naturally for 10 minutes. Quick-release any remaining pressure and remove the lid.

3. Drain any excess moisture from the vegetables. Transfer to a food processor; pulse to puree the vegetables. Gradually add the cream as you pulse the vegetables until they reach their desired consistency. Once the vegetables are pureed, transfer them to a serving bowl and stir in the sour cream. Taste for seasoning and add additional salt and sour cream if desired. Garnish with the nutmeg. Serve.

CHAPTER 22

Fabulous Fruits

Basic Unsweetened Applesauce
255

Spiced Peaches
255

Spiced Fruit-Infused
Barbeque Sauce
256

Special Occasion Chunky
Applesauce
257

Cranberry Sauce
257

Apple Butter
258

Dried Fruit Compote
258

Lemon Custard
259

Fruit Compote
260

Banana Cream Custard
261

Stuffed Apples
262

Pears Poached in Wine
263

Vanilla-Spice Pear Butter
264

Lemon Curd
265

Basic Unsweetened Applesauce

There's no need to core the apples to remove the seeds when you'll be using a food mill to process the cooked apples. For chunky applesauce, quarter the apples before you cook them. Once they're cooked, slightly mash the apples into the cooking liquid rather than processing them.

INGREDIENTS | YIELD: 5 CUPS

1 cup water
12 medium apples (about 3 pounds)

Applesauce Notes

Instructions are for a 6-quart pressure cooker. For a yield of 3 cups in a 4-quart pressure cooker, reduce the apples to 2 pounds and the water to ⅔ cup. For a yield of 6½ cups of applesauce in an 8-quart pressure cooker, increase the apples to 5 pounds and the water to 1⅔ cups.

1. Add the water to the pressure cooker. If using organic apples, rinse and quarter the apples. If not, rinse, peel, and quarter the apples. Add to the pressure cooker.

2. Lock the lid into place, bring to high pressure, and immediately remove from the heat; let the pressure release naturally for 10 minutes. Quick-release any remaining pressure.

3. Once the apples have cooled slightly, pass the apples and cooking liquid through a food mill. If you do not have a food mill, add the apples and cooking liquid in batches to a food processor or blender. Refrigerate covered for up to 10 days or freeze for up to 4 months.

Spiced Peaches

To make spiced peach butter, after Step 2, process the peaches and liquid in a blender or food processor until smooth and return to the pressure cooker. Simmer and stir over low heat for 30 minutes or until thickened enough to coat the back of a spoon.

INGREDIENTS | SERVES 6

2 15-ounce cans sliced peaches in syrup
¼ cup water
1 tablespoon white wine vinegar
⅛ teaspoon ground allspice
1 cinnamon stick
4 whole cloves
½ teaspoon ground ginger
Pinch cayenne pepper
Optional: 1 tablespoon candied ginger, minced
Optional: 3 whole black peppercorns

1. Add all of the ingredients to the pressure cooker. Stir to mix. Lock the lid into place and bring to low pressure; maintain pressure for 3 minutes. Remove the pressure cooker from the heat, quick-release the pressure, and remove the lid.

2. Remove and discard the cinnamon stick, cloves, and peppercorns if used.

3. Return the pressure cooker to medium heat. Simmer and stir for 5 minutes to thicken the syrup.

4. Serve warm or chilled. To store, allow to cool and then refrigerate for up to a week.

Spiced Fruit-Infused Barbeque Sauce

This sauce uses fruit instead of the tomatoes traditionally associated with barbeque sauce. Use it as a glaze the next time you grill steaks or chicken, or add some to pulled pork.

INGREDIENTS | YIELD: ABOUT 2 CUPS

1 large clove garlic, peeled and minced

1 jalapeño pepper, seeded and diced

1 1-inch piece fresh ginger, sliced

1 small onion, peeled and quartered

1 16-ounce can pitted tart cherries, drained

1 16-ounce can pitted plums, drained

¼ cup honey

3 tablespoons rice wine or white wine vinegar

1 tablespoon dark soy sauce

1 tablespoon brown sugar

2 whole allspice berries

2 whole cloves

1 3-inch cinnamon stick

Salt and freshly ground pepper, to taste

1. Add the garlic, jalapeño pepper, ginger, onion, cherries, plums, honey, vinegar, soy sauce, and brown sugar to a food processor. Pulse until chopped and mixed. Transfer to the pressure cooker.

2. Wrap the allspice berries, whole cloves, and cinnamon stick in a piece of cheesecloth, stir to secure, and add to the fruit mixture in the pressure cooker. Lock the lid into place. Bring to low pressure; maintain pressure for 15 minutes. Remove from heat and allow pressure to release naturally.

3. Remove the lid. Remove and discard the cheesecloth bundle. Stir the sauce. Taste for seasoning. Add additional honey, brown sugar, salt, and pepper, if needed. Cool to room temperature. Transfer to a covered container; refrigerate for up to 5 days or freeze until needed.

Special Occasion Chunky Applesauce

To sweeten the applesauce, stir in sugar, maple syrup, or honey to taste after you remove the lid from the pressure cooker. This applesauce adds a special flair to just about any pork meal.

INGREDIENTS | SERVES 6

8 Granny Smith apples

1 cup apple juice or cider

2 tablespoons fresh lemon juice

¼ cup sugar

⅓ cup light brown sugar, packed

½ teaspoon ground nutmeg

¼ teaspoon ground cinnamon

⅓ cup cinnamon hearts candy

1. Rinse, peel, core, and dice the apples. Add to the pressure cooker with apple juice or cider, lemon juice, granulated sugar, brown sugar, nutmeg, and cinnamon. Stir well. Lock the lid into place and bring to low pressure; maintain for 4 minutes. Remove from heat and allow pressure to release naturally for 10 minutes.

2. Quick-release any remaining pressure. Stir in the candy until it's melted and blended into the sauce, mashing the apples slightly as you do so. Serve warm or chilled. Can be stored for several days in the refrigerator.

Cranberry Sauce

You can make this cranberry sauce several days in advance, store it in the refrigerator, and then bring it back to temperature on the stove. For additional flavor, stir in some orange liqueur, bourbon, or brandy.

INGREDIENTS | SERVES 6

1 12-ounce bag fresh cranberries

1 cup sugar

½ cup water, apple juice, or pineapple juice

Pinch salt

1 tablespoon frozen orange juice concentrate

Optional: Cinnamon and ground cloves, to taste

1. Rinse and drain the cranberries. Remove and discard any stems or blemished cranberries.

2. Add the cranberries to the pressure cooker along with the sugar, water or juice, and salt. Lock the lid into place and bring to high pressure; maintain for 6 minutes.

3. Remove from heat and allow pressure to release naturally for 10 minutes. Remove the lid. Stir in the orange juice concentrate. Stir well, breaking the cranberries apart with a spoon or mashing them slightly with a potato masher.

4. Taste for seasoning and adjust if necessary, stirring in additional sugar if needed and the cinnamon and cloves if desired. Serve warm or chilled.

Apple Butter

To make red-hot apple butter, mix the cinnamon and allspice. Thirty minutes into the simmering time, stir in ¼ teaspoon ground cloves and 3–4 tablespoons Red Hots cinnamon candy.

INGREDIENTS | **YIELD: ABOUT 2 CUPS**

1 cup apple juice or cider

12 medium apples (about 3 pounds)

1½ teaspoons ground cinnamon

½ teaspoon ground allspice

⅛ teaspoon ground cloves

1½ cups sugar

Optional: 1 or 2 drops oil of cinnamon

1. Add the apple juice or cider to the pressure cooker. Wash, peel, core, and dice the apples. Lock the lid into place, bring to high pressure, and immediately remove from heat; let the pressure release naturally for 10 minutes. Quick release any remaining pressure.

2. Press cooled apples through a fine sieve or food mill, or process in a food processor or blender. Return apples and liquids to pressure cooker, add the cinnamon, allspice, cloves, and sugar.

3. Return the pan to medium heat and bring to a simmer. Simmer uncovered and stir until the sugar is dissolved. Reduce heat, simmer, and stir for 1 hour. Note that it's important that you frequently stir the apple butter from the bottom of the pan to prevent it from burning.

Dried Fruit Compote

If you plan to add sugar to the dried fruit compote, do so before the fruit has cooled so that it can be stirred into the fruit mixture until it dissolves. Honey can be served at the table.

INGREDIENTS | **SERVES 6**

1 8-ounce package dried apricots

1 8-ounce package dried peaches

1 cup golden raisins

1½ cups orange juice

1 cinnamon stick

4 whole cloves

Optional: Sugar or honey

1. Cut the dried apricots and peaches into quarters and add them to the pressure cooker along with the raisins, orange juice, cinnamon stick, and cloves. Lock the lid into place and bring to high pressure; maintain pressure for 3 minutes. Remove from heat and allow pressure to release naturally. Remove the lid.

2. Remove the cinnamon stick and cloves. Return to medium heat and simmer for several minutes. Serve warm or allow to cool, and then cover and store in the refrigerator until needed. Use within a week.

Lemon Custard

You can also prepare the lemon custard by fixing it in a 5-cup heatproof casserole dish that will fit on the rack inside the pressure cooker. Increase the pressure time to 20 minutes. Serve these custards dusted with powdered sugar or topped with fresh or cooked fruit.

INGREDIENTS | SERVES 6

½ cup sugar

1 tablespoon cornstarch

2 large eggs

2 egg yolks

1½ cups milk

1 cup heavy cream

2 medium lemons

2 cups water

1. Add the sugar and cornstarch to a bowl. Stir to combine well. Whisk in the eggs and egg yolks. Stir in the milk and cream. Grate the zest from one of the lemons and add it to the batter along with the juice from both lemons (about ¼ cup). Evenly divide between six ½-cup custard cups. Tightly cover the top of each custard cup with aluminum foil to prevent any water from getting into the cups.

2. Set the rack in the bottom of the pressure cooker and pour in the water. Place the custard cups on the rack, stacking them if you need to.

3. Lock the lid into place and bring to high pressure; maintain pressure for 12 minutes. Remove the pressure cooker from the heat, quick-release the pressure, and remove the lid.

4. Carefully lift the custard cups from the pressure cooker and place them on a wire rack. Remove the foil.

5. Let custard cool to room temperature. Once cooled, cover each cup with plastic wrap and chill overnight in refrigerator.

Fruit Compote

Serve with a dollop of whipped cream or increase the number of servings by using it as a topping for plain or lemon yogurt.

INGREDIENTS | SERVES 6

1 cup apple juice

1 cup dry white wine

2 tablespoons honey

1 cinnamon stick

¼ teaspoon ground nutmeg

Zest of 1 lemon

Zest of 1 orange

3 apples

3 pears

½ cup dried cherries, cranberries, or raisins

1. Add the apple juice and wine to the pressure cooker over medium-high heat. Bring to a boil. Stir in the honey until dissolved. Add the cinnamon stick, nutmeg, lemon zest, and orange zest. Reduce heat to maintain a simmer.

2. Wash, peel, core, and chop the apples and pears. Add to the pressure cooker. Stir. Lock the lid into place and bring to high pressure; maintain pressure for 1 minute. Remove the pressure cooker from heat, quick-release the pressure, and remove the lid.

3. Use a slotted spoon to transfer the cooked fruit to a serving bowl. Return the pressure cooker to the heat and bring to a boil; boil and stir until reduced to a syrup that will coat the back of a spoon. Stir the dried cherries, cranberries, or raisins in with the cooked fruit in the bowl and pour the syrup over the fruit mixture. Stir to mix. Allow to cool slightly, then cover with plastic wrap and chill overnight in the refrigerator.

Banana Cream Custard

Dark rum bumps up the flavor of this recipe, making it a rich, delicious way to use up ripe bananas. Think of this dessert as like a banana eggnog pudding.

INGREDIENTS | SERVES 6

Butter
2 slices bread, crusts removed
2 ripe bananas
2 tablespoons fresh lemon juice
1 cup heavy cream
2 large eggs
½ cup dark brown sugar, packed
1 teaspoon ground nutmeg
2 tablespoons dark rum
1 tablespoon vanilla
1 cup water

1. Butter the inside of a 5-cup casserole dish that will fit inside the pressure cooker on the rack; set aside. Add the bread to a blender or food processor; pulse to create soft bread crumbs. Remove and set aside.

2. Add the bananas and lemon juice to the blender or food processor; puree while gradually adding in the cream. Add the eggs; pulse to mix.

3. Add the brown sugar, nutmeg, rum, and vanilla; pulse until mixed. Stir in the reserved bread crumbs.

4. Pour the banana mixture into the prepared casserole dish. Cover and wrap tightly in aluminum foil.

5. Pour the water into the pressure cooker. Place the rack in the cooker. Set the foil-covered casserole dish on the rack. Lock the lid into place and bring to low pressure; maintain pressure for 22 minutes. Remove from the heat and allow pressure to release naturally.

6. Transfer the casserole dish to a cooking rack and remove the foil. Serve warm or chilled.

Stuffed Apples

You can replace the sugar with maple syrup or brown sugar if desired. Serve as dessert, with a scoop of vanilla or caramel swirl ice cream.

INGREDIENTS | SERVES 4

½ cup apple juice

¼ cup golden raisins

¼ cup walnuts, toasted and chopped

2 tablespoons sugar

½ teaspoon grated orange rind

½ teaspoon ground cinnamon

4 cooking apples

4 teaspoons butter

1 cup water

1. Put the apple juice in a microwave-safe container; heat for 1 minute on high or until steaming and hot. Pour over the raisins. Soak the raisins for 30 minutes. Drain, reserving the apple juice. Add the nuts, sugar, orange rind, and cinnamon to the raisins and stir to mix.

2. Rinse and dry the apples. Cut off the top fourth of each apple. Peel the cut portion and chop it, then stir the diced apple pieces into the raisin mixture. Hollow out and core the apples by cutting to, but not through, the apple bottoms.

3. Place each apple on a piece of aluminum foil that is large enough to wrap the apple completely. Fill the apple centers with the raisin mixture.

4. Top each with a teaspoon of the butter. Wrap the foil around each apple, folding the foil over at the top and then pinching it firmly together.

5. Pour the water into the pressure cooker. Place the rack in the cooker. Place the apples on the rack. Lock the lid into place and bring to high pressure; maintain pressure for 10 minutes.

6. Remove pressure cooker from heat, quick-release the pressure, and remove the lid. Carefully lift the apples out of the pressure cooker. Unwrap and transfer to serving plates. Serve hot, at room temperature, or chilled.

Pears Poached in Wine

Use Bartlett, Anjou, or Bosc pears. If you prefer, replace the cinnamon stick, ginger, and orange zest with a whole split and scraped vanilla bean. Whatever way you season them, these pears are delicious served over pound cake.

INGREDIENTS | SERVES 4

4 ripe, but still firm pears

2 tablespoons fresh lemon juice

1¼ cups dry wine

½ cup cream sherry

¼ cup sugar

1 3-inch cinnamon stick, halved

¼ teaspoon ground ginger

2 teaspoons orange zest, grated

Recipe Alternatives

Make this dessert alcohol free by replacing the wine and sherry with fruit juice; adjust the sugar accordingly. If you prefer to serve whole pears, peel the pears and cut off some of the bottom ends so they'll stand upright. After you've dissolved the sugar into the sauce, insert the rack into the pressure cooker and stand the pears upright.

1. Rinse and peel the pears and cut them in half. Use a spoon or melon baller to remove the cores. Brush the pears with the lemon juice.

2. Combine the wine, sherry, sugar, cinnamon, ginger, and orange zest in the pressure cooker. Bring to a boil; stir to blend and dissolve the sugar. Carefully place the pears cut side down in the pressure cooker. Lock the lid into place and bring to low pressure; maintain pressure for 3 minutes. Remove the pressure cooker from the heat, quick-release the pressure, and remove the lid.

3. Use a slotted spoon to transfer the pears to a serving bowl or to place them on dessert plates. If desired, return the pressure cooker to medium heat and simmer uncovered for several minutes to thicken the sauce. Remove and discard the cinnamon stick pieces. Spoon the sauce over the pears. Serve.

Vanilla-Spice Pear Butter

Bartlett pears are light green and are especially prevalent in the Pacific Northwest. Serve on scones or toasted English muffins.

INGREDIENTS | **YIELD: ABOUT 2 CUPS**

6 medium Bartlett pears
¼ cup dry white wine
1 tablespoon fresh lemon juice
¾ cup sugar
2 orange slices
1 lemon slice
2 whole cloves
1 vanilla bean, split lengthwise
1 cinnamon stick
¼ teaspoon ground cardamom
Pinch salt

1. Rinse, peel, and core the pears and cut them into 1-inch dice. Add the pears, wine, and lemon juice to the pressure cooker. Lock the lid into place and bring to low pressure; maintain pressure for 8 minutes.

2. Remove from heat and allow pressure to release naturally for 10 minutes. Quick-release any remaining pressure and remove the lid. Transfer the fruit and juices to a blender or food processor and puree.

3. Return the puree to the pressure cooker. Add the sugar. Stir and cook over low heat until sugar dissolves. Stir in the remaining ingredients. Increase the heat to medium and boil gently, cooking and stirring for about 30 minutes or until mixture thickens and mounds slightly on spoon.

4. Remove and discard the orange and lemon slices, cloves, and cinnamon stick. Remove the vanilla pod; use the back of a knife to scrape away any vanilla seeds still clinging to the pod and stir them into the pear butter. Cool and refrigerate covered for up to 10 days or freeze for up to 4 months.

Lemon Curd

This tart lemon dish is most commonly spread on toast. It can also be used to fill baked tart shells.

INGREDIENTS | SERVES 6

1⅓ cups sugar

3 large eggs

1 egg yolk

¼ cup butter, softened

¼ cup fresh lemon juice

1 teaspoon lemon zest, grated

2 cups water

Lemon Brunch Croissant

For each croissant, mix ½ teaspoon powdered sugar into 1 tablespoon cream cheese. Split a croissant and spread the sweetened cream cheese inside. Spoon some lemon curd to taste over the sweetened cream cheese. Fold the top of the croissant over the fillings. Serve.

1. Add the sugar to a blender or food processor. Process to create superfine sugar. Add the eggs, egg yolk, butter, lemon juice, and lemon zest. Process until well-mixed.

2. Prepare a 3-cup heatproof casserole dish that will sit on the rack of the pressure cooker by treating it with nonstick spray or coating the inside with butter. Strain the mixture from the blender or food processor into the dish. Cover tightly with aluminum foil.

3. Pour the water into the pressure cooker and insert the rack. Place the foil-covered casserole dish on the rack. Lock the lid into place and bring to low pressure; maintain pressure for 18 minutes. Remove the pressure cooker from the heat, quick-release the pressure, and remove the lid. Remove the casserole dish and place it on a wire rack.

4. Remove the foil from the casserole dish, being careful not to get any moisture clinging to the foil into the lemon curd. Use a small whisk or a fork to whisk the lemon curd.

5. The lemon curd can be served warm, but it will be somewhat runny. Cool, and then refrigerate covered for at least 4 hours to thicken the curd.

CHAPTER 23

Custards, Steamed Puddings, and Desserts

Banana Pudding Cake
267

Chocolate-Berry Bread Pudding
268

Cornmeal Cake
269

Creamy Coconut Rice Pudding
269

Lemon Cheesecake
270

Molten Fudge Pudding Cake
271

Plum Pudding
with Brandy Sauce
273

Peanut Butter and
Fudge Cheesecake
274

Coconut Custard
276

Glazed Lemon
Poppy Seed Cake
277

Date Pudding
278

Piña Colada Bread Pudding
279

Tapioca Pudding
280

Steamed Dessert Bread
281

Banana Pudding Cake

This is a delicious way to use up ripe bananas. You'll need to use a pressure cooker large enough to hold a 1-quart or 6-cup Bundt or angel food cake pan to make this recipe.

INGREDIENTS | SERVES 12

1 18¼-ounce package yellow cake mix

1 3½-ounce package instant banana pudding mix

4 eggs

4 cups water

¼ cup vegetable oil

3 small ripe bananas, mashed

2 cups powdered sugar, sifted

2 tablespoons milk

1 teaspoon vanilla extract

½ cup walnuts, toasted and chopped

Alternative Glaze

While the cake is still warm, slowly brush maple syrup over the outside of the cake. The syrup will sink into the cake somewhat, but the cake will remain sticky to the touch. The walnuts won't stick to the cake, however, so serve the nuts on the side or add them to the cake batter before you bake the cake.

1. Treat a 1 quart or 6-cup Bundt or angel food cake pan with nonstick spray. Set aside.

2. Add the cake mix and pudding mix to a large mixing bowl; stir to mix. Make a well in the center and add the eggs and pour in 1 cup water, oil, and mashed banana.

3. Beat on low speed until blended. Scrape bowl and beat another 4 minutes on medium speed. Pour the batter into the prepared pan. Cover tightly with a piece of heavy-duty aluminum foil.

4. Pour 3 cups water into the pressure cooker and add the rack. Lower the cake pan onto the rack.

5. Lock the lid into place and bring to high pressure; maintain pressure for 35 minutes.

6. Remove the pressure cooker from the heat, quick-release the pressure, and remove the lid.

7. Lift the cake pan out of the pressure cooker and place on a wire rack to cool for 10 minutes, then turn the cake out onto the wire rack to finish cooling.

8. To make the glaze, mix together the powdered sugar, milk, and vanilla in a bowl. Drizzle over the top of the cooled cake. Sprinkle the walnuts over the glaze before the glaze dries.

Chocolate-Berry Bread Pudding

You can somewhat cut the fat in Chocolate-Berry Bread Pudding by replacing the milk and cream with skim or 2% milk, but add one more egg to the batter if you do.

INGREDIENTS | SERVES 6

6 slices day-old challah or brioche

½ cup raspberry preserves

½ cup dried strawberries or prunes, diced

½ cup hazelnuts, chopped

½ cup cocoa

½ cup sugar

Pinch salt

2 tablespoons butter, melted

3 large eggs

2 cups whole milk

2 cups heavy cream

1 tablespoon vanilla

1 cup water

Challah and Brioche

Challah is a slightly sweet, yeast-leavened Jewish egg bread. Brioche is a similar sweetened French bread. The dough can be used as the base for myriad pastries. This dessert won't be as sweet if you use homemade white or French bread, but it will still be good.

1. If the crusts on the bread are dark remove them. If using fresh bread, lightly toast it. Spread raspberry preserves over the bread. Treat a 5-cup heatproof soufflé dish with nonstick spray.

2. Tear the bread into chunks. Layer half the bread in the bottom of the soufflé dish. Sprinkle with dried fruit and chopped hazelnuts. Add remaining bread preserves side down.

3. Whisk the cocoa, sugar, and salt together. Add butter and eggs; whisk to mix. Whisk in milk, cream, and vanilla. Pour half the cocoa mixture over the bread. Tap down the dish and wait several minutes for the bread to absorb the liquid. Pour in remaining cocoa mixture.

4. Tear off 2 large pieces of heavy-duty aluminum foil. Lay one piece of the foil over the top of the dish, crimping it slightly around the edges, and wrap it around the dish, folding it and tucking it under. Set the dish in the middle of the remaining piece of foil; bring it up and over the top of the dish and crimp to seal.

5. Pour water into the pressure cooker and add rack. Crisscross 2 long doubled pieces of foil over the rack to help you lift the dish out of the pressure cooker later. Place the covered soufflé dish over the crossed foil strips on the rack.

6. Lock lid into place and bring to high pressure; maintain for 15 minutes. Remove from heat and allow pressure to release naturally.

7. Remove the dish from the pressure cooker, remove the foil, and place on a rack until ready to serve or until it's cool enough to cover and refrigerate.

Cornmeal Cake

Serve warm with maple syrup or make a maple-infused butter by whisking pats of chilled butter into heated maple syrup. Eat leftovers for breakfast cornbread-style: by crumbling into a bowl of milk.

INGREDIENTS | SERVES 6

2 cups milk

¼ cup light brown sugar, packed

1 teaspoon orange zest, grated

½ cup fine yellow cornmeal

1 large egg

2 egg yolks

2 tablespoons butter, melted

2 tablespoons orange marmalade

1 cup water

1. Bring milk to a simmer over medium hear. Stir in the brown sugar; simmer and stir until the milk is at a low boil. Whisk in the orange zest and cornmeal. Simmer and stir for 2 minutes. Remove from heat. Whisk together the egg, egg yolks, butter, and orange marmalade. Stir into the cornmeal mixture. Treat a 1-quart soufflé or heatproof glass dish with nonstick spray. Add batter.

2. Pour water into the pressure cooker and add rack. Place soufflé dish on the rack. Lock lid into place and bring to low pressure; maintain pressure for 12 minutes. Remove from heat and allow pressure to release naturally for 10 minutes. Quick-release any remaining pressure and remove the lid. Transfer to a wire rack.

Creamy Coconut Rice Pudding

Garnish this pudding with a sprinkling of ground cinnamon and serve with a dollop of whipped cream.

INGREDIENTS | SERVES 6

1½ cups Arborio rice, rinsed and drained

2 cups whole milk

1 14-ounce can coconut milk

1 cup water

½ cup sugar

2 teaspoons ground cinnamon

½ teaspoon salt

1½ teaspoons vanilla

1 cup dried cherries, dried strawberries, or golden raisins

1. Add the rice, milk, coconut milk, water, sugar, cinnamon, and salt to the pressure cooker. Cook and stir to dissolve the sugar over medium-high heat and bring to a boil. Lock the lid into place and bring to low pressure; maintain for 15 minutes.

2. Turn off the heat, quick-release the pressure, and remove the lid. Stir in the vanilla and dried fruit. Replace the cover, but do not lock into place. Let stand for 15 minutes. Stir and serve.

Lemon Cheesecake

*Serve this rich, popular dessert topped with cherry pie filling or
sugared fresh blueberries, raspberries, or strawberries.*

INGREDIENTS | SERVES 8

Nonstick spray

12 gingersnaps or vanilla wafers

1½ tablespoons almonds, toasted

½ tablespoon butter, melted

2 8-ounce packages cream cheese, room temperature

½ cup sugar

2 large eggs

Zest of 1 lemon, grated

1 tablespoon fresh lemon juice

½ teaspoon natural lemon extract

1 teaspoon vanilla

2 cups water

Lemon Fresh

For a milder lemon flavor, replace the lemon extract with vanilla. For a strong lemon flavor, add a few drops of food-grade lemon oil or more lemon zest. When you shave the zest off of the lemon, make sure you avoid the white pith, which tastes bitter.

1. Use a pressure cooker with a rack that's large enough to hold a 7" × 3" springform pan. Treat the inside of the pan with nonstick spray.

2. Add the cookies and almonds to a food processor. Pulse to create cookie crumbs and chop the nuts. Add the melted butter and pulse to mix.

3. Transfer the crumb mixture to the springform pan and press down into the pan. Wipe out the food processor bowl.

4. Cut the cream cheese into cubes and add it to the food processor along with the sugar; process until smooth. Add the eggs, lemon zest, lemon juice, lemon extract, and vanilla. Process for 10 seconds.

5. Scrape the bowl and then process for another 10 seconds or until the batter is well mixed and smooth.

6. Place the springform pan in the center of two 16" × 16" pieces of aluminum foil. Crimp the foil to seal the bottom of the pan.

7. Transfer the cheesecake batter into the springform pan. Treat one side of a 10-inch square of aluminum foil with nonstick spray; lay over the top of the springform pan and crimp around the edges.

8. Bring the bottom foil up the sides so that it can be grasped to raise and lower the pan into and out of the pressure cooker.

9. Pour the water into the pressure cooker. Insert the rack. Set the springform pan holding the cheesecake batter on the rack.

Lemon Cheesecake (*continued*)

10. Lock the lid into place and bring to high pressure; maintain pressure for 8 minutes. Remove from heat and allow pressure to release naturally. Remove the lid.

11. Lift the covered springform pan out of the pressure cooker and place on a wire rack. Remove the top foil.

12. If any moisture has accumulated on top of the cheesecake, dab it with a piece of paper towel to remove it. Let cool to room temperature and then remove from the springform pan.

Molten Fudge Pudding Cake

Serve warm with a scoop of vanilla bean ice cream and garnish with fresh fruit or dust with powdered sugar.

INGREDIENTS | SERVES 6

4 ounces semisweet chocolate chips

¼ cup cocoa

⅛ teaspoon salt

3 tablespoons butter

2 large eggs, separated

¼ cup sugar, plus extra for the pan

1 teaspoon vanilla

½ cup pecans, chopped

¼ cup plus 2 tablespoons all-purpose flour

2 teaspoons instant coffee granules

2 tablespoons coffee liqueur

1 cup water

1. Add the chocolate chips, cocoa, salt, and 2 tablespoons butter to a microwave-safe bowl. Microwave on high for 1 minute; stir well. Microwave in additional 20-second segments if necessary, until the butter and chocolate are melted. Set aside to cool.

2. Add the egg whites to a medium-size mixing bowl. Whisk or beat with a mixer until the egg whites are foamy. Gradually add the ¼ cup of sugar, continuing to whisk or beat until soft peaks form; set aside.

3. Add the egg yolks and vanilla to a mixing bowl; use a whisk or handheld mixer to beat until the yolks are light yellow and begin to stiffen. Stir in the cooled chocolate mixture, pecans, flour, instant coffee, and coffee liqueur.

Molten Fudge Pudding Cake (*continued*)

4. Transfer a third of the beaten egg whites to the chocolate mixture; stir to loosen the batter. Gently fold in the remaining egg whites.

5. Treat the bottom and sides of a 1-quart metal pan with 2 teaspoons of the remaining butter. Add about a tablespoon of sugar to the pan; shake and roll to coat the buttered pan with the sugar.

6. Dump out and discard any extra sugar. Transfer the chocolate batter to the buttered pan.

7. Treat one side of a 15-inch piece of aluminum foil with the remaining teaspoon of butter. Place the foil butter side down over the top of the pan; crimp around the edges of the pan to form a seal.

8. Pour the water into the pressure cooker. Place the rack in the cooker. Create handles to use later to remove the pan by crisscrossing long, doubled strips of foil over the rack.

9. Place the metal pan in the center of the rack over the foil strips. Lock the lid into place and bring to low pressure; maintain pressure for 20 minutes.

10. Remove pressure cooker from heat, quick-release pressure, and remove the lid. Lift the pan out of the pressure cooker and place on a wire rack. Remove foil cover.

11. Let rest for 10–15 minutes. To serve, either spoon from the pan or run a knife around the edge of the pan, place a serving plate over the metal pan, and invert to transfer the cake.

Plum Pudding with Brandy Sauce

This traditional steamed Christmas pudding can be made up to a month in advance if you refrigerate it in a brandy-soaked cheesecloth in a covered container. If made ahead, steam it or heat it gently in the microwave before serving it with the brandy sauce.

INGREDIENTS | SERVES 10

1 cup prunes, snipped

1 cup dried currants

1 cup dried cranberries

1 cup raisins

1 cup candied lemon peel, minced

½ cup dark rum

1 cup butter, partially frozen

1½ cups all-purpose flour

1 cup dried bread crumbs

½ cup pecans, chopped

1 tablespoon candied ginger, minced

1 teaspoon baking soda

½ teaspoon salt

1 teaspoon ground cinnamon

¼ teaspoon ground nutmeg

¼ teaspoon ground cloves

3 eggs

2 cups light brown sugar, packed

3 cups water

1 cup heavy cream

¼ cup brandy

1. Add the prunes, currants, cranberries, raisins, candied lemon peel, and rum to a bowl. Stir to mix. Cover and let stand at room temperature for 8 hours.

2. Partially freeze ¾ cup butter. Add the flour, bread crumbs, pecans, ginger, baking soda, salt, cinnamon, nutmeg, and cloves to a large mixing bowl. Stir to mix.

3. Grate the butter into the flour mixture. Add the marinated fruit. Toss grated butter and fruit into flour mixture. Add eggs and 1 cup of brown sugar to a separate bowl; whisk to mix. Pour into the flour-butter-fruit mixture. Combine the two mixtures together.

4. Wrap the base of a 7- or 8-inch springform pan with heavy-duty aluminum foil.

5. Transfer the batter to the springform pan, pressing it down into the pan to eliminate any air pockets.

6. Tear off a 25-inch-long piece of heavy-duty aluminum foil and treat one side of one 8-inch end of the foil with nonstick spray. Place the nonstick spray-treated side of the foil over the top of the springform pan and then wrap the remaining foil under and over the pan again; crimp to seal.

7. Pour the water and place the rack into the pressure cooker. Crisscross long doubled strips of foil over the rack to create handles to use later to remove the pan.

8. Place springform pan on rack, over foil strips. Lock lid into place and bring to high pressure; maintain for 1 hour.

9. Remove from heat and allow pressure to release naturally. Remove lid. Lift pan from the pressure cooker and cool. Remove foil cover.

10. Let rest and cool for 15 minutes and then run a knife around the edge of the pudding to loosen it from the sides of the pan. Unmold the pudding and transfer it to a plate.

11. To make the brandy sauce, add remaining cup of brown sugar, cream, and remaining ¼ cup butter to a saucepan placed over medium-high heat. Simmer and stir until sugar dissolves, stir in the brandy. Simmer and stir for 10 minutes. Serve over the warm pudding.

Peanut Butter and Fudge Cheesecake

Adults and kids alike love peanut butter and chocolate, so this dessert will be a hit with everyone. Serve with a dollop of whipped cream if desired.

INGREDIENTS | SERVES 8

1 cup toasted, unsalted peanuts
½ cup vanilla wafers
1 tablespoon cocoa
3 tablespoons butter, melted
1 cup peanut butter
2 8-ounce packages cream cheese, softened
½ cup light brown sugar, packed
½ cup powdered sugar, sifted
2 tablespoons cornstarch
2 large eggs
¼ cup sour cream
1 12-ounce package semisweet chocolate chips
2 cups water

1. Add the peanuts, vanilla wafers, and cocoa to a food processor. Pulse to grind the peanuts and turn the vanilla wafers into crumbs. Add the butter. Pulse to mix.

2. Press into the bottom of a 7-inch springform pan. Set aside. Wipe out the food processor.

3. Add the peanut butter, cream cheese, and brown sugar to the food processor. Process until smooth.

4. Add the powdered sugar and cornstarch to a small bowl; stir to mix well. Add to the food processor with the eggs and sour cream. Process until smooth.

Peanut Butter and Fudge Cheesecake (*continued*)

5. Remove the lid and stir in the chocolate chips. Transfer the batter to the springform pan.

6. Wrap the base of the springform pan with heavy-duty aluminum foil. Tear off a 25-inch-long piece of heavy-duty aluminum foil and treat one side of one 8-inch end of the foil with nonstick spray. Place the nonstick spray-treated side of the foil over the top of the springform pan and then wrap the remaining foil under and then over the pan again; crimp to seal.

7. Pour the water and place the rack into the pressure cooker. Crisscross long, doubled strips of foil over the rack to create handles to use later to remove the pan.

8. Place the springform pan on the rack over the foil strips. Lock the lid into place and bring to high pressure; maintain pressure for 22 minutes.

9. Remove from heat and allow pressure to release naturally. Remove the lid. Lift the pan from the pressure cooker and place it on a wire rack. Allow to cool slightly. Refrigerate at least 4 hours before serving.

Coconut Custard

This dessert is delicious as is, but it's also great when combined with other flavors, too. You can serve it topped with some hot fudge or with fresh fruit.

INGREDIENTS | SERVES 8

1 cup milk

1 14-ounce can coconut milk

1 10-ounce can sweetened condensed milk

½ teaspoon vanilla

3 eggs

3 egg yolks

2 cups water

1. Add the milk, coconut milk, and sweetened condensed milk to a saucepan. Heat it over medium heat until it's steaming and begins to reach a low boil.

2. Stir in the vanilla. In a separate bowl whisk the eggs together with the egg yolks.

3. Whisk a couple of tablespoons of the milk mixture into the eggs and then stir the eggs into the milk mixture.

4. Reduce heat to low; cook and stir for 4 minutes or until the mixture begins to thicken.

5. Treat a 6-cup soufflé dish with nonstick spray. Pour the heated custard into the treated dish.

6. Cover the dish with a piece of heavy-duty aluminum foil; crimp the edges to form a seal around the dish.

7. Pour the water and place the rack into the pressure cooker. Crisscross long, doubled strips of foil over the rack to create handles to use later to remove the pan.

8. Place the pan on the rack over the foil strips. Lock the lid into place and bring to high pressure; maintain pressure for 30 minutes.

9. Remove from heat and allow pressure to release naturally for 30 minutes. Quick-release any remaining pressure. Remove the lid.

10. Lift the pan from the pressure cooker and place it on a cooling rack. Once the custard has cooled, remove the foil. Use a paper towel to dab any moisture that may have formed on the surface of the custard. Cover the dish with plastic wrap and refrigerate until ready to serve.

Glazed Lemon Poppy Seed Cake

Make this cake ahead of time. The flavor improves if you wrap it in plastic wrap and store it for a day or two before you serve it.

INGREDIENTS | SERVES 8

½ cup butter, softened
1 cup sugar
2 eggs, separated
1 teaspoon vanilla
2 lemons
1¼ cups all-purpose flour
1 teaspoon baking soda
1 teaspoon baking powder
¼ teaspoon salt
⅔ cup whole milk
⅓ cup poppy seeds
2 cups water
½ cup powdered sugar, sifted

1. Add the butter and sugar to a mixing bowl; beat until light and fluffy. Beat in the egg yolks, vanilla, grated zest from 1 lemon, and juice from 1 lemon.

2. Mix together the flour, baking soda, baking powder, and salt. Add the flour and milk in 3 batches to the butter mixture, mixing after each addition. Stir in the poppy seeds.

3. Add the egg whites to a chilled bowl. Whisk or beat until stiff. Fold the egg whites into the poppy seed batter.

4. Treat a 4-cup soufflé dish or Bundt pan with nonstick spray. Transfer the batter to the pan.

5. Treat a 15-inch square of heavy-duty aluminum foil with nonstick spray. Place the foil, treated side down, over the pan; crimp around the edges to seal.

6. Pour the water and place the rack into the pressure cooker. Crisscross long, doubled strips of foil over the rack to create handles to use later to remove the pan.

7. Place the pan on the rack over the foil strips. Lock the lid into place and bring to low pressure; maintain pressure for 40 minutes.

8. Remove from heat and allow pressure to release naturally. Remove the lid. Lift the pan from the pressure cooker and place it on a cooling rack. Remove foil cover.

9. To make the glaze, whisk the juice and grated zest from the remaining lemon together with the powdered sugar. Transfer the cake to a serving platter and drizzle the glaze over the top.

Date Pudding

This is a rich, decadent dessert in the tradition of an English sticky toffee pudding. You can double the number of servings if you layer the pudding in parfait glasses with caramel sauce, chopped toasted pecans, and whipped cream.

INGREDIENTS | SERVES 8

2½ cups dates, pitted and snipped

1½ teaspoons baking soda

1⅔ cups boiling water

2 cups dark brown sugar, packed

½ cup butter, softened

3 large eggs

2 teaspoons vanilla

3½ cups all-purpose or cake flour

4 teaspoons baking powder

Pinch salt

Quick Caramel Sauce

Add 1½ cups packed brown sugar, ½ cup butter, and 3 cups of heavy cream to a saucepan over medium heat. Bring to a boil, stirring constantly. Reduce heat and maintain a simmer for 6 minutes, continuing to stir. Refrigerate leftovers in a covered container for 2 weeks, or until the expiration date given on the heavy cream container.

1. Add the dates to a mixing bowl and toss them together with the baking soda. Pour the boiling water over the dates. Set aside.

2. Add the brown sugar and butter to a food processor. Process to cream them together and then continue to process while you add the eggs and vanilla.

3. Use a spatula to scrape the brown sugar mixture into the bowl with the dates. Stir to mix.

4. Add the flour, baking powder, and salt to a bowl; stir to mix. Fold into the date and brown sugar mixture.

5. Wrap the base of a 7- or 8-inch springform pan with heavy-duty aluminum foil. Treat the pan with nonstick spray.

6. Press the batter into the springform pan. Tear off a 25-inch-long piece of heavy-duty aluminum foil and treat one side of one 8-inch end of the foil with nonstick spray. Place the treated side of the foil over the top of the springform pan and then wrap the remaining foil under and then over the pan again; crimp to seal.

7. Pour the water and place the rack into the pressure cooker. Crisscross long, doubled strips of foil over the rack to create handles to use later to remove the pan.

8. Place the springform pan on the rack over the foil strips. Lock the lid into place and bring to low pressure; maintain pressure for 50 minutes.

9. Remove from heat and allow pressure to release naturally. Remove the lid. Lift the pan from the pressure cooker and place it on a cooling rack.

Piña Colada Bread Pudding

If desired, you can add 1 tablespoon butter and 2 tablespoons brown sugar to the juice drained from the pineapple. Simmer and stir over medium-low heat until it thickens and then serve over the bread pudding.

INGREDIENTS | SERVES 8

1 16-ounce can cream of coconut
½ cup heavy cream
½ cup whole milk
3 large eggs
½ cup butter, melted
¾ cup sugar
1½ teaspoons rum flavoring
¼ teaspoon ground nutmeg
1 20-ounce can pineapple chunks, drained
1¼ cups coconut
8 cups French bread, torn into 2-inch cubes
1½ cups water

1. Add the cream of coconut, cream, milk, eggs, butter, sugar, rum flavoring, and nutmeg to a large bowl. Whisk to mix thoroughly. Stir in the drained pineapple and coconut. Fold in the bread cubes.

2. Treat a 5-cup soufflé dish with nonstick spray. Transfer the bread pudding mixture into the dish. Pour in the water and place the rack into the pressure cooker.

3. Crisscross long, doubled strips of foil over the rack to create handles to use later to remove the pan.

4. Treat one side of a 15-inch-square piece of heavy-duty aluminum foil with nonstick spray.

5. Lay the foil, treated side down, over the soufflé dish and crimp the edges to seal.

6. Tear off another piece of heavy-duty foil to completely wrap the soufflé dish to ensure the seal. Place over the crisscrossed pieces of foil.

7. Lock the lid into place and bring to high pressure; maintain pressure for 12 minutes. Remove pressure cooker from heat, quick-release pressure, and remove lid.

8. Remove pan from the pressure cooker, uncover, and place on a wire rack to cool. Serve warm, at room temperature, or chilled.

Tapioca Pudding

Add another dimension to this dish by combining it with other flavors. You can stir in some toasted pecans, chocolate chips, or coconut. Top it off by serving with a dollop of whipped cream.

INGREDIENTS | SERVES 4

½ cup small pearl tapioca

1¾ cups water

⅓ cup sugar

1 tablespoon butter

2 large eggs

⅛ teaspoon salt

1½ cups milk

1 cup heavy cream

1 teaspoon vanilla

1. Combine the tapioca and ¾ cup water in a small bowl; cover and let soak overnight.

2. Add the sugar, butter, eggs, and salt to a bowl; beat until smooth. Stir in the milk, cream, and vanilla. Drain the tapioca and stir into the milk mixture.

3. Treat a 1-quart stainless steel bowl with nonstick spray. Pour the tapioca mixture into the bowl. Cover the bowl tightly with heavy-duty aluminum foil.

4. Pour the remaining cup of water into the pressure cooker and add the rack. Crisscross long, doubled strips of foil over the rack to create handles to use later to remove the pan.

5. Center the covered pan holding the tapioca mixture on the foil strips on the rack.

6. Lock the lid into place and bring to low pressure; maintain pressure for 12 minutes. Remove the pressure cooker from the heat, quick-release the pressure, and remove the lid.

7. Lift the pudding out of the pressure cooker. Let rest for 15 minutes and then remove the foil cover. Stir. Taste for flavor and add more vanilla if desired. Chill until ready to serve.

Steamed Dessert Bread

Serve this dessert bread with sweetened cream cheese or butter. Toast leftovers by placing slices on the oven rack or a cookie sheet in a 350°F oven for 5 minutes.

INGREDIENTS | SERVES 8

½ cup unbleached all-purpose flour
½ cup stone-ground cornmeal
½ cup whole wheat flour
½ teaspoon baking powder
¼ teaspoon fine salt
¼ teaspoon baking soda
½ cup maple syrup
½ cup buttermilk
1 large egg
butter
2 cups water

1. Add the flour, cornmeal, whole wheat flour, baking powder, salt, and baking soda to a mixing bowl. Stir to combine.

2. Add the maple syrup, buttermilk, and egg to another mixing bowl or measuring cup. Whisk to mix and then pour into the flour mixture. Mix until a thick batter is formed.

3. Butter the inside of a 6-cup heatproof pudding mold or baking pan. Add enough batter to fill the container ¾ full.

4. Butter one side of a piece of heavy-duty aluminum foil large enough to cover the top of the baking dish. Place the foil butter side down over the pan and crimp the edges to seal.

5. Pour the water and place the rack into the pressure cooker. Crisscross long, doubled strips of foil over the rack to create handles to use later to remove the pan.

6. Place the pan on the rack over the foil strips. Lock the lid into place and bring to low pressure; maintain pressure for 1 hour.

7. Remove from heat and allow pressure to release naturally. Remove lid. Lift pan from pressure cooker and place on a cooling rack. Remove foil.

8. Test the bread with a toothpick; if the toothpick comes out wet, place the foil over the pan and return it to the pressure cooker to cook longer. If the bread is done, use a knife to loosen the bread and invert it onto the cooling rack. Serve the bread warm.

Ingredient Sources

AMERICAN SPOON
American Spoon Foods specialty foods, such as:
Cherry Juice, Fruit Butters, Fruit Preserves, Maple Syrup, Spoon Fruits
www.spoon.com

BIRDS EYE FOODS
Frozen Vegetable Blends
www.birdseyefoods.com

BOCA
Frozen Ground Burger Crumbles meat substitute
www.bocaburger.com

BROWNWOOD ACRES FOODS, INC.
Tart cherry juice concentrate
www.brownwoodacres.com

CASCADIAN FARM
Organic frozen hash browns; vegetables
www.cascadianfarm.com

CROWN PRINCE
Boiled baby clams and other canned seafood
www.crownprince.com

KING ORCHARDS
Tart cherry juice concentrate
www.mi-cherries.com

NUTTY GUYS
Dried fruit; nuts
www.nuttyguys.com

MINOR'S
Broth bases
www.soupbase.com

MRS. DASH
Mrs. Dash Salt-Free Seasoning and Grilling Blends
www.mrsdash.com

MUIR GLEN
Organic canned tomatoes
www.muirglen.com

PILLSBURY
Refrigerated Peel-and-Unroll Pie Crusts
Refrigerated Pizza Crust
Refrigerated Biscuits and Dinner Rolls
Frozen Pie Crust
Frozen Biscuits
www.pillsbury.com

REDI-BASE
Broth bases
www.redibase.com

ROSINA FOOD PRODUCTS, INC.
Frozen Italian specialty food products
www.rosina.com

SEA STAR SALT
Celtic gray (sea) salt; fleur de sel
www.seastarseasalt.com

THE SPICE HOUSE
Freeze-dried shallots
Spices
www.thespicehouse.com

WELLSHIRE FARMS
Nitrate-free bacon, corned beef, ham, and other meats
www.wellshirefarms.com

APPENDIX B

Equipment Sources

CHICAGO METALLIC BAKEWARE
Chicago Metallic Professional and Professional
Nonstick Bakeware
www.chicagometallicbakeware.com

CUISINART
Cuisinart has a wide selection of countertop
appliances and cookware:
**Cuisinart 6-quart Programmable Electric
Pressure Cooker**
**Cuisinart CleanWater Countertop Filtration
System**
Cuisinart (countertop) Microwave Oven
Cuisinart PowerPrep Plus 14-Cup Food Processor
**Cuisinart Brick Oven Toaster Oven with
Rotisserie**
www.cuisinart.com

FAGOR
Electric Multi-Cooker
www.fagoramerica.com

HAWKINS FUTURA
Pressure cookers
www.hawkinscookers.com

KAISER BAKEWARE
Baking sheets
www.kaiserbakeware.com

MAGAFESA
Pressure cookers
www.magefesausa.com

MANTTRA
Pressure cookers
www.manttra.com

PLEASANT HILL GRAIN
A full-service distributor for a wide variety of helpful
cooking appliances, which include:
BAMIX Hand Mixer (immersion blender)
Berkey Stainless Water Purifier System
B/R/K Pressure Cookers
Kuhn Rikon Pressure Cookers
Nutrimill Grain Mill
www.pleasanthillgrain.com

PRESTO
Pressure Cookers
www.gopresto.com

REYNOLDS CONSUMER PRODUCTS COMPANY
Reynolds Handi-Vac Vacuum Sealing System
www.reynoldskitchens.com

SILIT
Pressure cookers
www.silit.com

TAYLOR PRECISION PRODUCTS LP
Taylor Digital Oven Thermometer/Timer
www.taylorusa.com

T-FAL
Pressure cookers
www.t-falusa.com

WMF
Pressure cookers
www.wmf-usa.com

Pressure Cooking Time Charts

Keep in mind that the times given in the charts are only for the time the food is cooked under pressure. Once the lid is locked firmly and securely into place, it can take 5 to 40 minutes for the pressure itself to build. The time it takes for the pressure to build depends on a number of factors: how well your particular pressure cooker conducts heat, the burner setting, the amount of food in the pressure cooker, and the temperature of that food. For example, colder or frozen ingredients in the pressure cooker will affect the temperature of the liquid you add and will take longer to come to pressure.

Beans

The time required to pressure cook beans can depend on the beans and how dry they are. How the beans are stored, or even the humidity during the time the beans are exposed to the air, can lengthen or shorten their cooking time.

Getting beans ready to cook begins with going over them and discarding any broken or shriveled beans. Also, always rinse and drain the beans before you soak or cook them.

As a general rule, you'll want to cook each cup of beans in 4 cups of water or broth and 2 teaspoons of oil. The oil is necessary to prevent foaming, which can clog the pressure cooker regulator. You can add other ingredients—like herbs or vegetables—along with the beans, but don't add salt until after the beans are cooked because it will hinder the cooking.

Soaking beans in water overnight removes much of the sugar molecules (specifically the oligosaccharides raffinose and stachyose) that cause excessive gas and other digestive problems for many people. Anise seeds, coriander seeds, and cumin are often added to bean dishes because they're natural carminatives, or additives that reduce the formation of or aid in the expulsion of digestive gas.

Regardless of whether you presoak the beans or cook them immediately, it's generally best to err on the side of undercooking them. If necessary, you can finish cooking them by simmering them in the cooking liquid. For most dishes, beans should be cooked until they're tender, not mushy.

TABLE C-1

BEANS			
Bean Type (1 cup)	**Cooking Time (Soaked)**	**Cooking Time (Unsoaked)**	**Yield**
Black Beans	25–30 minutes	28–32 minutes	2 cups
Cannellini	18–22 minutes	33–38 minutes	2 cups
Chickpeas (garbanzo beans)	35–40 minutes	50–60 minutes	2½ cups
Great Northern (white beans)	25–30 minutes	30–35 minutes	2¼ cups
Lentils	n/a	8–10 minutes	2 cups
Pinto	20–24 minutes	30–35 minutes	2¼ cups
Navy Beans	22–25 minutes	30–35 minutes	2 cups
Red Beans	22–25 minutes	30–35 minutes	2 cups
Soybeans	26–33 minutes	33–40 minutes	1¼ cups

Rice and Grains

As a general rule, when prepared in the pressure cooker, rice and grains cook best in a large quantity of liquid. A combination of natural and quick pressure release is then used to finish the cooking. If further cooking is needed once the rice or grain has been stirred and fluffed, simmer until tender. Once rice or grains are cooked to the desired result, the excess liquid is drained. Keep in mind that rice or grains should be slightly undercooked if they'll be added to soups, stews, or casseroles.

White Long-Grain or Basmati Rice

Long-grain white rice and basmati rice require different cooking methods than other types of rice or grains. Also, when they're cooked in the pressure cooker, these types of rice will be slightly stickier and moister than when they're cooked on the stovetop. Cook the rice on high for 3 minutes and then remove the pressure cooker from the heat and let the pressure release naturally for 7 minutes. Quick-release any remaining pressure before removing the lid.

When cooking white long-grain or basmati rice, do not fill the pressure cooker more than half full. The butter or oil is necessary to prevent the rice from foaming, which can clog the pressure cooker's pressure regulator.

TABLE C-2

WHITE LONG-GRAIN AND BASMATI RICE		
Rice Amount	**Liquid + Butter or Oil**	**Yield**
1 cup	1½ cups + 1 tablespoon	3 cups
1½ cups	2¼ cups + 1 tablespoon	4–4½ cups
2 cups	3 cups + 2 tablespoons	5½–6 cups
3 cups	4¼ cups + 2 tablespoons	7½–8 cups

Other Types of Rice and Grains

In most cases, 1 cup of rice (other than white rice) or grain is cooked in 3¼ cups of liquid along with 1 tablespoon of butter or oil.

TABLE C-3

OTHER TYPES OF RICE AND GRAINS				
Rice or Grain Type	**Special Cooking Instructions**	**Pressure**	**Time**	**Pressure Release Method**
Arborio Rice	Sauté in butter or oil until opaque; add liquid.	High	6 minutes	Quick pressure release
Black Japonica, Brown, Red, and Wehani Rice		High	10 minutes	Natural pressure release for 10 minutes, then quick pressure release
Wild Rice		High	20 minutes	Natural pressure release for 10 minutes, then quick pressure release
Amaranth	2¼ cups liquid for each cup of grain	High	6 minutes	Quick release pressure, then simmer to evaporate excess liquid
Kamut		High	20 minutes	Natural pressure release for 10 minutes, then quick pressure release
Quinoa	1½ cups quinoa + 2¼ cups liquid	High	2 minutes	Natural pressure release for 10 minutes, then quick pressure release
Wheat Berries		High	30 minutes	Natural pressure release for 10 minutes, then quick pressure release

Vegetables

When you cook vegetables in the pressure cooker, you'll need to add at least ½ cup water or other liquid along with the vegetables so that the cooker will come to pressure. Vegetables should always be well washed. Unless indicated otherwise in the table, peeling is optional.

Quick pressure release is used for all vegetables. Because they cook quickly, it's better to err on the side of caution and undercook the vegetables and then cover them and let them steam to finish cooking.

TABLE C-4

VEGETABLE			
Food	**Amount**	**Pressure**	**Cooking Time**
Artichokes	4 medium	High	7 minutes
Artichokes	4 large	High	9 minutes
Beans, Green or Yellow Waxy	1½ pounds, cut into 2-inch pieces	Low	2 minutes

VEGETABLE (continued)			
Food	Amount	Pressure	Cooking Time
Beets	Medium	High	24 minutes
Broccoli	Large florets	High	2 minutes
Cauliflower	Large florets	High	2 minutes
Carrots	Baby (or 2-inch pieces)	High	8 minutes
Carrots	½-inch slices	High	3 minutes
Greens	Collard, Kale, cut into 1-inch strips	High	5 minutes
Onions	Baby, peeled	High	3 minutes
Parsnips	Peeled, 2-inch pieces	High	4 minutes
Parsnips	Peeled, ½-inch slices	High	2 minutes
Potatoes, White	Medium, quartered	High	6 minutes
Potatoes, Red New	2–3 ounces each	High	7 minutes
Potatoes, Sweet	2-inch cubes	High	6 minutes
Squash, Acorn	Halved and seeded	High	8 minutes
Squash, Butternut	Peeled and sliced	High	4 minutes
Squash, Yellow Crookneck or Zucchini	1-inch slices	High	3 minutes

If you're pressure cooking unthawed frozen vegetables, add 1 or 2 minutes to the cooking time.

Meats

The longer you intend to pressure cook meats, the more liquid you'll need to add to the pressure cooker. For example, for most cuts of meat you'll need to add at least 1 cup of liquid if you'll be cooking the meat for 45 minutes or less, or at least 1½ cups of liquid for longer cooking periods.

Times given are an approximation. If there is any doubt as to whether the meat is cooked through, use a meat thermometer to determine the internal meat temperature.

TABLE C-5

CHICKEN		
Description	Cooking Time	Pressure Release Method
Whole, up to 4 pounds	25 minutes	Quick
Breast, bone-in, 3 pounds	10 minutes	Quick

CHICKEN (continued)		
Description	Cooking Time	Pressure Release Method
Breast, boneless, 2 pounds	6 minutes	Quick
Legs, bone-in	9 minutes	Quick
Thighs, bone-in	12 minutes	Quick
Thighs, boneless	10 minutes	Quick

TABLE C-6

BEEF			
Cut	Size	Cooking Time	Pressure Release Method
Pot Roast, Bottom Round	3–3½ pounds	99 minutes	Natural
Brisket	2½–3 pounds	55 minutes	Natural
Corned Beef Brisket		24 minutes per pound	Natural
Short Ribs	2–3-inches thick	50 minutes	Natural
Stew	2-inch cubes	10 minutes	Natural

TABLE C-7

LAMB			
Cut	Size	Cooking Time	Pressure Release Method
Shanks	4 12-ounce	24 minutes	Natural
Shoulder	2-inch cubes	25 minutes	Natural

TABLE C-8

PORK			
Cut	Size	Cooking Time	Pressure Release Method
Chops, Loin, bone-in	1-inch thick	Brown first, 11 minutes	Quick
Shoulder Roast, Boneless	3 pounds	55 minutes	Natural
Spareribs	2-rib pieces	22 minutes	Quick
Spareribs	3-rib pieces	28 minutes	Quick

TABLE C-9

VEAL			
Cut	Size	Cooking Time	Pressure Release Method
Shoulder Roast, Boneless		10 minutes per pound	Natural
Cubes for stew	2-inch	10 minutes	Natural

Index

A

Acorn squash, 108
Anchovies, 241
Apple juice, 88, 234, 257, 258, 260, 262
Apples, 10, 41, 50, 96, 98, 104, 180, 239, 255, 257, 258, 260, 262
Applesauce, 100, 236
Apricot, 14, 53, 61, 158, 180, 201, 258
    preserves, 87
Artichoke, 193, 223
Asparagus, 174, 194, 242

B

Bacon, 240
Balsamic vinegar, 97
Bananas, 261, 267
Barbecue sauce, 96
Barley, 151, 176, 190, 216
Beans, 181, 184, 209, 219
    black, 28, 129, 152, 179
    kidney, 31, 134, 166, 177
    lima, 240
    pinto, 160, 177
    red, 186
    white, 99, 161, 175, 181, 185, 226-27
Beef, 27, 32, 36, 37, 42, 81, 82, 83, 84, 85, 86, 87, 88, 89, 90, 91, 92, 106, 107, 108, 110, 111, 112, 113, 114, 133, 135, 138, 141, 146, 148, 153, 154, 158, 165, 168, 206-7, 213, 227, 228, 232, 233
Beer, 68, 83, 167
Beet greens, 251
Beets, 137, 237, 238
Biscuits, 71
Blueberry, 19
Brandy, 273-74
Bread, 261
    challah or brioche, 268
    French, 279
Broccoli, 241, 242
Butter, 237, 247
Buttermilk, 281

C

Cabbage, 32, 88, 107, 112, 178, 206-7, 220, 239
Caesar salad dressing, 202
Cake mix, yellow, 267
Cantaloupe, 29
Carrots, 84, 86, 91, 92, 95, 205, 238, 244, 251
Celery, 247
Cheese
    Cheddar, 52, 192, 213, 217
    Colby, 192
    mozzarella, 110, 192
    Parmesan, 248
Cherries, 260, 269
Chicken, 34, 26, 38, 55, 56, 57, 58, 59, 60, 61, 62, 63, 64, 65, 66, 130, 139, 142, 145, 155, 159, 160, 161, 163, 164, 166, 167, 187, 188, 194, 198, 200, 202, 204, 215, 226-27
Chickpeas, 23, 178, 191, 229
Chilis, 60, 84, 113, 165
Chocolate chips, semisweet, 271-72, 274-75
Citrus, 15
Clams, 169
Cocoa, 268, 271-72, 274-75
Coconut, 203, 279
    cream of, 279
    milk, 58, 269, 276
Coffee, 272
Collard greens, 218
Cooking methods, 4-5
Corn, 17, 163, 204, 213, 219, 241
Cornbread stuffing mix, 134
Cornmeal, 51, 240, 269
Crab, 118
Cranberries, 10, 18, 41, 53, 74, 101, 184, 234, 257, 260, 273-74
Cream, 77, 78, 118, 135, 161, 188, 189, 214, 244, 247, 252, 253, 259, 261, 268, 279, 280
    cheese, 24, 33, 214, 270-71, 274-75
Curry, 59, 66, 140, 187, 236

D

Dates, 278
Duck, 222

E

Eggplant, 24, 79, 115, 171, 173, 199
Eggs, 52, 79, 200, 232, 233, 259,
    261, 265, 267, 269, 270-71, 272,
    276, 277, 278, 279, 280, 281
Enchilada sauce, 84, 90
Endive, 193, 211
Equipment, 2-3

F

Fennel, 162, 208, 250
Figs, 72, 97, 180
Fish, 117, 118, 119, 120, 121, 122, 123,
    124, 125, 126, 127, 161, 162, 190
Flour, 278, 281

G

Garam masala, 56, 136
Garlic, 245
Ginger, 60
Gingersnaps, 270-71
Grape leaves, 30

H

Ham, 47, 94, 103, 109, 149, 152, 186,
    211, 216, 217, 218, 220
Hamburger buns, 100
Horseradish, 244

K

Kale, 147, 249
Ketchup, 38, 40, 85, 106, 131, 185

L

Lamb, 114, 132, 137, 150, 158, 223,
    227
Leeks, 162, 163, 208
Lemon
    extract, 271
    juice, 62, 65, 242, 247, 259, 265,
        271, 277
Lentils, 150, 179, 187

M

Mango, 17
Mayonnaise, 59
Milk, 268, 269, 276, 280
    sweetened condensed, 276
Mincemeat, 20
Miso paste, 122
Mushroom, 44, 63, 73, 77, 108, 148,
    151, 168, 172, 176, 199, 212, 224-
    25, 228, 229

N

Noodles, 146-47, 155. *See also*
    Pasta

O

Oats, 47, 53
Okra, 76, 204

Olive oil, 242, 253
Olives, 126, 215, 223
Onion, 12, 63, 87, 88, 89, 90, 92, 96,
    101, 114, 171, 185
Orange, 62, 222

P

Paprika, 63, 64, 133
Parsley, 124
Parsnip, 247, 253
Pasta, 175, 178, 188, 189, 190, 192,
    194, 213. *See also* Noodles
    sauce, 110, 232, 233
Peaches, 21, 255, 258
Peanut butter, 274-75
Peanuts, 274-75
Pears, 180, 260, 263, 264
Peas, 26, 149, 174, 184, 188, 205,
    214, 219
Pecans, 234
Pepper, 16, 90, 90, 101, 111, 138,
    160, 161, 166, 171, 173, 177, 179,
    183, 188, 191, 198, 199, 206-7,
    213, 216, 243, 256
Pesto, 58
Pickling spice, 92
Pineapple, 102, 103, 279
Plums, 39, 256
Poppyseeds, 277
Pork, 94, 95, 96, 97, 98, 99, 100, 101,
    102, 103, 104, 106, 109, 113, 115,
    131, 135, 140, 154, 234
Potatoes, 29, 46, 48, 49, 50, 52,
    58, 63, 68, 70, 71, 86, 91, 95,
    104, 108, 123, 131, 141, 145,
    148, 156, 161, 162, 163, 169, 211,

212, 217, 219, 220, 236, 237, 244, 245, 249

Pressure cooker
   history, 2
   tips and troubleshooting, 6-7
Pressure release methods, 3-4
Prunes, 61, 96, 201, 273-74
Pudding mix, instant banana, 267

Q

Quinoa, 193

R

Radishes, 252
Raisins, 103, 260, 262, 269, 273-74
Rice, 109, 111, 129, 136, 153, 154, 174, 196, 197, 198, 199, 200, 201, 202, 203, 204, 205, 206-7, 208, 209, 212, 215, 227, 269
Romano cheese, 75
Root beer, 95
Rum, 180, 261, 273-74, 279
Rutabagas, 253

S

Saffron, 142, 196
Salad greens, 187
Salsa, 213
Saltpeter, 92
Sauerkraut, 68, 95
Sausage, 44, 46, 49, 50, 51, 52, 76, 101, 108, 109, 134, 147, 152, 186, 189, 212, 214, 226-27
Scallops, 215

Shrimp, 109, 125, 196, 215
Sour cream, 65, 245, 250, 253, 274-75
Spinach, 38, 218
Strawberries, 13, 18, 268, 269
Sub buns, 110
Sweet potatoes, 101, 201, 243
Swiss chard, 197, 248

T

Tapioca, pearl, 280
Tarragon, 78
Thai green curry paste, 143
Tomato, 11, 12, 33, 37, 41, 42, 43, 55, 57, 69, 70, 79, 111, 112, 113, 117, 118, 120, 126, 133, 144, 151, 156, 164, 165, 166, 169, 172, 177, 181, 193, 213, 223, 226-27, 230-31, 249
Turkey, 68, 69, 70, 71, 72, 73, 74, 75, 76, 77, 78, 79, 107, 156, 219
Turnip greens, 253
Turnips, 244, 250, 251, 252

V

Vanilla, 264
Veal, 224-25, 230-31

W

Wheat berries, 183
Wine, 127, 222, 223, 228, 229, 239, 250, 260, 263, 264

Y

Yams, 236
Yogurt, 66, 72

Z

Zucchini, 181, 183, 197, 233